AF600650

CONFESSORS OF RELIGIOUS

A DISSERTATION

Submitted to the Faculty of Canon Law of the Catholic University of America in partial fulfillment of the requirements for the Degree of

DOCTOR OF CANON LAW

By

ROBERT EMMET McCORMICK, J. C. L.

Priest of the Archdiocese of New York

THE CATHOLIC UNIVERSITY OF AMERICA
WASHINGTON, D. C.

1926

Nihil Obstat:

✠ Thomas J. Shahan, S. T. D.,

Censor Deputatus.

Washingtonii, D. C., die 7 Iunii, 1926.

Imprimatur:

✠Michael J. Curley,

Archiepiscopus Baltimorensis.

Baltimorae, die 7 Iunii, 1926.

TABLE OF CONTENTS

PART II.

Confessors of Female Religious

APPENDICES

INTRODUCTION.

THE CONFESSOR OF RELIGIOUS.

DEFINITION.

The confessor of religious is the duly appointed priest having special approbation or jurisdiction from the proper superior to hear the confessions of religious. The word *confessor* has gone through an evolution in meaning from its use in the early Church until it now has an entirely different force than that of its primary significance. Confessors at the beginning of the Church were not only martyrs who gave their lives for Christ but also those who openly confessed Our Lord before tyrants and the enemies of the faith and who suffered punishment and torment but died a natural death.[1] This word acquired another meaning by being applied to chanters, who were in the lower grades of the clericate,[2] because in chanting the Scriptures they frequently pronounced the word *confiteri*. Gradually the term *confessor* came to mean *confessarius* or the penitent confessing his sins in sacramental confession to a priest who was called the *confessor*.[3] Peculiarly the name confessor was sometimes given to a monk who for the expiation of crimes "entered monastic confession" or penance, forsaking the life of the world.[4]

The confessor of religious was sometimes designated by the

---

1 Du Cange, *Glossarium ad Scriptores Mediae et Infimae Latinitatis*, t. II, col. 950 ff; Facciolati, *Totius Latinitatis Lexicon* I, 442; Andrews, *Latin-English Lexicon*, p. 340.

2 Du Cange, *op. cit.*, p. 952.

3 Du Cange, *op. cit.*, p. 952, quotes in support of this the following, "*Qui peccata sua confitetur sacerdoti*"—Chronicon. Mellicense, p. 328, col. 11; In Reg. Reformat. Monast. Mellicense, "*Confessarius autem, nude, pure, humiliter ac breviter confiteatur culpas suas & Confessor habens intentionem latissimam absolvendi . . . . subjungat; Dominus Noster Jesus Christus, etc.*"

4 Du Cange, *loc. cit.*

term *sacerdos confessionis* as is found in the rule of the Order of Sempringham[5] and in the book of the Order of St. Victor of Paris.[6] This lack of uniformity in terminology is found even in the sixteenth and seventeenth centuries, when the Council of Trent[7] applied to confessors of religious the term *confessor,* while Clement VIII in 1593[8] used the word *confessarius.* The former term was reverted to by Clement X, who applied it to both the ordinary and extraordinary confessor of women religious.[9] This term *confessor* was also accepted by succeeding Pontiffs Innocent XIII,[10] and Benedict XIII[11] until Benedict XIV in his constitution "Ad Militantes"[12] once more used *confessarius* in application to the ordinary and extraordinary confessors of nuns. In his constitution "Pastoralis Curae" of August 5, 1748,[13] the words *confessor* and *confessarius* were applied without distinction and even simultaneously in the same paragraph by this Pontiff. But from that time on he and his successors brought about uniformity in terminology by always using the word *confessarius*[14] which is found in the decree "Quemadmodum"[15] and is now the accepted term in the Code of Canon Law.

Division.

Since the law in regard to the confessors of male religious developed in different phases and different periods than those of the confessors of female religious the general division of this work is based upon the fact of this divergence. In each section

5 *Regula Ordinis Sempringensis,* c. 5; cf. Holsten, *Codex Regularum,* II, 471.
6 MS, c. 31; cf. Du Cange, *op. cit.,* 952.
7 Sess. XXV, c. 10, *De Regularibus et Monialibus;* Ehses, *Concilium Tridentinum,* t. 9, p. 1082.
8 Decree, *Cum Sanctissimus,* May 26, 1593, § 3; FJC n. 177.
9 Const. *Superna,* June 21, 1670, § 4; FJC n. 246.
10 Const. *Apostolici ministerii,* May 23, 1723, § 21; FJC n. 280.
11 Const. *In Supremo,* Sept. 23, 1724, § 17; FJC n. 283.
12 March 30, 1742, § 20; FJC n. 236.
13 FJC n. 388.
14 Benedict XIV, Const. *Quamvis Justo,* Apr. 30, 1749, §§ 13, 16; FJC n. 398; Const. *Apostolici ministerii,* Dec. 9, 1749; FJC n. 405.
15 S. C. EE et RR, Dec. 17, 1890; Col. S. C. P. F. (ed. 1907), n. 1745.

the history of the law from its origin and development under monastic rule is offered as the preparation for subsequent advances in legislation which preceded the Code. The canonical treatment naturally falls into two parts, *"The Confessor of Male Religious"* and *"The Confessor of Female Religious"* and the minor divisions within each section are made for the purpose of a clear presentation in a logical order. The main division of the second part in regard to female religious is made from the viewpoint of approbation and the attempt will be made to present the rules of law for confessors requiring special approbation to be followed by those concerning confessors who are exempt from the law of special approval. On disputed questions the clear statement of conflicting opinions with their supporting arguments will be offered and a choice made of that which seems the better, but for the practical solution of the individual case which may arise solid canonical principles of action will be advanced.

Purpose.

The law of the confessor of religious has been the subject of much dispute both before and after the Code and CHELODI[16] states that probably more ink has been spilt on the solutions of the difficulties that canon 522 offers than on any other canon of the Code. The importance of a clear and concise statement of the difficulties with the equally clear solution of these both theoretically and practically is the goal towards which this present dissertation is directed in the hope that the consciences of confessors, religious, superiors and local ordinaries, with whom the law is concerned, may find peace in the definite knowledge of their rights and obligations.

16 *Jus de Personis,* n. 258.

CHAPTER I.

PRE-CODE DEVELOPMENT OF THE LAW.

PRAENOTANDA.

In the historical treatment of this question only those rules and laws will be traced, which have reference to the confessor to whom the religious confessed in the sacrament of penance to receive absolution from their sins. It is necessary therefore to preface this chapter with the distinction between the sacramental confession made by the religious and the confession of faults or the *capitulum culparum* which is required by some religious rules. The latter is not sacramental and consists in the public admission in the religious chapter of external violations of the rules and constitutions, or of disturbances caused through negligence in the public recitation of the office, or of any excesses committed in the refectory, etc.[1] The procedure generally followed is that the monk, when rebuked by his prior, exclaims "mea culpa" and then prostrates himself at the feet of the latter seeking pardon. At the command of the prior he arises and, when requested, humbly gives his reason.[2] Not only did the right of accusing others of fault belong to the monks of the

1 *Capitula Monachorum: "Si quis negligenter sonitum fecerit, aut aliud quid excesserit in Refectorio, mox a Priore veniam petat;" B. Caroli Magni Opp.* pars 1 sectio 1; n. 41, MPL 97, 386; cf. Woulter, *Praecipua Ordinis Monastici Elementa,* p. 380.

2 *Capitula Monachorum,* n. 13, *Cum a quocunque Priore suo increpatus quis monachorum fuerit "mea culpa" primo dicat, dehinc prosternens se illius pedibus cum cappa, si habuerit, veniam petat. Et tunc jubente Priore, surgat et unde interrogatus fuerit, rationem humiliter redat.;"* MPL XCVII, 382; cf. *Udalrici Consuetudines Cluniacenses, lib.* II, cap. 17, 18; MPL CXLIX, 708, cf. *Constitutiones Ordinis Praedicatorum,* Dist. II, n. 818 ff.

community in chapter,[3] but sometimes even the obligation of doing so was imposed in virtue of the vow of obedience. This distinction between sacramental confession and the *capitulum culparum* must be kept in mind in considering the prescriptions of monastic rules and constitutions in regard to confessions and confessors.

Article I. In Monastic Rules.

1. African Monasticism.

The Rule of St. Anthony.

As Mackean says, asceticism and mystical tendencies were very prevalent in the Egyptian Church. The desire of inward purity in this world as a preparation for the next, together with the longing to follow in the footsteps of Christ supplied the tendency towards living in the desert, a country of equable climate. This formed the fuel of the monastic movement, which St. Anthony's example and influence ignited.[4] To him, then, is to be attributed the foundation of Christian Monasticism and more especially of the hermit or anchorite life in the Desert of Thebes, about the year of 270 A. D.[5] Although he had many followers he did not draw up a definite rule of life for them. The rule attributed to him had its origin most likely in the second half of the Fourth century and was composed probably by some of his disciples.[6] In the twenty-fifth clause this rule forbids the hermits to confess their bad thoughts to all men and only to those who could save their souls.[7]

This, of course, offers no conclusive proof as to the exist-

---

[3] *Goffridi Abbatis Vindocinensis, Opuscula XIV, "Ordinamus itaque et ordinando sub nomine sanctae obedientiae praecipimus, ut alter alterius culpam sic in capitulo notificet quatenus eum minari non praesumat, nec increpet . . . Liceat unicuique qui accusatur aut humiliter culpam agnoscere, vel si culpabilis minime fuerit, se non audacter, sed patienter excusare etc.;"* MPL CLVII, col. 228 ff.

[4] Mackean, *op. cit.*, p. 70; Heimbucher, *Die Orden und Kongregationen*, I, 93 ff.

[5] Pourrat *op. cit.*, p. 80.

[6] Heimbucher, *op. cit.*, 1, 96.

[7] St. Benedict of Aniane, *Codex Regularum;* MPL, CIII, 424.

ence of a special confessor for the hermits but it seems to refer to priests endowed with the power of the keys, for they alone could save souls stained with mortal sin.

The Rule of St. Pachomius.

With the elimination of the more crude elements of the hermit life, a new form arose attributed to St. Pachomius (345, A. D.) the disciple of St. Anthony. He was the author of the cenobitical or community life for the early Egyptian monks. His rule translated by St. Jerome is not authentic, yet it may well contain some of his principles for it was written during the century in which he himself lived.[8] The superiors of the different houses under this rule, corrected all faults committed therein, but if it was a question of a sin not embraced by the rule the monks referred it to the Fathers of the monastery.[9] It is not certain that these Fathers were priests. Although Pachomius was of the opinion that his monks should not receive sacerdotal consecration, he nevertheless received priests as his disciples, on the condition that they should not aspire to any distinction in the community.[10] It was perhaps to these priests that the confession of sins, other than infractions of the rule, was to be made.

2. Oriental Monasticism.

The Rule of St. Basil.

The next step in monastic development leads to the East and Cappadocia, where the rule of St. Basil the Great, Bishop of Caesarea is found in force. This great writer of the church made an intimate study of monastic life and, desiring to do away with the eremetical system, incorporated his ideal of monastic government in the most important of his works, the *Regulae Brevius Tractatae* and the *Regulae Fusius Tractatae.* These rules written about 356 A. D. presuppose, as do all his monastic

---

8 St. Benedict of Aniane, *op. cit.*, MPL, CIII, 416.
9 Ladeuze, *Le Cenobitisme Pakhomien*, p. 393.
10 Ladeuze, *op. cit.*, p. 279.

writings, that the monastic community is already in existence.[11] Following the catechetical method in his rule, in response to the two hundred and eighty-eighth question of the Shorter Rules, as to whom the monks should confess their sins, whether to all or only certain persons, the words are found, "*Peccata iis confiteri necesse est, quibus mysteriorum Dei concredita dispensatio est.*"[12] RAUSCHEN is inclined to the opinion that these dispensers of the mysteries of God, here mentioned were not priests and that it is doubtful whether these cloister confessions or at least some of them involved sacramental confession.[13] He leaves the matter rest there without giving any reason for his opinion, weakening it with the words, "at least some of them," thereby admitting the converse, that some of these confessions were sacramental. If they were sacramental these confessions would demand the existence of the priest confessor. CLARKE defends the same view from another angle acknowledging the presence of priests in the monasteries, who celebrated the Sacrament of the Eucharist, but claiming that a careful reading of the rules and a glance at later Greek monachism leads to the conclusion that the duty of hearing such confessions was not assigned to the monk priests as such and that St. Basil ordered his monks to confess to the senior brethren or at least to some of them.[14] Neither of these arguments is supported by any substantial proof and in view of weighty reasons to the contrary, the negative view seems entirely untenable.

Thus DOM BESSE states that this passage is noteworthy as being the most explicit evidence in favor of sacramental confession preserved for us in the monuments of primitive monastic tradition.[15] It is POURRAT's contention that these words of St. Basil recommend the practice of confession in the monastery to the brethren who were priests, and that this private

---

11 Morison, *St. Basil and His Rule*, p. 17.

12 *Regulae Brevius Tractatae;* MPG, XXXI, 1077, 1078; MPL, XXXII, 728.

13 Rauschen, *Eucharist and Penance*, p. 239.

14 Clarke, *St. Basil the Great*, p. 97 (ed. 1913).

15 Besse, *Les Moines d'Orient anterieurs au Concile de Chalcedoine (an. 451 A. D.)*, p. 209, note 1,

administration of the Sacrament of Penance, apart from outward solemnity, was not long in becoming general in the monasteries of the East.[16] This view also finds favor with MORISON, who states that, "there can be no reasonable doubt that St. Basil expected such confessions to be made to priests for the reference to the dispensation of the mysteries of God" and the reference to the Sacrament of Baptism (Reg. Brev. 288) would seem quite conclusive. He argues for this from the fact that in St. Basil's day, if confession was to be made to an individual, it should have been made to a bishop or priest.[17] That the custom of the Church in the East was to confess to priests seems evident from the fact that after the Decian Persecution (249-251), priest penitentiaries were appointed in different places,[18] whose existence is all the more forcibly proven by the fact of their suppression at Constantinople, by Nectarius, in the year 391.[19] Secret confession to priests was in truth the recognized and all but universal practice of the Church, the "Apostolic rule" as St. Leo termed it (A. D. 459).[20] The common practice, as Morison states, favored sacerdotal absolution and the monks would be most unwilling to incur a reputation for irregularity in their administration of the Sacrament of Penance. That the clergy therefore who were to hear these confessions should be chosen with extreme care is what should be naturally expected.[21] To these authorities can be added the name of ABBE MARIN who not only proves the existence of the confessor of the monks under the rule of St. Basil but also that this office was held by the superior, one of whose graver

---

16 Pourrat, *op. cit.*, p. 95.

17 Morison, *op. cit.*, p. 74.

18 Watkins, *A History of Penance*, I, 486.

19 Watkins, *op. cit.*, 315, 316, 349; Sozomenus, *Historia Ecclesiatica*, MPG, LXVII, 1547; Rauschen, *op. cit.*, p. 196.

20 Leo I, March 6, 459 (Letter to the Bishop of Compania) *Magna indignatione*, *BRT* I, n. 19, p. 80; Denzinger, *Enchridion Symbolorum*, n. 145 (134).
"*Apostolica regula—reatus conscientia sufficit solis sacerdotibus indicare confessione secreta;*" cf. O'Donnell, *Penance in the Early Church*, p. 97.

21 Morison, *op. cit.*, p. 64.

duties was to hear the weekly confessions of his monks.[22] This confession was not merely for spiritual direction but had a sacramental character and was confession properly so called, participating in the Sacrament of Penance. Abbots not vested with the priesthood sometimes usurped this right but their action was always condemned by the councils.[23]

As a rule, however, the superiors were priests. The register of the Synod of Constantinople of 536 A. D. shows that all superiors of monasteries there present were priests. This is also in conformity with the Greek *Euchologium,* which presupposes the superior to be both priest and monk.[24] The cogency of the arguments advanced in favor of this opinion compared to the weakness of those offered by the contrary view force the conclusion that the confessor of the oriental monks following the Basilean rule was a priest and at the same time their superior. Since the rule of St. Basil prevailed over all the others in the East and is retained today by all oriental monks,[25] Eastern monasticism need not be considered any further.

3. Occidental Monasticism.

Rule of St. Benedict of Nursia.

The rule of St. Benedict of Nursia was written most likely in 530 A. D. at Monte Cassino. It has been the foundation for all subsequent monastic legislation throughout the centuries until the present. The rule of St. Benedict was not the new creation of his mind for he was aided in its composition by the rules of St. Pachomius, St. Basil and the 211th letter of St.

---

22 The number of monks often exceeded 1,000, necessitating weekly confession and no monk was allowed to extend this time beyond 15 days; Marin, *Les Moines de Constantinople, etc.,* p. 95.

23 Neither can the practice which later arose of people confessing to monks not in priestly orders and due to an exaggerated reverence prove anything against the practices of the monks of St. Basil's day within the monasteries; cf. Morison, *St. Basil and His Rule,* p. 76.

24 Marin, *op. cit.,* p. 96.

25 Montalambert, *The Monks of the West,* I, 328, footnote; Smith, *Christian Monasticism from the Fourth to the Ninth Centuries,* p. 59.

Augustine of Hippo of Africa,[26] but in the matter of dircet quotation he is most indebted to the Institutes and Conferences of Cassian.[27] His rule however surpassed them all as a practical code of legislation.[28] Reference is made in this rule to confession of sins hidden in the soul. This confession was to be made to the *Abbot* or the *Spiritual Seniors,* who knew how to cure their own wounds and not to reveal those of others.[29]

Does this refer to Sacramental confession? DE LATTE in his modern commentary supports the negative view, interpreting the words "spiritual seniors" as meaning those who had an important part in the government of souls.[30] He argues that this rule is parallel in purpose to the fifty-first instrument of good works,[31] or the fifth degree of humility[32] in which the monks are advised to confess their thoughts to the Abbot. These latter two parts of the rule have been the basis of dispute among commentators and the weight of authority makes the view, that they do not imply sacramental confession, the more probable. It must be remembered, however, that these quotations refer to revelation of bad thoughts only. This is very indefinite, and might imply imperfections whereas the first quotation speaks

---

26 St. Augustine wrote no rule for men, but the one which bears his name is based on the 211th letter to his nuns (a. d. 423).

27 John Cassian, an ascetical writer of Southern Gaul (about the year of 429), refers to the confession of thoughts to the senior monk. The latter, however, was not the sacramental confessor, for this was a sort of "culpa confession" for the sake of mortification. (cf. Gazaeus, *Cassiani Opera Omnia,* p. 53; MPL XLIX, 161: Watkins, *op. cit.,* 1,400.) The same seems to be the case in the rule of the monastery of Kilros built in 448. This rule is the most ancient monument of occidental monachism in existence. (cf. Holsten, *Codex Regularum,* II, p. 65; I, index, p. XXXI.)

28 Butler, *Benedictine Monachism,* p. 164 ff; Pourrat *op. cit.,* p. 243; Heimbucher, *op. cit.,* p. 211 ff.

29 *Regula Benedicti,* ch. 46; "*Si animae vero peccati causa latens fuerit; tantum abbati aut spiritualibus senioribus patefaciant qui sciant curare sua et aliena vulnera non detegere et publicare.*" MPL, LXVI, col. 649.

30 De Latte, *Commentary on the Rule of St. Benedict,* p. 300, ff.

31 *Rule of St. Benedict, ch. IV;* cf. St. Benedict of Aniane, *Concordia Regularum,* MPL CIII, col. 802; Woelfflin, *Regula Benedicti,* p. 14, n. 30; *Rule of St. Benedict,* (Eng. Version, Birmingham 1844), p. 14.

32 MPL LXVI, col. 219.

explicitly of sins hidden in the soul. Therefore it does not seem that a strict parallel exists between these passages implying identity in meaning.

The better view is that the passage in question refers to sacramental confession to priests.[33] The purpose of St. Benedict in this rule was that confession should be made not only to the Abbot but also to the Spiritual Father (the name used by the ancient Greeks and more recent Latins to designate the confessor) because at that time not all Abbots were priests. St. Benedict required of these Spiritual Fathers the greatest secrecy which properly belongs to sacramental confession. MARTENE quotes in support of this view such commentators as ST. HILDEGARD, BERNARD OF CASSIA, NICHOLAS OF FRACTURA, RICHARD OF ST. ANGELO, PETER BOHERIUS, JOHN CRAESBEEK and ANTHONY PEREZ.[34]

Evidently then the forty-sixth chapter cannot be interpreted in the same way as the fourth and seventh chapters, which refer to a sort of "culpa confession." And so the conclusion is evident that the forty-sixth chapter in its prescription to the monks to confess the sins hidden in their souls to their Abbot or Spiritual Seniors prescribes sacramental confession. Since this confession was to be made not only to the Abbot but to other priests, confessors of the same order, to whom they could have recourse especially in the case where the Abbot had not priestly orders, the existence of confessors supplementary to the Abbot seems evident.

BENEDICTINE REFORMS.

Benedictine Monachism, which did away with the very austere asceticism of the African and Oriental forms, soon at-

---

33 St. Benedict received priests who desired to live in the monastery, but would not permit them to exercise the functions of their priestly office without permission of the Abbot, who could request ordination for his monks for the service of their own church. (*Regula Magistri*, MPL CIII, 1313, 1315, 1323.)

34 The latter three held against sacramental confession in the quotations of the fourth and seventh chapters, while they interpret the quotation of the forty-sixth chapter in its favor. cf. Martene, *Regula Benedicti Commentata*, MPL LXVI, Col. 696.

tracted thousands to its monasteries which had sprung up in the different countries of Europe. But at the same time that the Benedictines strengthened their power and extended their organization in an extraordinary manner, the first symptoms of dissolution and decadence manifested themselves. Earthly potentates built monasteries in their territories to gain the good will of Heaven and those who could not take the habit sought to receive part of the heavenly favor attached to the habit by enriching the men that wore it or their institution. With riches then corruption entered the Benedictine Order and becoming habituated in luxury and the pleasures that it brings, laxity in observance of the rule was engendered.[35] The necessity of reform was recognized by St. Benedict, Abbot of Aniane, who died in 821 A. D. He obliged all the monasteries of the Frankish Empire to return to the primitive rule of St. Benedict of Nursia. He left two monastic writings, the *Codex Regularum Monasticorum et Canonicorum*[36] and a *Concordia Regularum,* i. e., a concordance of these rules with that of St. Benedict. This saintly Reformer of the religious life made no specific statement in regard to confessors other than that contained in the original rule[37] but he gave the impetus which culminated in the more definite reforms of the next centuries.

Thus the monastery of Cluny, France, saw the inauguration of such a reform in 910 and in the constitutions of the order drawn up about 1000 A. D. the Abbot is still the confessor of his own monks[38] with the exception that at death the prior could be chosen for that purpose.[39] In England under the reform of St. Dunstan of Glastonbury about 944 A. D., the Abbot was the regular confessor together with those priests of his monastery whom he delegated for that purpose.[40] An abuse arose during the latter part of the twelfth century among the

35 Marchand, *Moines et Nonnes,* p. 90 ff.
36 MPL CIII, 423-702.
37 MPL CIII, 713-1380.
38 *Udalrici Consuetudines Cluniacenses,* lib. II, c. 26; MPL CXLIX, 712.
39 ibid., lib. III, c. 28; MPL CXLIX, 770.
40 *Sancti Dunstani Regularis Concordia;* MPL CXXXVII, 482; cf. Martene, *Regula Benedicti Commentata,* MPL LXVI, 696.

monks of the Abbey of St. Laumer, France, of confessing to the bishops and their delegated priests instead of their abbot, a practice which PETER OF BLOIS, of the same abbey, condemns as an unjust violation of the prescriptions of their Fathers.[41] These Abbots must have been priests, for he states clearly elsewhere that confession must be made to priests.[42] About the same time at Paris in the Abbey of St. Victor the Abbot is found appointing a monk as confessor, to whom his brethren could confess.[43]

Orders Following the Benedictine Rule.

The rule of the Cistercian Order, founded by St. Robert of Molesme in 1090 on the Benedictine rule, mentions only the Abbot as confessor.[44] St. Robert de Arbrissel in the rule of the ORDER OF FONTEVRAULT, about 1117 A. D., in which the Abbess was superioress of both nuns and monks,[45] prescribed confession to the Prior but to other priests if fear prevented the revelation of their sins to their superior.[46] The CARTHUSIAN ORDER founded by St. Bruno in 1084 received its first written rule from the Abbot Guigo about 1127. Although it was not a branch of the Benedictine Order yet the rule of St. Benedict was one of the main elements upon which it was based.[47] Here again the Prior or his delegate was the weekly confessor of the monks.[48] It is evident then that both under the original rule of St. Benedict, and under the constitutions of the different reformed Bendictine abbeys and also those of other orders which took the rule of St. Benedict as their whole or partial norm of life, the Abbot

---

41 Petri Blesensis, *Liber de poenitentia;* MPL CCVII, 1095.

42 Petri Blesensis, *De Confessione Liber,* MPL CCVII, 1077.

43 Lea, *History of Confession and Indulgences,* I, 199.

44 *Liber Institutorum, Capituli Generalis Ordinis Cisterciencis,* dist. 6, c. 14; cf. Martene, *op. cit.,* in MPL LXVI, 679.

45 Heimbucher, *Die Orden und Kongregationen;* I, 477 ff; Weber, *Cath. Encycl.* VI, 130 ff.

46 *Praecepta Recte Vivendi,* c. XXII; MPL CLXII, 1084.

47 Webster, *Cath. Encycl.* III, 388.

48 *Consuetudines Guigonis* (Stat., c. 7); Martene, *Regula Benedicti Commentata;* MPL LXVI, 696.

held the office of regular confessor of his monks and as a rule delegated other priests for that purpose.

The Rule of St. Columban.

In Ireland even before the time of *Columban* the practice of private confession and reconciliation of the monasteries had found its way into lay circles.[49] The year of 530 brings to light the *Penitential of Finian,* in which as a general rule the Abbot was a priest; and he or any other priest on his behalf heard confessions and assigned penances.[50] The same is found in the *Preface on Penance of Gildas* (about 560 A. D.) while in the *Penitential of Columban* the office of the priest is clearly in evidence.[51] Moreover the Abbot of the sixth century in Ireland exercised jurisdiction without scruple.[52]

During this century, the same office which St. Basil and the Greek Monks had performed in the East as the apostles of private confession was sponsored in Gaul, by *St. Columban,* the greatest figure of Irish monastic legislation. (543-615.)[53] Once more the Abbot is seen as the confessor of his own monastic subjects as is evident from the advice of St. Columban to his monks to make confession to their Abbot secretly before receiving Communion if they had committed sins of impurity.[54] This evidently refers to the confession of mortal sins, for these alone would prevent the reception of Holy Communion. This implies also that the Abbot was in priestly orders for only those with the sacerdotal character could remit sins of their very nature grave.

When the *Regula Coenobalis* is consulted, this will become

49 Rauschen, *Eucharist and Penance,* p. 239.

50 *Poenitentiale Vinniani;* Haddan and Stubbs, *Councils and Ecclesiastical Documents Relating to Great Britain and Ireland,* I, 114; Watkins, *op. cit.,* II, 609 ff.

51 Ch. IV; Haddan and Stubbs, *op. cit.,* I, 114; Watkins, *op. cit.,* p. 604, 612, 617.

52 Watkins, *op. cit.,* I, 270 ff.

53 Pourrat, *Christian Spirituality,* p. 256.

54 *Columbani Regula Monachorum,* c. LXXX; cf. Holsten, *op. cit.,* I, 279 ff; MPL LXXX, 209-216.

more evident,[55] since it prescribes confessions to priests only.[56] This confession was to be made daily by youths.[57]

The rule of St. Columban then confirms as necessary the unity of confessor required by the other rules already considered.

The Rule of St. Chrodegang.

Another advance in confessional discipline is marked in the rule of St. Chrodegang, Bishop of Metz (742-766), who obliged his diocesan clergy to live in community and gave them the name of *Canons Regular*. He not only exhorts them to confess to the priests of God but prescribes weekly confession to the bishop or prior.[58] Confession to their own bishop was demanded of the clergy twice during the year, i. e., once during Lent and again between the middle of August and the first day of November. If confession was necessary during these periods and permission was granted by their bishop or if outside of these times necessity existed and they desired to confess, they could make their confession to another bishop or some other priest whom their bishop had delegated.[59] Thus there can be seen in episcopal legislation for the secular clergy the tendency toward unity of confessors. The practice of the monastery was beginning to receive favor outside of its walls.

The Franciscan Rule.

The thirteenth century was of quite some importance in the development of confessional discipline. During this century the Mendicant Order of Friars first claims our attention. St. Fran-

---

55 This rule was not written primarily for monks strictly so-called, but for all the inmates of the monastery; cf. Watkins, *op. cit.*, pp. 614, 618.

56 Ch. X; MPL LXXX, col. 222.

57 Metlake, *American Ecclesiastical Review*, vol. XLIX, p. 543.

58 *Regula Canonicorum Chrodegangi*, ch. 32; Harduin, *Acta Conciliorum*, IV, 1187; MPL, 89, col. 1072.

59 *Regula Canonicorum Chrodegangi* (*editio altera*), ch. 14; MPL. LXXXIX, col. 1104; cf. Lea, *op. cit.*, I, 187.

cis of Assissi in 1207 gathered about himself a few disciples, the nucleus of a great order which ramified into the Friars Minor or Franciscans and the Conventual Friars Minor in 1517 and the Capuchins in 1528. In his first rule approved verbally by Pope Innocent III in 1209 and afterwards in 1215 by the Fourth Lateran Council there is found no mention of confession to a superior and the only requirement is that of confession to the priests of the order, or, if this be impossible, to other discreet Catholic priests.[60]

The most important change, however, that the rule of St. Francis introduced was the reservation, for the first time, of sins within the order. That is to say, the reserved sin could not be absolved by the confessor, but the penitent had to make application to a higher tribunal, i. e., the superior. If the superior was a priest, he could absolve and enjoin penances. But St. Francis, who felt unworthy to approach closer to the service of God than the diaconate, made provision for superiors who might not be priests. In the latter case, the superior was to impose the penance through the priest of the order who heard the confession.[61] This rule and practice received the papal approval of Pope Honorius III in his constitution, *Solet annuere* of Nov. 29, 1223.

The Augustinian Rule.

The Rule of St. Chrodegang together with the Statutes of the Council of Aix-la-Chapelle (816) had formed the norms for the community life of canons. During the succeeding centuries

---

60 *First Rule of St. Francis of Assissi*, ch. XX; cf. *Works of St. Francis by a Religious of the Order*, p. 44; *Second Rule*, cf. Monier, *A History of St. Francis*, p. 334.

61 *Regula Bullata St. Francisci*, ch. VII—"*Si qui fratrum, instigante inimico, mortaliter peccaverint, pro illis peccatis, de quibus ordinatum fuerit inter fratres, ut recurratur ad ministros provinciales, teneantur praedicti fratres ad eos recurrere quam citius sine mora. Ipsi vero ministri si presbyteri sunt cum misericordia injungant illis poenitentiam. Si vero presbyteri non sunt, injungi faciant per alios pedire.*" Honorius III, Const. *Solet annuere*, Nov. 29, 1223; BRT III, n. 67, p. 396.

these were found unsatisfactory and the so-called Rule of St. Augustine was compiled.[62] The present orders that trace their rule of life to that of St. Augustine are the Praemonstratensians, whose rule does not refer to the sacramental confessor, the Augustinians and the Order of Preachers or Dominicans.[63]

Rule of the Augustinian Regulars.

At the beginning of the thirteenth century, William of Paris, (1105-1202), of noble French birth, who became a secular canon at St. Genevieve du Mont and after Suger's reform a canon regular and sub prior of that monastery, received later the dignity of Abbot of the Augustinian Regular Canons at Eskill, Denmark. He states that confession is both necessary and useful especially for religious. Therefore, he prescribed that Abbots or Priors or other superiors in their absence demand, at least once a month, of the confessors appointed to hear the confessions of the monks, the names of those monks confessing to them.[64]

The Dominican Rule.

One of the foremost religious orders to adopt this revised Augustinian rule was the Order of Preachers, or Dominicans.[65] There is nothing in this rule directly bearing on confessors but the Acts of the General Chapter of Paris, 1236, commanded that suitable confessors be appointed in all their houses.[66] Priors could reserve to themselves some determined cases of mortal sin.[67] Here, also, the superior is no longer the only confessor of the religious subject to him.

---

62 *Epistola 211* formed the basis. MPL 33, col. 962 ff.; Schaaf, *The Cloister*, p. 25. Pourrat, *Christian Spirituality*, p. 165.

63 Montalambert, *Monks of the West*, I, 328; Crusenius, *Monasticon, Augustinianum*, p. 93 ff.

64 *Additiones Gulielmi Parisiensis ad Constitutiones Cardinalis Gallanis;* Harduin, VI b, 1978.

65 Schaaf, *The Cloister*, p. 25.

66 *Acta Capitulorum Generalium Ordinis Praedicatorum*, Paris 1236; cf. *Constitutiones Ordinis Praedicatorum*, p. 9.

67 ibid. *Prologue, n.* 11, p. 15.

Article II.

In Local Legislation.

The trend of the eighth century was not only towards private confession to priests, but towards confession by each person to his own proper priest. Thus *St. Egbert,* Bishop of York, England, from 732-736, commanded not only all clerics in monasteries but even lay people to go to their own proper priests at Christmas time for confession. This he claimed had been the custom since the time of Pope Vitalian 570.[68] It was most likely this movement towards the unity of confessor that has been noticed also in the different religious rules that caused the *Great Synod of Rome,* held on November 15, 826 by Pope Eugenius II, to demand that the Abbots of all monasteries should become priests. This was done primarily that he might hear the confessions of his subjects and thus keep them from sin.[69]

The prescription of the unity of confessor had already been made for the secular clergy, when its violation caused the *Provincial Council of Paris, June* 6, 829 attended by the bishops of Rheims, Sens, Tours and Rouen to decree that the already established practice of clerics or priests confessing to monastic priests and declining the ministry of their own bishops and priests canons was wrong. Monks were only to hear the confessions of members of their own order living in the same monastery.[70]

In England there was demanded of the diocesan clergy by the Council of London in the year of 1200, at least semi-annual confession, i. e., once in Advent and again in Lent, to priests appointed for that purpose in the individual deaneries.[71] And so gradually the monastic practice and rule of confessing to defi-

68 *Egberti Dialogus, Interrogatio* XVI; Mansi, XII, 482; Haddan and Stubbs, *op. cit.,* III, 413; MPL LXXXIX, 442.

69 *Synodus Romana* an. 820, ch. XXVI; Mansi XIV, 1007; Hefele, *Conciliengeschicte,* IV, p. 49.

70 *Concilium Parisiense* VI; ch. XLVI; Mansi XIV, 565; Harduin, IV, 1323; Hefele, *op. cit.,* IV, 65.

71 *Concilium Londoniense,* ch. VI; Mansi, XXII, 715.

nite and appointed priests was prescribed for the secular clergy. On the other hand the Synod of Salzburg, 1274, prohibited religious from confessing outside of their order[72] and monks and canons were refused by the Synod of Lambert in the year of 1330 permission to confess to one another.[73]

Article III.

Papal Enactments.

1. Before Clement VIII.

Privileges Granted to Religious.

The monastic practice had so influenced the times that during the Middle Ages the unity of confessor was established for the whole world. As a result Urban II (1088-1099) decreed that it was not lawful for a priest to receive a penitent committed to the charge of another without the permission of the latter unless the penitent was in ignorance of the one to whom he first confessed.[74] The Fourth Lateran Council went further by making annual confession to their own proper priest, a matter of obligation upon all the faithful, who had attained the use of reason.[75] This strictness of discipline was mitigated for the faithful by the privilege given to the Mendicant Friars and the Dominicans to hear the confessions of all the faithful who came to them.[76] But even before these privileges were

72 Hefele, op. cit., VI, p. 170.

73 Hefele, ibid. p. 632.

74 c. 3, D, VI, *de poenit;* cf. Vermeersch, *Per.*, V, p. (1); Choupin, *Recents Decrets du Saint Siege*, p. 30; and *L'Etat Religieux*, p. 200.

75 c. 10, X, *de poenitentiis et remissionibus*, V, 38; Mansi XXII, 1007; Denzinger, *Enchiridion Symbolorum*, n. 437; Wernz, *Jus Decretalium*, III, n. 738; Vermeersch, *op. cit.*, p. (2); Choupin, *Nature etc. l'Etat Religieux*, p. 201; cf. Azpilcueta, *Enchiridion sive Manuale Confessariorum et Poenitentium*, cap., XXI, p. 558.

76 Boniface VIII (1294-1303), c. 2, *de sepulturis*, III, 7, *in Clem;* Van Espen, *Jus Ecclesiasticum Universum*, Pars II, tit. VI, ch. 5, n. 10 (ed. 1732) p. 95—Quotes the text of the privilege given by Gregory IX to English Bishops, in 1227; cf. *Il Monitore Ecc.*, (March, 1925) series IV, vol. VII, p. 82.

given for the use of the faithful, Gregory IX (1227-1234) exempted from the law of confessing to their own proper priest both bishops and religious superiors including minor exempt prelates, granting to them the right to choose, without permission of their superiors, a discreet confessor.[77] This was the first relaxation, with papal sanction, of the strict confessional discipline for religious. For the other regular male religious the rigor of the previous requirements was maintained as the general rule at all times.[78] The prescription, that the superiors should hear the confessions of their subjects was contained even in some rules having papal approval.[79] Despite the fact, that these prelates had themselves received so great a concession of freedom in confessional matters, they were unwilling to mitigate in the least the very strict practice of making their subjects confess to them even if unwilling. This abuse was so pronounced that Gregory IX on August 21, 1231 issued a decree to all the prelates of the world commanding that this practice be stopped.[80] Benedict XI (1336-1346), to settle disputes which had arisen, explained the decree of Boniface VIII to the effect that those religious who by their constitutions had to confess to their superiors could not be absolved in virtue of the faculties of the Mendicant Orders,[81] unless their superiors had given them permission to confess to such confessors. Those confessions made without this permission were invalid.[82]

Some few privileges were granted to individual orders of choosing on two occasions, i. e., once during life and at the time of death, a confessor, who thereby received faculties to absolve from censures. As a rule these confessors were of the same order and chosen only with permission of the superior.

---

77 c. 16, X, *de poenitentiis,* V, 38.

78 *Synod of Salzburg* 1274; cf. Hefele, op. cit., VI, 170; *Synod of Lambert,* ibid., p. 632.

79 *Declaration of the Rule, of the Brothers of the Order of SS. Trinity to Redeem Captives,* by Clement IV, Const. *In Ordine,* Dec. 7, 1267; BRT III, n. 26, p. 791, ch. 7.

80 c. 16, *de excessibus praelatorum,* V, 31; cf. Scherer, *Handbuch des Kirchenrechts,* II, p. 767.

81 Const. *Inter Cunctas,* c. 1, *de privilegiis,* V, 7, *in Extravag. com.;* Scherer, ibid.

82 Boudinhon, *Canoniste Contemporain,* vol. 36, p. 699, 701.

Such were the concessions given by Eugene IV to the Brothers of the Blessed Virgin of Mt. Carmel, February 16, 1432[83] and to the Hermits of St. Peter of Pisa, February 22, 1437;[84] by Sixtus IV to the Dominicans and the Friars Minor, July 26, 1479;[85] by Julius II, April 2, 1512 to Regular Canons of the Congregation of San Salvador, of the Order of St. Augustine;[86] and by Leo X to the Camaldolese monks of St. Michael de Murano, July 4, 1513.[87] The restriction of confessing to priests of the same order was removed in some other privileges, as for instance in that granted to the Brothers of St. Francis de Paula by Sixtus IV, on May 27, 1474.[88] They had the privilege of choosing any confessor whether regular or secular, whose faculties of absolution thereby extended to all cases of excommunication, interdict and suspension, even if reserved to the archbishop by law or by himself. Such confessors could absolve as often as necessary.

The concession of making confession to any secular or regular priest was made by many pontiffs to various societies engaged in works of charity.[89] Sixtus IV gave to Dominican Prelates, August 2, 1480 the right to go to any confessor when on a journey and extended this privilege to their subjects on that condition that they have the permission of their superiors to use it.[90] All these privileges were exceptions to the general law of the unity of confessor and did in no way mitigate the general discipline. In fact, the reverse is very much in evidence,

---

83 Const. *Romani Pontificis,* BRT V, n. III, p. 5.

84 Const. *Provenit,* BRT op. cit., n. 15, p. 30.

85 Const. *Sacri Praedicatorum,* BRT loc. cit., n. 25, p. 280, 283; Roderici, *Resolutiones Quaestionum Regularium,* Res. XXXII, p. 257.

86 Const. *Inter caeteros;* BRT V, n. 36, p. 522, § 30.

87 Const. *Etsi a Summo;* BRT, V, n. 3, p. 553, § 47.

88 Const. *Sedes apostolica;* BRT V, p. 214.

89 By Innocent VIII, to the Confraternity under the Invocation of St. John Baptist, Beheaded; cf. Const. *Inter desiderabilia,* Aug. 23, 1490; BRT, op. cit.; By Leo X, to those taking care of the poor and sick of the Hospital of the Blessed Virgin in Rome; cf. Const. *Salvatoris Nostri;* July 19, 1515, BRT, op. cit., V, n. 16, p. 643, § 14; By Paul III to the Archconfraternity of the Blessed Virgin Mary of the Visitation, for the care of orphans; Const. *Altitudo Divinae Providentiae,* Feb. 7, 1541; cf. BRT op. cit., VI, n. 34, p. 309.

90 Const. *Supplicari, Bullaria Fratrum Praedicatorum, III,* n. 9, p. 592; cf. Vermeersch, *De Religiosis* II, n. 222, p. 469.

for many were forbidden to confess outside of their order as was first prohibited to the Brothers of St. Francis de Paula by Julius II on July 28, 1506.[91] This was reaffirmed for the Jesuits by Paul III on September 18, 1549.[92] In like manner Pius V on July 21, 1571 refused the Dominicans the privilege of choosing a confessor according to the bull *Cruciatae* and reserved the absolution of their subjects to the prelates of the order.[93] And even during the seventeenth century there is found the same prohibition for the Canons Regular of the Congregation of The Holy Cross in Portugal laid down by Urban VII September 10, 1625[94] and extended by this Pontiff to the Benedictine Monks of Portugal on May 30, 1629.[95]

2. From Clement VIII to the Decree "Quemadmodum."

A. *Exclusion of Superiors as Community Confessors.*

The Jesuits were obliged from time to time to make a manifestation of conscience to their superiors. According to St. Ignatius this could be done either in confession or outside of it.[96] Since the Jesuit General Claudius Aquaviva had prohibited all superiors to use confessional knowledge for external direction, the question arose as to whether the manifestation of conscience was permissible in sacramental confession. The Spanish Jesuits submitted this question to the Inquisition. It was transmitted to Sixtus V in 1590. This difficulty afforded the occasion for the second paragraph of Clement VIII's decree *Sanctissimus Dominus*.[97] Moreover, another restriction had been placed upon the consciences of the Regulars by the two prevalent reservation of cases. The Carthusian Abbots had even

91 Const. *Virtute conspicuos;* BRT V, n. 13, § 22, p. 439.

92 Const. *Licet debitum;* BRT VI, n. 65, § 10, p. 395.

93 Const. *Romani pontificis;* BRT VII, n. 198, § 2, p. 295; Vermeersch, *Per.* V, p. (2).

94 Const. *Romani pontificis;* BRT XIII, n. 59, p. 396.

95 Const. *Romanus Pontifex;* BRT XV, n. 334, p. 63; Choupin, *L'Etat Religieux*, p. 202; *Razon y Fe*, 37 (1913), 375, §§ 15, 16.

96 Honore, *Le Secret de la Confession*, p. 86; Kurtscheid, *Das Beichtsiegel*, p. 118.

97 Kurtscheid, *loc. cit.*

gone so far as to reserve all grave sins of their subjects,[98] with the result that the liberty of confession was greatly restricted. It was to exterminate such abuses that Clement introduced a change in discipline in his famous decree *Sanctissimus Dominus* of May 26, 1593.[99]

Clement, reducing the possible reservations to nine in number, forbade superiors to hear the confessions of their subjects unless it was a question of a reserved sin or when the subject freely and spontaneously approached him for that purpose.[100]

The superiors were to appoint in the individual houses two or more confessors according to the greater or lesser number of subjects. These confessors, who were to be learned, prudent and charitable, had the power to absolve from non-reserved cases. Moreover, the faculty to absolve from reserved cases was to be granted to such confessors, whenever a case should occur, in which the confessor, who was to be the first to judge in such matters, thought that this faculty should be granted to him.[101] The superiors were to retain the power of defining certain grave penalties to be imposed by the confessors for more grave sins even if not reserved.[102] Upon refusal by the superior of a requested faculty to absolve from any reserved case the confessor could absolve without any further request.[103]

But, as LEHMKUHL[104] states, it does not follow from this that the superior could never legitimately refuse the faculty of absolving from reserved cases or that the confessor, if the superior had denied the faculty, could always safely absolve. For if the relapse should become the external occasion of sinning or cause some other damage, especially to the community, there would be the obligation for the penitent of approaching the superior. Therefore in such circumstances, the confessor could not absolve without having obtained the faculty.

---

98 Benedict XIV, *De Synodo Dioecesana*, lib. V, c. V, n. 2.
99 Decree, *Sanctissimus*, intro.; FJC, n. 177.
100 ibid., § 1, 2.
101 ibid., § 3.
102 ibid., § 5.
103 ibid., § 7.
104 *Theol. Mor.* (1910), II, n. 540.

This decree had full force for all regulars despite all contrary constitutions, immemorable customs, rules, chapters, privileges and concessions.[105] This was the most important step towards liberty of conscience that the penitential discipline for regulars has manifested up till this time.

This decree was followed shortly afterwards by another "*Cum ad regularem,*" of March 19, 1603, containing a prescription for the novices of a general confession on entrance,[106] and a bi-monthly confession thereafter.[107] The duty of hearing these confessions was committed to the novice master alone. All superiors, however, even if only local, could hear these confessions twice a year or appoint a priest for that purpose.[108] These prescriptions were soon incorporated in the constitutions of different orders.[109] Urban VIII gave to regular confessors, once refused by their superiors, the faculty of absolving in a special case from reservations.[110] Finally the Congregation of Bishops and Regulars on August 16, 17, 1866 commanded all superiors of small communities to appoint a resident confessor from the religious of their own order with the faculty of absolving from cases and censures reserved in the order.[111]

B. *Privileges Granted to Individual Institutes.*

1. The Choice of a Confessor.

Although Clement VIII excluded superiors from the office of confessor of their own religious, he left the choice of the con-

---

105 Decree, *Sanctissimus,* § 7; FJC, ibid.

106 Clement VIII, Decree, *Cum ad regularem;* BRT, V, n. II, § 7, pp. 412-415; cf. Vermeersch, *De Religiosis,* II, n. 43, p. 137; confirmed by Urban VIII, Oct. 26, 1624, BRT, XIII, p. 215.

107 Clement VIII, ibid., § 9.

108 ibid., § 10; cf. *Collectanea Sacrae Congregationis de Propaganda Fide* (ed. 1907), n. 2064, note 1.

109 *Constitutiones Fratrum Sancti Ordinis Praedicatorum, Distinctio* I, *De Novitiis,* ch. IV, n. 4; cf. Holsten, *Codex Regularum,* IV, p. 39; cf. *Constitutiones* (editio 1886, Paris), n. 236; for Jesuits, cf. Leo XII, Const. *Plura inter,* July 11, 1826; *cf. Bullarii Romani Continuatio,* VIII, n. 155, n. 438.

110 Vermeersch, *Periodica,* V, p. (3); Boudinhon, *Canoniste Contemporain,* 36, p. 704.

111 Vermeersch, *De Religiosis* II, n. 228, p. 485; Boudinhon, *loc. cit.*

fessors of the community entirely in their hands. Since the decree *Sanctissimus* sufficiently provided for the liberty of conscience of religious, this same Pontiff in virtue of his constitution *Romani Pontificis* of November 23, 1599[112] denied the use of the privilege of the bull *Cruciatae* and other particular indults to all members of religious orders and other institutes. His intention was that in these matters of confessional administration the religious should be subject to the disposition of their prelates.[113] This became the general rule of ecclesiastical discipline. Exceptions, however, were made by different Pontiffs for certain reasons. Thus Benedict XIV on March 30, 1742, revoked a particular statute laid down in the general chapters of the Capuchins which forbade confession outside of their own order. This was causing much hardship for those who were legitimately engaged outside of their convent with the permission of their superiors. These could be validly and licitly absolved only by a confessor of the same order approved by their superior.[114] Benedict granted to these Capuchins who were outside of their convent with the permission of their superior the right to confess, freely and lawfully in the absence of a priest of their own order, to any secular priest approved by the local ordinary or to any regular priest approved by his proper superior. These confessors thereby received the faculty to absolve from cases and censures reserved in the order. In the latter case they were to impose the penance and the obligation of going to their regular superior and again asking absolution.[115] The same permission was given July 4, 1862, by the Sacred Congregation of Bishops and Regulars after an audience with Pius IX, to the Regulars of the Order of the Sacred Heart of Mary belonging to the suppressed apostolic college of the Blessed Virgin Mary, in the Diocese of Guadalajara.[116] This

112 BRT X, p. 550, §§ 2, 3.

113 The Jesuits were not permitted to confess to any priest who had not received faculties from their superiors. cf. Leo XII, Const. *Plura inter,* § 2; cf. *Bullarii Romani Continuatio,* VIII, n. 155, p. 438.

114 Const. *Quod communi;* § 1; BRT, I, n. 49, p. 175.

115 ibid. § 2.

116 Bizzarri, *Collectanea in Usum Sacrae Congregationis Episcoporum et Regularium,* p. 155.

decree differed from the concession to the Capuchins in that both regular and secular confessors had to be approved by the local ordinary. This privilege extended even to those ejected religious of the same institute, who were living in community, provided that they did not have four confessors of their own order among them.

2. Jubilee Confessors.

Another evidence of the tendency of the Church towards leniency is manifested in the right of the Jubilee Confessor granted to religious. It was Boniface VIII, who first confirmed the ancient Jewish practice of the jubilee, required an interval of one hundred years between jubilees and granted certain indulgences.[117] This was reduced to fifty years by Clement V, January 7, 1343,[118] because of the fact that the span of human life was so short as to make it impossible for the faithful to hope to see a jubilee in their generation.[119] Paul II, 1390, established the interval as twenty-five years, which is retained today.[120] Jubilees are divided into ordinary and extraordinary since the year of 1475. An ordinary jubilee is one held for a year in Rome and then extended to the whole world and an extraordinary jubilee is granted by the Pope to Rome and the whole world at the same time on certain major solemnities or peculiar necessities of the Church.[121]

It remained, however, for Clement V to first concede to regulars the right of a choice of confessor so that they might obtain the jubilee indulgence. These confessors, once approved by the local ordinary, when chosen by the regular penitents received faculties to absolve from all sins, censures and punishments no matter how they were inflicted or reserved and even those contained in the bull *Coena Domini*. This faculty could

117 c. l. V, *de poenitentiis*, 9, *in Extravag. com.*; cf. *Razon y Fe* (1904), 8, p. 512.
118 c. 2, V, *de poenitentiis*, 9, *in Extravag. com.*
119 Thurston, Art. Jubiloo, *Cath. Encyclo.*, VIII, p. 553.
120 Bull, *Ineffabilis providentia;* BRT, V, p. 200 ff.
121 Noldin, *De Sacramentis*, n. 330, p. 382; McCarthy, *Am. Ecc. Rev.* (1924), LXX, p. 564 ff.

be exercised for religious only on one occasion during the jubilee.[122] This received confirmation from Benedict XIV by its verbal incorporation November 11, 1740, into his letter on the jubilee *Laetiora apostolicae servitutis.*[123] Benedict XIV granted greater leniency in his constitution, *Convocatis* of Dec. 5, 1749, by giving to the penitentiaries and confessors appointed in Rome for the jubilee power to absolve, in the internal forum only, any regulars of any order, congregation or institute confessing to them even under prohibition of their superiors or constitutions to confess outside the order. The absolution had to be given by those appointed and not through others. Their faculties extended to all occult excommunications and censures even if reserved to the Holy See in any way, including those contained in the bull *Coena Domini* and also from all grave and heinous sins even reserved to the Holy See. All the requirements of the law in regard to enjoining penances were to be fulfilled.[124] For the convenience of regular communities of all orders, congregations and institutes the number of confessors for the jubilee was to be increased and the same faculties mentioned above given to them.[125] This was extended to the whole world by his encyclical letter *Benedictus Deus,* of December 26, 1750.[126]

The only reservations that remained in force during the jubilee were public censures. But Leo XII removed even this restriction in 1824.[127] It is to be noted that the rules for jubilees, whether ordinary or extraordinary, were given by Benedict XIV and these must be observed even today in every respect, unless a special pronouncement with contrary prescriptions emanates from the Holy See.[128]

It is evident from the exclusion of the superior as the

---

122 Const. *Unigenitus Dei,* May 14, 1655; BRT XVI, n. 2, p. 4.

123 *Bullarii Romani Continuatio,* I, n. 1, § 4, p. 2.

124 Const. *Convocatis; Bullarii Romani Continuatio,* III, pt. 1, n. 20, 25, p. 154 ff; cf. FJC, n. 402.

125 ibid., n. I.

126 FJC, n. 409.

127 Const. *Annum auspicatissimum,* Oct. 21, 1824; *Bullarii Continuatio,* VIII, n. 67, p. 253.

128 *Decreta Authentica Sacrae Congregationis Rituum,* n. 353, March 15, 1852; cf. Tanquerey, *Theol. Mor.* I, 382.

regular confessor of his own subjects, and the limitation of the number of reservations within the order together with the permission to confess outside of the order granted to some institutes and the jubilee privileges, that the constant tendency of the Church was towards leniency.

3. From the Decree "Quaemadmodum to the Code of Canon Law.

A. *Special legislation for religious men of simple vows.*

Congregations of priests of simple vows were ruled by the same law as regulars but other male religious of simple vows were not subject to the discipline of the unity of confessors.[129] Therefore male lay religious, subject to the Bishop, could validly confess to any confessor, approved for the faithful by the Bishop. It was the mind of the Holy See that male lay religious subject to exempt religious superiors should be given the same facilities by the appointment of confessors.[130] The Council of Trent had made regulations for the ordinary and extraordinary confessor of female religious[131] and Benedict XIV in his famous constitution, *Pastoralis Curae*[132] did much to lighten the hardships of confession for female religious but it was not until the decree *Quemadmodum* of Leo XIII edited December 17, 1890, by the Congregation of Bishops and Regulars that male lay religious became the subjects of special legislation in regard to confessional discipline.

Legislation of this character is prompted by abuses. Religious superiors previous to this decree forced their subjects to manifest their consciences to them.[133]

As a result the decree strictly prohibited any manifesta-

129 S. C. EE et RR, Dec. 11, 1903; Vermeersch, *Per.*, I, n. 50, p. 131; Boudinhon, *CC*, 36, p. 704, 705.

130 Vermeersch, *Per.*, V, p. (3); Choupin, *L'Etat Religieux*, p. 203.

131 *Sess. XXV, De Regularibus*, c. 10; Ehses, *Concilium Tridentinum*, t. 9, 1082.

132 FJC. n. 388.

133 S. C. EE et RR., Decree, *Quemadmodum*, Dec. 17, 1890, Intro.; Col. S. C. P. F. (ed. 1907) n. 1745; Vermeersch, *De Rel.* II, n. 230, p. 488.

tion of conscience. Upon violation of this prescription superiors were to be denounced by their subjects to the major superior. If the latter was guilty the denunciation was to be made to the Congregation of Bishops and Regulars. Subjects, on the other hand, for the sake of counsel, could of their own free will manifest their consciences to their superiors.[134] Some superiors had even prohibited their subjects from receiving Holy Communion. To remove this abuse the Decree Quemadmodum stated that the granting of permission or the prohibition to go to Communion belonged to the confessor unless since his last confession the subject had given scandal to the community. All superiors violating these mandates would incur "ipso facto" apostolic punishments.[135] This decree only affected institutes which were purely lay in character and not those which had as members many priests.[136]

B. *Superiors prohibited to hear confessions of their subjects.* There had grown up in the City of Rome itself the custom in some religious communities, seminaries and colleges of the superiors hearing the confessions of their subjects living with them in the same house. From this many inconveniences and numerous grave abuses could arise for on the one hand the liberty of the students was restricted and the integrity of confession endangered while, on the other hand, the superiors were less free in the government of the community and exposed to suspicion of using the knowledge received in confession or of being better disposed towards the students who confessed to them.

To avoid these evils the Congregation of the Holy Office by the express command of Leo XIII strictly forbade such superiors, whether major or minor, to hear the confessions of their students, living in the same house with them, except in a rare case of necessity, in which they felt burdened in conscience to

---

134 ibid. § 1.
135 ibid. §§ 5, 8.
136 Decl. S. C. EE et RR Apr. 5, 1891, ad 2; cf. Vermeersch, *op. cit.*, n. 231, p. 492.

do so.[137] This, however, did not derogate anything contained in the apostolic constitutions and especially the constitution, *Cum ad Regularem,* published March 19, 1603, by Clement VIII, for novices of religious orders;[138] nor did it change the legislation for religious congregations of simple and perpetual vows living in community and approved by the Church.[139]

C. *Confession Outside of the Monastery.*

Exempt regulars, as was seen above, when living in their monastery or house could only address themselves to those confessors appointed for that office by the regular prelate. In fact a certain number of religious received these powers to hear the confessions of the community. But they could be absolved from reserved cases only by the superior or his delegate having the required faculties. Even when on a voyage or in a case of urgency, if the confessor companion, whom he addressed, did not have the faculty to absolve from reserved cases the obligation remained on the penitent of presenting himself to the superior to accuse himself of his fault or to a confessor having the required powers to obtain absolution directly. The Congregation of Bishops and Regulars stated that Lazarists could not without the permission of their superiors go to an approved priest not of their own institute when there was one of their own congregation easily accessible.[140] Some secular and regular priests began to ask Rome for the faculty to absolve from the cases reserved in the religious institutes. The Sacred Penitentiary, when it judged opportune, accorded on certain conditions the "*pagella,*" that is an indult with special faculties.[141]

But finally in 1902 on May 14 the Sacred Penitentiary in reply to the questions of a secular priest in regard to such confessions stated:

I. If the superiors and other confessors had been away

137 *S. R. U. Inquisitionis* (*S. Officii*) July 5, 1899; cf. Vermeersch, *De Religiosis,* II, n. 232, p. 496; Col. S. C. P. F. n. 2057; Bucceroni, *Casus Conscientiae,* II, p. 79.

138 *S. U. R., Inquisitionis,* Aug. 23, 1899; Vermeersch. *op. cit.,* p. 497.

139 *S. U. R. Inquisitionis,* Dec. 20, 1899; Vermeersch, *op. cit.,* p. 498.

140 S. C. EE et RR, Sept. 28, 1881; Boudinhon. *CC* 36, p. 706.

141 Choupin, *L'Etat Religieux,* p. 204.

from the religious house at least one day and it was hard for the religious to be without absolution any longer he could be validly and licitly absolved by any suitable extraneous priest approved for confessions, whom he approached.[142]

II. Priests who had received the "*pagella*" or faculties granted by the Penitentiary to absolve religious of any order, who had the permission of their superiors to confess, could absolve from all cases no matter how they were reserved in the order.

III. Regular confessors of the same order, if approved to hear the confessions of religious of the order, could also absolve from these cases if they had the same faculty.

IV. Superiors when granting permission for their subjects to confess to such confessors could not impose the restriction "provided you observe the customs of the order on reservations," for by the very permission the confessor could absolve in virtue of his faculties received from the Sacred Penitentiary, independently of the will of the superior.

V. This could not be extended to the case where a religious on a journey went without the express faculty of his superior to an extraneous confessor unless the latter had special faculties from the Holy See to absolve from such cases reserved in the order.[143]

Some further privileges were granted for particular conditions and circumstances. For example, priests going to the Chinese missions could hear the confessions of all accompanying them, including regulars, during the course of the entire journey. They were required to have the approbation of their superior, if regulars, or the proper ordinary of the diocese from which they came, to which they were going or through which they were passing.[144]

---

142 *Sacrae Penitentiariae, Resp.* May 14, 1902, ad. 1; cf. Col. S. C. P. F. (ed. 1907), n. 2141; cf. Vermeersch, *De Rel.* II, n. 234, p. 499; Boudinhon, *La Confession Des Religieux, CC.* (1913) vol. 36, p. 702 ff; Choupin, *op. cit.*, p. 204.

143 *S. Penit.*, ibid. n. 2-5: cf. Ferreres, *Razon y Fe* (1903), vol. 7, p. 117, ff; (1913), vol 37, p. 376.

144 *S. C. Propagandae Fidei; Pluries petitum,* Feb. 4, 1907; Vermeersch, *De Religiosis* II, n. 278 (ter), p. 597.

Another concession was made in 1911 when Pius X gave to Cardinals the faculty of hearing confessions of religious of both sexes all over the world and of absolving from all sins and censures except those censures reserved in a most special way to the Holy See or those inflicted for the revelation of the secrets of the Holy Office.[145]

D. *Choice of a Confessor.*

Despite all these concessions the discipline for regulars did not give entire liberty for the choice of confessors. Assuredly this system had its advantages but was also the source of many grave inconveniences. All these restrictions in regard to the choice of the confessor could often be fatal for souls in a matter where full liberty of confessing is, God aiding, the surest guarantee of the good dispositions of penitent. To remove these difficulties the Holy See modified and ameliorated the discipline in force up till that time by the communication of Pius X of the 8th of February, 913.[146] This was not published in the official *Acta Apostolicae Sedis* but given to each confessor of Rome individually. By virtue of this, all confessors approved by the Ordinary of Rome had the faculty to absolve religious of all orders approaching him even without the permission of the superior and moreover there was no necessity of recourse. On the 5th of August of the same year Pius extended this faculty through the Sacred Congregation of Religious to all the confessors of the world approved by their local Ordinaries.[147] This decree accomplished a complete change in the law for regulars. Although the constitutions of religious institutes concerning the regular confessors and confession at definite times still had full force, nevertheless this decree suppressed the ancient limitations and restrictions and gave all members of all religious orders, congregations and institutes full freedom to choose their

---

145 *Ex audientia* SSmi D. N. Pii PP. X; *Gratia* Dec. 20, 1911; cf. Vermeersch, *Per.* VII, n. 737, § 1, p. 251.

146 Vermeersch, *Per.* VII, n. 702, p. 175; Boudinhon, CC, 36, p. 698; Lehmkuhl, *Theol. Mor.*, II, p. 299; Choupin, *op. cit.*, p. 212.

147 *Acta Apostolicae Sedis* (1913), V, p. 431.

confessors at other times. The authority of the confessor lay solely in the fact that the penitent came to him.[148] As a result regulars could validly and licitly confess to all their confreres or any secular or regular having episcopal approbation. The permission of the superior required by the famous constitution, *Inter Cunctas* of Benedict XI on the Mendicant privileges was no longer necessary.[149] Although no censures were suppressed by this decree the reservation of sins and censures in the order seemed to have lost all force in practice. The power of absolution held only for the internal forum. The decree was silent about cases reserved to the Pope and it was deduced that the confessor could absolve religious from those, from which he could absolve the faithful. If, however, the confessor received his jurisdiction from a regular superior he could absolve also from episcopal reserved cases. This held even if he was not officially constituted as the confessor of his confreres in the order.[150] This decree concerned the religious exclusively and it could be applied to all religious without exception.[151] Novices also had this privilege of choice of confessor,[152] and confessors of the Oriental rite could hear confessions of religious of the Latin rite and vice-versa.[153]

This decree marks the climax of pre-code legislation on the confessor of regulars and has been practically incorporated into the Code in the canons which will be treated in the subsequent chapters.

148 Boudinhon, *loc. cit.*
149 c. I, *de privilegiis*, V, 7, *in Extravag. com.*
150 Vermeersch, *Per.* VII, p. 174.
151 Choupin, *op. cit.*, p. 218.
152 S. C. De Rel. May 3, 1914, ad. 2; A A S, VI, 232; Vermeersch, *Per.* VIII, n. 15, p. 39.
153 S. C. de Rel. ibid. ad 1.

CHAPTER II.

CONFESSORS OF CLERICAL INSTITUTES.

Article I.

Appointed Confessors.

Although in most rules of religious orders there was the prescription that there should be besides the Superior other priests appointed to whom the religious could confess, nevertheless it was not until the decree *Sanctissimus* of Clement the VIII that the appointment of other confessors became an obligation upon all regular superiors. Clement demanded that the number of appointed confessors should be two or more proportionate to the number of subjects. The Sacred Congregation of Bishops and Regulars August 16-17, 1866, demanded that even in small communities superiors should appoint one confessor from the same order having the faculty of absolving from cases and censures reserved within the order.

Exempt clerical congregations followed the same rules as the religious orders and their superiors appointed the confessors and delegated jurisdiction to hear the confessions of their subjects while non-exempt congregations were subject to the Bishop in these matters.

The Code makes no distinction and requires that confessors be appointed in the same way for all clerical institutes.

CANON 518.

§ 1. In singulis religionis clericalis domibus deputentur plures pro sodalium numero confessarii legitime approbati, cum potestate, si agatur de religione exempta, absolvendi etiam a casibus in religione reservatis.

In the houses of every clerical institute there shall be deputed, in proportion to the number of subjects, several legitimately approved confessors with power, if it be a question of an exempt Institute, to absolve from the cases reserved in the Institute.

Definition of terms.

I. *An Institute*—every society, approved by legitimate ecclesiastical authority, the members of which tend to evangelical perfection, according to the laws proper to their society, by the profession of public vows, whether perpetual or temporary, the latter renewable after the lapse of a fixed time.[1]

II. *A Clerical Institute*—every institute, the majority of whose members receive the order of priesthood; otherwise it is a lay institute.[2]

This canon, 518, refers to all clerical institutes including even non-exempt congregations.[3]

THE APPOINTMENT OF CONFESSORS.

These confessors must be appointed in every house of clerical institutes.[4]

Appointment means the designation of the confessor which is generally done after examination and verification of fitness[5] and the grant of faculties.

The number of confessors to be appointed is not definitely determined by the Code. Following the rule of Clement VIII[6] the Code demands a number proportionate to the number of the members in the community. There should be at least two appointed, for the canon uses the word *plures* and according to the rule of law "*Pluralis locutio, duorum numero est con-*

1 Can. 488. I (All translations of canons referring to religious are taken from the authorized english translation, entitled, *Canonical Legislation Concerning Religious*, Rome, 1924.)

2 Can. 488, 4°.

3 Genicot, *Institutiones Theologiae Moralis* (ed. 10, 1922), n. 337, IV.

4 Can. 488, 5°.

5 Augustine, *A Commentary on Canon Law*, III, p. 152.

6 Decree, *Sanctissimus*, May 26, 1593; FJC n. 177 § 3.

tenta."[7] Therefore, superiors would not satisfy their obligation by only appointing one confessor in the individual clerical houses. The assignment of a certain number of religious to each confessor, as the exclusive confessor of that group, seems to be against the spirit of the law.[8] It breaks down the liberty of conscience which the Code is trying so hard to safeguard. The number of those members upon which this computation is to be based includes all the professed, novices, and other persons dwelling day and night in the religious house by reason of service, education, hospitality or health.[9] Both the exempt religious superior[10] for his own institute and the local Ordinary for non-exempt institutes[11] can delegate, as confessors of the individual houses, priests of the secular clergy or another institute. But the implicit meaning of the canon is that these confessors should be appointed from the same house and institute, whether exempt or non-exempt, for they are to reside habitually in the same house.[12] It would be well for the competent superiors to delegate this power also to retreat masters.

1. *In Exempt Clerical Institutes.*

The exempt superior cannot reserve to himself the office of hearing the confessions of his subjects within the cloister, but is bound to appoint other confessors.[13]

The canon states that the priests must be "*legitime approbati.*" Legitimate approbation is the grant of jurisdiction to hear confessions validly and licitly. The faculty to hear confessions belongs to the internal forum, but the granting of that faculty is an act of public jurisdiction in the external forum, the result of jurisdiction proper.[14] Therefore, approval can be given and appointment made by one who enjoys jurisdiction.

---

7 R. J. in VI°, Reg. XL; Decree, *Sanctissimus,* loc. cit.; cf. Blat, II pars II, n. 579.
8 cf. Augustine, III, p. 153.
9 Can. 514, § 1; cf. Augustine, *loc. cit.*
10 Can. 875, § 1.
11 Can. 874, § 1.
12 Decree of S. C. EE et RR, Aug. 17, 1866; Vermeersch, *De Rel.* II, n. 228, p. 485.
13 Can. 518 § 2; 891; Fanfani, *loc. cit.*
14 Augustine *op. cit.,* III, p. 153.

The principles governing the granting of this approbation are contained in the following canon.

CANON 875.

§ 1. In religione clericali exempta ad recipiendas confessiones professorum, novitiorum aliorumve de quibus in Can. 514, § 1, jurisdictionem delegatam confert quo que proprius eorundem Superior, ad normam constitutionum; cui fas est eam concedere etiam sacerdotibus e clero saeculari aut alius religionis.

Power of Delegating Jurisdiction for Exempt Religious.

Superiors who can delegate this jurisdiction, are major superiors, possessing jurisdiction in the external forum, i. e., the Superior General or Provincial of an exempt order and the Abbot of each independent monastery.[15] But "The Abbot Primate and Abbots Presidents," as AUGUSTINE[16] rightly states, "are not empowered to give faculties either for the order or respective congregation; neither can the cloistral priors or guardians except by sub-delegation, grant such faculties." On the other hand, appealing to the constitution, "*Romani Pontificis*" of Pius V[17] Augustine claims that, according to the better opinion held by the majority, both conventual priors and guardians, have this power of granting jurisdiction, since this constitution "expressly mentions the conventual priors as endowed with the same faculties as the Ordinaries with regard to absolution and dispensation."[18] This cannot be admitted, since a reading of the constitution reveals no express mention of the conventual prior as having such faculties. Moreover, the canon now under consideration states explicitly that the proper superior "*ad normam constitutionum*" has this power and therefore the con-

15 Can. 488, 8°; cf. Blat, *op. cit.*, III, *pars* I, n. 198; Augustine, *A Commentary on Canon Law,* III, p. 154.

16 *op. cit.*, p. 154, note 5.

17 Aug. 6, 1571; FJC n. 139; Augustine does not quote the place where this constitution can be found nor its date, but the one of Aug. 6, 1571, is the only one of many, which Pius V introduces with these same words, that could possibly refer to the point in question.

18 Augustine, *loc. cit.*

stitutions of each institute must be consulted to determine just what superiors have ordinary jurisdiction over their subjects and can in virtue of this power delegate confessional jurisdiction. The prescriptions of these constitutions must be followed in this matter.[19]

The Constitutions of the Friars Minor of the year 1922[20] grant this power of delegating faculties, for confessions of the religious of the order, to the Minister General and the Provincial but without any mention of the guardians.

The constitutions can, moreover, take away from superiors the power of delegating jurisdiction to hear the confessions of their subjects, which common law has given them. This is deduced from Canons 199 § 1, 873 § 2, and 875 § 1, which leave the determination of the power to delegate entirely to the constitutions. Thus local superiors of the Friars Minor cannot delegate to other Friars the faculty to hear the confessions of their subjects, although they certainly have that power by common law. But if a restriction of this power is intended the constitutions should explicitly say so.[21]

The phrase of Canon 875 § 1 "*jurisdictionem delegatam confert quoque proprius eorundem superior*" implies because of the word "*quoque*" that the persons mentioned in Canon 875 § 1 and 514 § 1, can confess to confessors approved by the Ordinary of the place as well as those approved by the religious superior.[22]

Method of Delegating Such Jurisdiction.

The superior can delegate directly by personally appointing the confessor to hear confessions of his subjects. Indirect delegation on the other hand would suffice, e. g., if a superior gave a religious subject to him the faculty to choose a confessor for himself during a journey. The chosen priest, even if of another institute, or the secular clergy, and even if he be not approved

19 cf. Fanfani, *op. cit.*, n. 127; Blat, *op. cit.*, n. 198.
20 *Constitutiones Generales Ordinis Fratrum Minorum*, n. 346.
21 CpR, (1923) IV, p. 341; (1926) VII, p. 40.
22 Cf. Blat, III, *pars* I, n. 198; Fanfani, *op. cit.*, n. 127.

by the bishop, has thereby faculties from the religious superior for that confession. This delegation may be permanent or only temporary; for all or only for one or another of his subjects.[23] This delegation should be given expressly either by word of mouth or in writing. The code does not permit tacit or presumed delegation to hear confessions.[24]

Powers of Delegated Confessors.

Some of these confessors of exempt institutes must be given the faculties to absolve from all cases reserved within the order, even if reserved with censure.[25] It is not necessary that all appointed confessors have such faculties since the canon uses the word "*plures.*" The requirement that a number of confessors receive these faculties is sufficiently fulfilled by granting such faculties to at least two confessors, ("Pluralis locutio, duorum numero est contenta"),[26] who therefore comprise the minimum number. This delegated jurisdiction is personal as is evident from Canon 875 § 1 and, since it is not restricted to any place, confessions of those religious for whom these confessors were appointed can be heard even outside of the monastery. No additional faculties from the local Ordinary are required.[27] Such a delegated priest has faculties for the whole order if they were granted by the General and for the members of a province if by a Provincial.[28]

Since faculties over cases reserved within the order must be given to the confessors appointed for the house in virtue of Canon 518 § 1 and are given "a jure" to the confessor to whom the religious approach for the peace of their conscience in virtue of Canon 519 reservation within the order has practically lost all force.[29]

23 Fanfani, *De Jure Religiosorum*, n. 127; Blat, III, *pars* I, n. 202.
24 Can. 879, § 1; Vermeersch-Creusen, *Epit.* II, n. 147; Fanfani, *loc. cit.*, Blat, *loc. cit.*
25 Can. 518, § 1.
26 R. J. in VI°, Reg XL; cf. Blat, *op. cit.*, II, *pars* II, n. 579.
27 cf. Lehmkuhl, *Theol. Mor.* II, n. 511.
28 *Constitutiones O. F. M.*, n. 347.
29 Can. 896; Dargin, *Reserved Cases according to the New Code*, p. 22.

Since these appointed confessors receive their faculties from the exempt religious superior, their power of absolution is not affected by episcopal reservations. In regard to reservations by common law they will have to observe the prescriptions of the Code for the absolution of the faithful.[30]

Penitents Who Can Be Absolved in Virtue of This Delegation.

The old law which was based upon the constitution "*Superna*" of Clement X published on June 21, 1670[31] and the Council of Trent[32] granted to regular prelates and the confessors of the same order, the right to hear in their monasteries and colleges, the confessions of those, who were truly of the family and lived there, but not of the servants. That is to say those who continually lived and boarded there, staying within the walls of the monastery, partook of the exemption from the diocesan bishop and were subject to the jurisdiction of the regular prelate. Therefore their absolution did not depend upon the jurisdiction and approbation of the bishop.[33] The code, however, is much more lenient and extends this privilege of confession to regular confessors to those enumerated in Canon 514, § 1. Therefore, not only the professed and novices can confess to these confessors, but even servants, students, guests and the sick. It is required that these persons stay in the religious house day and night. The religious house includes the entire premises and even a number of buildings as long as the religious actually possess and inhabit them.[34]

Since they must stay there day and night, the following can be considered as subjects in the sense of this canon, i. e., boarding students, guests coming to visit relatives, sick persons cared for by the religious, whether they are relatives or not and especially if the religious have an hospital on their premises.

30 Fanfani, *op. cit.*, n. 131.
31 FJC n. 246, § 4.
32 *Sess. XXV, De Ref.* c. 11; Ehses, *Concilium Tridentinum*, IX, p. 1082.
33 Lehmkuhl, *Theol. Mor.* II, n. 512.
34 Augustine, *op. cit.*, p. 144.

It is not necessary that an entire day should have passed as long as they stay there after sundown and over night or even have the intention to stay there for that length of time. Therefore postulants or others having the required intention, can confess from the moment that they enter.[35] This is the almost universal opinion.

De Meester[36] contradicts, requiring that they stay some time longer than a night. But this opinion finds it hard to place a definite limit upon the exact length of time that the above mentioned persons must stay. Therefore, in the practical use of this faculty, it will come to the same conclusion as the first opinion since any other method of limiting the time would be impractical.

Those who would not be able to use this faculty would include day scholars,[37] and workers who live outside the monastery.[38]

2. *In Non-Exempt Clerical Institutes.*

It belongs to the local Ordinary to appoint confessors for the individual houses of these institutes and grant them faculties to hear the confessions of the community according to the prescriptions of Canon 518, § 1.[39] There must be two confessors at least, appointed for every house as in exempt institutes. The legitimate approbation for confessors of non-exempt institutes since it is synonymous with jurisdiction must be received from the Ordinary of the place where the confessions are to be heard. These faculties do not hold outside of the territory of the delegating bishop.

For non-exempt institutes in regard to episcopal reservations and reservations by common law the confessor must ob-

---

35 Fanfani, *De Jure Religiosorum*, n. 127; Vermeersch-Creusen, *Epit.*, n. 581; Cocchi, *Commentarium in Codicem Juris Canonici*, l. II, *pars* II, n. 28; Chelodi, *Jus de Personis*, n. 251.

36 *Juris Canonici Compendium*, II, p. 406.

37 Papi, *Religious in Church Law*, p. 148; Augustine, *loc. cit.*

38 S. C. EE et RR, July 21, 1848; cf. Bizzarri, p. 564 ff.

39 Can. 874 § 1; cf. can. 875 S 1; Fanfani, *De Jure Religiosorum*, n. 127.

serve the prescriptions of the Code for the absolution of the absolution of the faithful.[40]

ARTICLE II.

THE SUPERIOR AS CONFESSOR.

CANON 518.

§ 2. Superiores religiosi, potestatem audiendi confessiones habentes, possunt, servatis de iure servandis, confessiones audire subditorum, qui ab illis sponte sua ac motu proprio id petant, at sine gravi causa id per modum habitus ne agant.

The prohibition contained in this canon prevents religious superiors from becoming the regular confessors of their own religious, unless there is a grave reason to justify this.

The Superiors—This canon uses the generic term and therefore includes all religious superiors, endowed with the power of hearing confessions whether this power be ordinary, as in the case of an exempt institute, (Can. 501, § 1) or delegated by a special privilege of the Pontiff or by the Ordinary.[41] The canon then extends to major superiors such as, the Abbot Primate, the Abbot superior of a monastic congregation, the Abbot of an independent monastery, even though it form part of a monastic congregation, the Superior General of the whole Institute, the Provincial Superior, their Vicars and all others who have powers equivalent to those of Provincials;[42] and also to minor superiors[43] but not to those who are not superiors properly so-called in the sense of the canon.[44]

The Subjects—By these words are to be understood subjects properly so-called, i. e., those habitually and fully under the power of their respective superior. The Pontifical Com-

---

40 Fanfani, *op. cit.*, n. 131.
41 Larraona, CpR, (1920), vol. I, 54.
42 Can. 488, 8°.
43 Goyeneche, CpR. (1923) vol. IV, p. 341.
44 Larraona, *loc. cit.*

mission for the Authentic Interpretation of the Code stated September 29, 1918, that the prescriptions of Canon 518, § 2, must be observed by superiors in regard to student subjects, who form a section somewhat distinct from the community. The words of the Commission are "*Quoniam Studentes partem a Communitate aliquo modo sejunctam efformant, respectu eorum observandus est Can.* 518, § 2." [45] This was not published in the *Acta Apostolicae Sedis,* and therefore does not bind universally, but it is an indication of the mind of the legislator on this matter.

The prohibition of this law does not extend to those religious who occasionally stay at the house or within the province, if it be a question of a major superior, provided they remain fully subject to another proper superior of equal rank;[46] nor to day students at any time; or boarding students during their vacations and holidays.[47]

Conditions required to hear the confessions of subjects.—By way of exception the superior may lawfully receive the confessions of his own subjects upon fulfillment of the following requirements.

I. The subject must spontaneously and freely approach for that purpose, in which event he can be validly and licitly absolved by the superior having the required power to hear confessions. Commentators before the Code disputed as to whether these words "*sponte sua ac motu proprio*" of the Decree *Sanctissimus* of Clement VIII[48] were to be taken copulatively, i. e., both freedom and the initiative being required on the part of the religious, or disjunctively, which implies that although the subject must be free in his approach, nevertheless that counsel or exhortation on the part of the superior were

[45] LQS LXXIV (1921), 439.
[46] Larraona, *loc. cit.*
[47] Vermeersch-Creusen, *Epit.* I, n. 588.
[48] May 26, 1593, § 2; FJC n. 177.

not excluded.[49] This difficulty no longer exists in the code for Can. 518, § 3, expressly forbids anything on the part of the superior contrary to § 2.

CANON 518.

§ 3. Caveant Superiores ne quem subditum aut ipsi per se aut per alium vi, metu, importunis suasionibus aliave ratione inducant ut peccata apud se confiteatur.

Superiors must take care not to induce, personally or through others, by force, by fear, or by importunate persuasion, or by any other means any of their subjects to confess their sins to them. This is an authentic interpretation of § 2 and demands that the words "sponte sua ac motu proprio" of § 2 be taken copulatively. A spontaneous and free confession implies, therefore, that the subject is not led to confess through violence, threats, coaxing, or any other reason.[50] Theoretically, a simple suggestion or persuasion which is not importunate in a particular case, is not excluded, yet prudence dictates the better course of abstinence from such advice.[51] When, however, none of these means of pressure are brought to bear upon the subject, the superior can, with a safe conscience, hear the proposed confession of a subject provided the following condition is also fulfilled.

II. Even when the subject is perfectly free in his approach, the superior cannot hear his confessions habitually without grave reason. The words *per modum habitus* seem to imply in this case a permanent method of action which becomes a custom, so that a superior can be considered the ordinary or almost

---

49 Suarez, *De Religione,* tr. VIII, l. II, c. 15, n. 5; and Bizzarri, (2 ed.), p. 247, read in this decree the words *sponte aut motu proprio;* while Vermeersch, *De Religiosis,* II, n. 222, p. 470, gives the words *sponte ac proprio motu,* which is the wording contained in the "*Fontes Juris Canonici,* of Cardinal Gasparri, n. 177, and accepted by the Code in the present canon under consideration; Lehmkuhl, *Theol. Mor.* II, p. 314, note 1; cf. Larraona, *op. cit.* p. 55.

50 Blat, *Commentarium Textus Codicis Juris Canonici,* l. II, *pars,* II, n. 579.

51 Blat, *loc. cit.;* Larraona, CpR, I, p. 54, note 10, p. 55, 56.

the ordinary confessor of this particular subject.[52] On the contrary, occasional confession, although during certain periods, e. g., in temporary and extraordinary temptations or in time of grave sorrow, etc., it happens often, cannot be said to be *per modum habitus.*[53] In order that these confessions be heard habitually reasons which are in reality grave must be insisted upon. Any reasonable cause whatsoever would not suffice. This is evident from the fact that grave causes were not required by Clement VIII in his decree "Sanctissimus"[54] so that the superior could hear such confessions habitually if the subject approached him freely every time. The decree of the Holy Office, however, went further and the reception of occasional confession was permitted only in a rare case when he felt burdened in conscience to hear it.[55] The code is more lenient than the decree of the Holy Office and yet stricter than Clement VIII. The insertion of the words *sine gravi causa* leads to the conclusion that this was not done without reason by the legislator. It is therefore clear that the gravity of the reason must be insisted upon in order to permit superiors to hear the confessions of their subjects habitually.[56] An absolutely grave reason, which would be sufficient in all cases is not required and a relatively grave cause would suffice to hear the confessions of subjects.

To form a judgment as to the gravity of the reason, therefore, it is necessary to consider the circumstances of the person and the conditions of the religious house.[57] Such grave reasons would be the lack of priests in the house;[58] too great a distance from another suitable confessor; the desire to confess according to the prescriptions of the constitutions to a priest of his own institute even though other confessors, whether

---

52 Blat, *loc. cit.*
53 Choupin, *op. cit.*, p. 210; Larraona, *op. cit.* p. 56.
54 FJC, n. 177, § 2.
55 *S. R. U. Inquisitionis (S. Officii)*, July 5, 1899; cf. Vermeersch, *De Rel.* II, n. 232, p. 496; Col. S. C. P. F., n. 2057; Bucceroni. *Casus Conscientiae,* II, p. 79.
56 cf. Chelodi, *Jus de Personis*, n. 256, p. 397, note 1, 2; Larraona, CpR, I, p. 56.
57 Larraona, *loc. cit.*
58 Vermeersch-Creusen, *Epit.*, I, n. 588.

secular or regulars of another institute, are not far distant; a serious repugnance to confess to the other priests of the same institute;[59] scrupulosity; the serious affirmation of penitents worthy of faith that they get some special spiritual advantage from confession to their superiors.[60]

It might seem that the superior of the religious house does not so greatly differ from the superior of a seminary or secular college or the novice master that the same rigor should be used in judging the gravity of the cause for an habitual confession to the religious superior as in permitting an occasional confession to the master of novices or the superior of a seminary or college according to Canon 891. But it is evident from the reasons for the law, as given in the decree of the Holy Office,[61] that the gravity of the reason must be more strictly estimated in colleges and religious novitiates.[62] Even though, as LARRAONA says, there is an absolutely or relatively grave cause present, habitual confession to a superior can be more easily permitted if it is clearly evident in the external forum, (1) that the subject is entirely free, (2) that there does not arise therefrom, due to the subject's age, character or condition, the least occasion for suspicion of greater kindness towards the penitent and hence of the envy or emulation of others or murmuring at this mixing of the internal and external forum.[63]

Servatis de jure servandis—The rules laid down in the Code for the administration of the sacrament of penance must be observed by the superior. He must have the required jurisdiction; should impose suitable penances; is bound by the seal of confession and cannot use confessional knowledge for the external government in any way, etc. (Can. 885-908).[64] The superior must also conform to the prescriptions of a particular law on these matters.[65]

---

59 Larraona, CpR, I, p. 57; Choupin, *op. cit.*, p. 210.

60 Papi, *Religious in Church Law*, p. 50; Larraona, *loc. cit.;* Choupin, *op. cit.*, pp. 210, 211.

61 S. O., July 5, 1899; ASS XXXII, 64.

62 Larraona, CpR, I, p. 56.

63 Larraona, *loc. cit.*

64 Augustine, *A Commentary on Canon Law*, III, p. 155.

65 Blat, *op. cit.*, II, pars II, n. 579.

The Code then still continues the exclusion of the superior as the regular confessor of his own religious, as was first introduced by Clement VIII, but now permits habitual confessions to superiors only for really grave reasons.

CHAPTER III.

CONFESSORS OF LAY INSTITUTES.

Until the decree *Quemadmodum* of Leo XIII in the year of 1890, there were no special and definite regulations for confessors of male lay religious. This decree put them on a par with women religious in regard to both ordinary and extraordinary confessors and now the Code grants them practically the same rights as female religious.

CANON 528.

Etiam in laicalibus virorum religionibus deputetur, ad normam Can. 874, § 1, 875, § 2, confessarius ordinarius et extraordinarius; et si religiosus aliquem specialem confessarium expostulet, illum Superior concedat, nullo modo petitionis rationem inquirens neque id aegre se ferre demonstrans.

This is a summary of paragraphs four and seven of the Decree *Quemadmodum*.[1]

A lay institute is one in which the majority are not priests. These may be exempt or non-exempt.[2]

A. *The Number of These Confessors.*

For each house of lay male religious there should be at least one ordinary and one extraordinary confessor presented by the superior or the local Ordinary accordingly as the institute is exempt or not. The number of ordinary and extraordinary confessors should be proportionate to the number of brothers and the necessities of the different places.[3]

1 S. C. EE et RR, Dec. 17, 1890; cf. Col. S. C. P. F. (ed. 1907) n. 1745; Vermeersch, *De Rel.* II, n. 230.

2 C. 488, 4°.

3 Fanfani, *op. cit.* n. 129; Brandys, *op. cit.* n. 152. Blat, *op. cit.*, 1, II, *pars*, II, n. 591.

It is left to the Ordinary or superior to determine the number of confessors to be appointed for their respective houses.[4] Only the novices and not the professed members of the community are obliged to present themselves to the extraordinary confessor, when he comes to hear the confession of the house. They are to get at least his blessing, if they do not wish to confess.[5] The superiors should see to it that all their subjects, both novices and professed, confess weekly.[6]

B. *Appointment of Confessors.*

(1) *In exempt institutes.* The superior proposes the confessor, who must receive jurisdiction from the Ordinary of the place in which the religious house is situated, according to the prescriptions of canon 875, § 2. Such superiors have only dominative and not jurisdictional power,[7] but particular privileges in this matter are not abrogated.[8] The local Ordinary must approve the presented confessor. The right of presentation obliges to this unless the one presented is unfit.

(2) *In non-exempt institutes.* The Ordinary of the place in which the confessions are heard is to grant jurisdiction to the ordinary and extraordinary confessor, according to Canon 874, § 1.

These confessors, whether of exempt or non-exempt institutes, can be chosen either from the secular or religious clergy and must obtain jurisdiction from the Ordinary of the place where the confessions are to be heard. Religious priests, however, should not use this delegation without at least the presumed permission of their superior. The use of this delegation without this permission would not affect the validity of the absolution but only make it unlawful. No special jurisdiction is required for the confessions of male lay religious and there-

4 Vermeersch, Creusen, *Epit.* I, n. 589.
5 C. 566, § 2, 4°; cf. Bastien, *loc. cit.;* Vermeersch-Creusen, *loc. cit.;* Papi, *op. cit.,* p. 63; Shafer, Ordensrecht, p. 121.
6 Can. 595. § 1; 3°; Brandys, *op. cit.,* n. 152.
7 Schäfer, *Ordensrecht,* p. 121.
8 Vermeersch-Creusen, *Epit.* I, n. 589.

fore they can confess to any confessor approved for the faithful. When an ordinary confessor has been designated the religious should confess to him habitually, but this is merely for the sake of the external order and does not, in any way, influence the validity of the absolution.[9]

C. *Faculties for Reserved Cases.*

Since even exempt lay superiors have not ordinary jurisdiction in the internal forum they cannot make reservations.[10] Therefore the confessors who are appointed, will not need faculties for reservations within the institute as is required in Canon 518, § 1, for confessors of exempt clerical institutes.[11] But the prescriptions of the code for the absolution of the faithful must be observed by confessors of non-exempt institutes in regard to episcopal reservations and by confessors of all institutes in order to absolve from reservations by common law.[12]

D. *Requested Special Confessor.*

Should a religious ask for a special confessor, the superior must grant the petition. The confessor should, of course, be chosen from those having the usual faculties to hear confessions from the local Ordinary.[13] If the religious requests one not having faculties, these must be obtained for him. This confessor can be requested because of particular circumstances, e. g., sickness (even though it be not grave as in Can. 523, for religious women), but the canon primarily applies to the confessor to whom he desires to confess habitually as his special

---

9 Bastien, *Directoire Canonique a l'Usage des Congregations a Voeux Simples*, (Troisieme edition, 1923), n. 350; Papi, *Religious in Church Law*, p. 55, f; Biederlack-Fuhrich, *De Religiosis*, n. 50; Vermeersch-Creusen, *Epit.* II, n. 589; Schäfer, *Ordensrecht*, (ed. 1923) p. 121, Leitner, *Handbuch des Katholischen Kirchenrechts*, (*dritte Lieferung, Das Ordensrecht*), p. 348; Brandys, *Kirchliches Rechtsbuch*, n. 152.

10 Can. 893, §1.

11 Biederlack-Fuhrich, *op. cit.*, n. 50; Cocchi, *op cit.*, II *pars* II, n. 47.

12 Fanfani, *op. cit.*, n. 131.

13 Papi, *op. cit.*, p. 63; Vermeersch-Creusen, *Epit.* I, n. 598; Brandys, *loc. cit.;* Bastien, *op. cit.*, n. 350.

ordinary confessor as granted to female religious for their peace of conscience and greater progress in the spiritual life.[14] The canon does not speak of the motive necessary to confess habitually but by analogy with Can. 519 one can presuppose this to be tranquillity of conscience, e. g., if he has great confidence in the virtue and learning of the confessor; if he would receive better direction and greater spiritual profit or if he finds it easier to confess to him.

The superior cannot inquire into the motive of the request or in any way show displeasure at it. If abuses are evident they should be brought to the attention of the ordinary who can intervene directly.[15]

This habitual special confessor should be readily granted by the superior to those brothers who ask for him.[16]

It is to be added, however, that notwithstanding the appointment of confessors for the community, the members of lay institutes of men, enjoy the privilege of confessing for the peace of their conscience to any priest who has the ordinary faculties of the diocese, and the permission of the superior is not necessary as will be explained in a subsequent chapter on Canon 519. A fuller explanation of the prescriptions of law on the ordinary and extraordinary confessor will be found in the chapters on the ordinary and extraordinary confessors of women religious. (Can. 520, § 1, 521, § 1).

---

[14] Can. 520 § 2; Blat. *op. cit.*, II *pars* I, n. 590.
[15] Bastien, *loc. cit.*
[16] Vermeersch-Creusen, *loc. cit.*

CHAPTER IV.

CONFESSORS OF NOVICES.

I. The Ordinary Confessor.

CANON 566.

§ 2. In religionibus virorum, salvo praescripto Can. 519:

1° Pro novitiorum numero unus vel plures habeantur ordinarii confessarii, salvo praescripto Can. 891;

Like religious, novices can for the peace of their conscience confess to priests approved by the local ordinary, in virtue of Canon 519. This gives them no right to go out for that purpose, but if a priest with such faculties visits the convent, they can go to confession to him there.

These prescriptions also apply to novices of lay brothers, but not students after first tonsure, though they remain under the charge of a master.[1]

The ordinary confessor is to hear the confessions of all those novices living in the novitiate.[2] Where there are few novices it is the mind of the legislator that only one ordinary confessor be appointed. The computation of the number which would demand more is left to the free will of the superior. Twenty seems to suffice and sixty to demand that more than one be appointed. In such conditions the superior can licitly appoint more than two.[3]

A. *In Clerical Institutes.*

Both the confessors appointed for them by their superiors and also confessors having diocesan faculties can validly hear

1 Fanfani, *op. cit.* n. 214. This is a Dominican custom.

2 Can. 520, § 1; cf. Schäfer, *Ordensrecht*, p. 184; Blat, II, *pars* II, n. 635. Fanfani, *De Jure Religiosorum*, n. 213.

3 Vermeersch-Creusen, *Epit.* I, n. 663; Bastien, *Directoire Canonique*, p. 352,

the confessions of the novices.[4] In exempt clerical institutes it is the regular prelate who has the right and power to appoint and delegate jurisdiction to the confessors of his novices.[5]

CANON 566.

§ 2, 2°. Confessarii ordinarii, si agatur de religione clericali, in ipsa novitiatus domo commorentur;

The ordinary confessors for the novitiates of clerical institutes shall live in the novitiate house itself.

The novice master before the Code had the exclusive right and duty to hear the confessions of all the novices, but this has been completely changed to a prohibition.

CANON 891.

Magister novitiorum eiusque socius, Superior Seminarii collegiive sacramentales confessiones suorum alumnorum secum in eadem domo commorantium ne audiant, nisi alumni ex gravi et urgenti causa in casibus particularibus sponte id petant.

The master of novices and his assistant must not hear the confessions of their subjects living in the same house, unless the subjects for a grave and urgent reason in particular cases spontaneously request it.

This refers to the novice master and his assistant and not to others in the religious institute. These words must be taken taxatively. Therefore this prohibition does not include the spiritual director of the professed[6] who, according to the common practice, is appointed in many clerical institutes. For the spiritual director does not exercise disciplinary power as is required for the external regime of the novitiate.[7]

The canon does not forbid the master of novices to hear confessions of the professed or others who are not novices nor

---

4 Vermeersch-Creusen, *Epit.* I, n. 588, 663; Chelodi, *Jus de Personis*, n. 269.

5 Can. 875, § 1; Schäfer, *Ordensrecht*, p. 185.

6 *Praefectus seu Magister Spiritus*, cf. can. 588,

7 Can. 561.

to novices who are not subject to him. Despite the prohibition the confessions of novices heard by the novice master would be valid and even licit if the following conditions are fulfilled.

(1) *A spontaneous request by the subject.*—Therefore, the novice master could not by force, threats or importunate persuasion or anything of the kind, induce a novice to confess to him.[8]

(2) *A grave and urgent cause,* e. g., for his tranquillity of conscience; the necessity of absolution from a grave sin or even the desire to rightly dispose himself for Communion. In the latter case the novice could not do this when he can easily find another to whom he can tell his scruples and sins.[9] FANFANI states that even the desire of receiving special counsel and other reasons of a like nature would suffice.[10]

(3) This can be done, however, *only in particular cases* when the subject asks it spontaneously and therefore not habitually, since an urgent cause is required, which presupposes immediate necessity. If on one or another occasion the ordinary or extraordinary confessor is absent it would seem to constitute a particular case.[11] These causes must be more strictly estimated under this canon than in the use of Can. 518, § 2,[12] in virtue of which a religious might confess to his superior.[13]

Under no circumstances may the novice master become the regular confessor of his novices, for that is directly contrary to the spirit and letter of the law, "*Certum est, quod is committit in legem, qui, legis verba complectens, contra legis nititur voluntatem,*"[14] for Canon 891 states explicitly, "*nisi ex gravi et urgenti causa in casibus particularibus.*"[15]

---

8 Cf. can. 518.
9 Vermeersch-Creusen, *Epit.* II, n. 170.
10 Fanfani, *op. cit.* n. 214.
11 Fanfani, *loc. cit.* Vermeersch-Creusen, *loc. cit.*
12 Chelodi, *Jus de Personis,* n. 269.
13 Larraona, CpR, I, p. 56.
14 R. J. in VI°, Reg. 88.
15 Choupin, *L'Etat Religieux,* p. 211.

B. *In Lay Institutes.*

In these institutes, whether exempt or not, the local ordinary gives the jurisdiction to the confessor. In those institutes subject to him he selects the confessor and makes the appointment, but in exempt lay institutes the superior presents the confessor to the Ordinary.[16]

CANON 566.

§ 2, 2°. Confessarii ordinarii, si agatur de religione . . . laicali, saltem frequenter ad domum novitiatus accedant, novitiorum confessiones audituri;

The novices should have the opportunity of going to confession frequently and therefore this canon requires that the ordinary confessors of the novices of lay institutes should, at the least, go to the novitiate frequently to hear the confessions of the novices. This certainly implies that he should visit the novitiate for this purpose at least once a week[17] and, as most authors hold, even two or three times a week.[18]

The necessity of frequent approach can also be a cause for appointing more confessors than the number of novices itself might warrant. Thus, the appointed confessors could be content with weekly approach on different days.[19] This applies, of course, only to lay institutes, clerical institutes, the confessors live in the community, and therefore such questions as to visits cannot arise.

II. Extraordinary Confessor.

CANON 566.

§ 2, 4°. Quater saltem in anno detur novitiis confessarius extraordinarius, ad quem omnes accedant saltem benedictionem recepturi.

16 Can. 875, § 2; Cf. Bastien, *Directoire, Canonique*, n. 352; Brandys, *Kirchliches Rechtsbuch*, n. 41. Leitner, *Handbuch* (*Dritte Lieferung*) p. 48; cf. p.

17 Can. 595, § 1, 3°; Brandys, *Kirchliches Rechtsbuch*, n. 42.

18 Vermeersch-Creusen, *Epit.* I, n. 663; Arregui, *Summarium Theologiae Moralis* n. 604.

19 Vermeersch, *loc. cit.*

At least four times in the year, the novices are to be given an extraordinary confessor to whom all are to present themselves at least to receive his blessing. This is done so that no talk may arise as to those who would otherwise approach him to confess. It is not required that the same confessor go four times a year. Therefore, at the time of retreat the retreat master could be the extraordinary confessor, provided all go to him, whether to confess or only to receive his blessing. Of course there is no obligation of confessing to the extraordinary confessor.[20]

It is not required that the confessors of the novices be distinct from those of the professed.

III. Supplementary Confessors.

CANON 566.

§2, 3°. Praeter confessarios ordinarios, designentur aliqui confessarii, quos novitii in casibus particularibus adire libere possint, nec Magister aegre id se ferre demonstret;

Besides the ordinary confessors, other confessors must be designated to whom in particular cases the novices may freely have recourse. The Master of novices may not manifest any displeasure, if a novice approaches one of these confessors. Free approach can either be had by permitting the novice to go to the confessor or, as is more comformable, to regular observance, to see to it that the confessor requested by novice, comes to him in the customary place for confessions of novices.[21]

In clerical institutes they can be appointed from those staying in the house and can be approached by the novices or called by the novice master.[22]

---

20 Vermeersch-Creusen, *loc. cit.;* Blat, ibid; Brandys, *Kirchliches Rechtsbuch*, n. 41; cf. Treatment on Ordinary and Extraordinary confessors of women. The same principles apply.

21 Fanfani *op. cit.* n. 213; Bastien, *op cit.* n. 353.

22 Blat, LL, *pars* II, p. 622.

These confessors are not ordered to go to the house even frequently. However, approach to them should not be too difficult lest the law be evaded.[23]

The novices are to approach these confessors *only in particular cases,* i. e., as individuals, and not habitually.[24]

---

23 Vermeersch-Creusen, *Epit.* I, n. 663.

24 cf. Commentary on Canon 521, § 2, p.

CHAPTER V.

CONFESSORS FOR PEACE OF CONSCIENCE.

Although some religious orders had the privilege of confessing outside of their order, it was left to Pius X to extend this to all male religious. On February 8, 1913, this Supreme Pontiff granted to all confessors, approved by the Ordinary of Rome, the faculty of hearing the confessions of and of absolving religious men of any institute whatsoever, who came to them, without asking permission of their respective superiors.[1] This faculty was extended to all confessors in the world on August 5th of the same year.[2] These confessors had power to absolve from all sins no matter how reserved in the order; their faculties coming direct from the Pope. This was a very great boon for religious men[3] and formed the basis for our present canon.

CANON 519.

Firmis constitutionibus quae confessionem statis temporibus praecipiunt vel suadent apud determinatos confessarios peragendam, si religiosus, etiam exemptus, ad suae conscientiae quietem, confessarium adeat ab Ordinario loci approbatum, etsi inter designatos non recensitum, confessio, revocato quolibet contrario privilegio, valida et licita est; et confessarius potest religiosum absolvere etiam a peccatis et censuris in religione reservatis.

The Subjects Who Can Use This Canon. This faculty is extended directly by the canon to all religious men without exception, of any order, congregation or institute whatsoever; whether religious of solemn vows or simple; whether exempt or

1 Vermeersch, *Per.* VII, p. (24); This communication was not published in the official "Acta Apostolicae Sedis" but made known to the confessors of the City by printed card. cf. Vermeersch, *ibid.*, p. 179.

2 S. C. *De Rel.*, AAS, V, 431; cf. Vermeersch, *op. cit.*, p. 173; Lehmkuhl, *Theol. Mor.* II, n. 514; Choupin, *L'Etat Religieux*, p. 212.

3 Choupin, *op. cit.*, p. 214.

not; whether priests, monks or brothers, for those are religious who take vows in any institutes.[4] Novices are not religious properly so-called, for they do not take vows, but this privilege extends to them also, no matter what their order or congregation.[5] Moreover, the Code grants the same right to pious associations or societies [6] whose members imitate the manner of life of religious by living in community under the government of superiors and according to approved constitutions, but without being bound by the usual three vows. They are not properly a religious institute and their members cannot be properly designated by the term religious. Such a society may be clerical or lay, pontifical or diocesan.[7]

The Code expressly mentions the exempt religious as being the recipients of this privilege. They alone are free from episcopal jurisdiction. Therefore, it is only about these religious that difficulties can arise in regard to confession to a priest approved by the local Ordinary. It was also the common interpretation of authors before the Code that they were included in this privilege.[8]

Without prejudice to the constitutions—FATHER PAPI[9] seems to be wrong in his interpretation of this part of the canon, when he states that the constitutions must be observed whenever the "peace of conscience" does not require the use of this faculty. Since most authors hold that sufficient motive for peace of conscience is had in every serious confession, religious could, in virtue of this view, habitually avoid confession to the appointed confessors. That, however, is foreign to the mind of the legislator. The true meaning is, that the constitutions pre-

---

4 Can. 488, *In canonibus qui sequuntur, veniunt nomine: 7°. Religiosorum, qui vota nuncupantur in aliqua religione. . . .*

5 Can. 566 § 2; *S. C.* De Rel. *Roma et Aliarum,* ad 1; May 3, 1914; AAS, VI, 232; cf. Chelodi, *Jus De Personis,* n. 256; *Ir. Ecc. Rec.* (1914) IV p. 103; Leitner, *Handbuch,* (*Dritte Lieferung*), p. 350.

6 Can. 675, *Regimen determinatur in uniuscuiusque societatis constitutionibus; sed in omnibus serventur, congrua congruis referendo, can.* 499-530.

7 Can. 673, § 1.

8 Vermeersch, *Per.* VII, p. (30); Choupin, *op. cit.,* p. 218.

9 *Religious in Church Law,* p. 51; also *The Government of Religious Communities,* p. 130.

scribing confessions at definite times and to determined confessors, still remain in force despite the fact that religious can go at any time to the confessor of Canon 519 for their peace of conscience.[10] In fact this canon strengthens the constitutions in these prescriptions and the use of the faculty of going to these confessors does not dispense from the precept of the constitutions.[11] The unity of direction is not only useful but necessary, especially for the younger religious and those who are subject to temptations so that unless they are sustained and directed by the prudent hand of a constant spiritual physician they might lose perseverance in virtue.[12] It is evident from the history of the discipline that the constitutions were to be observed in this matter despite the fact that a religious could confess outside the order. In the Code this is summarized in the words *firmis constitutionibus,* which prescribe confessions at definite times and to determined confessors. There is nothing to prevent a religious from going besides to another confessor for the peace of his conscience.

This view is supported by almost all commentators.[13]

Occasional confessions in virtue of Canon 519 beyond the prescription of confession at determined periods, can be permitted as exceptions. But Canon 519 in no way supposes that the confessor to whom the religious approaches of his free will is to be converted into the special ordinary confessor of that religious,[14] without the permission of superior.[15]

---

10 Fanfani, *De Jure Religiosorum,* n. 127, dubium, II; Vermeersch-Creusen, *Epit.* I, n. 588.

11 Goyeneche, CpR. (1924) V, p. 28 ff.

12 Genicot, *Theol. Mor.*, II, n. 336.

13 Biederlack-Fuhrich, *De Religiosis,* n. 48; Creusen, *Religieux et Religieuses* (1924), n. 89, p. 76; Jansen, *Ordensrecht,* p. 150; Vermeersch-Creusen, *Epit.* I, n. 588; Augustine, *A Commentary on Canon Law,* III, p. 157; Blat, *Commentarium Textus C. I. C.*, I *pars* II, n. 580; Choupin, *L'Etat Religieux,* p. 210; Chelodi, *Jus de Personis,* n. 256; Goyeneche, CpR. III, 78-81; V, 28-29; Leitner, *Handbuch des Katholischen Kirchenrechts,* p. 249.

14 Vermeersch-Creusen, *Epit.* I, n. 588; Genicot, *Theol. Mor.* II, n. 336.

15 Creusen, *Religieux et Religieuses,* n. 89; Cocchi, *op cit.*, II, *pars* II, n. 36.

Religious superiors can and should urge the observance of the prescriptions for regular confessions to determine confessors since this is their duty by reason of Canon 595, § 1, 3°.[16]

The religious must approach the confessor. The word *adeat* implies that the confession made to a confessor approved by the local ordinary, will be valid and licit if the religious takes the initiative, but the Code does not attempt to define what constitutes such an approach. His approach can take place in many ways, e. g., either within or outside of the house, if the confessor is directly sought when the occasion offers. Of course the word "adeat" gives the religious no right to summon the confessor,[17] but even if this should be done the confession would be valid since no peculiar jurisdiction is required for the confessions of religious men as for female religious. Neither can a religious in virtue of this canon exact that the superior should call such a confessor;[18] nor disregard the observances of the institute; nor demand permission to go out; nor leave the house for this purpose, without such permission, when the constitutions or customs prescribe that he ask it.[19] The violation of the preceptive rule of not going out would not render the confession illicit.[20]

The superior, then, is not bound to accede to the request to go out especially if the religious is unwilling to tell the motive, i. e., for confession. Those religious observing the papal cloister cannot be given permission to go out. The superior of other religious may grant it for this reason alone.[21]

If, on the other hand, there is no abuse, the superior would act against the intention of the Church by arbitrarily prohibiting religious to go out for the sake of confession, especially if they should have the opportunity of going out either by reason

---

16 Goyenche, CpR (1922) III, p. 81.
17 cf. explanation of Canon 522.
18 Fanfani, *loc. cit.;* Vermeersch-Creusen, *Epit.* I, n. 588; Creusen, *Religieux et Religieuses,* n. 89.
19 Papi, *op. cit.,* p. 51.
20 Chelodi, *Jus Personale,* n. 256.
21 Reply of S. C. De Rel. Dec. 1, 1921 to the Bishop of Innsbruck; Hilling, *C. I. C. Interpretatio,* p. 39.

of their ministry or some other legitimate cause permitted by the rules and constitutions.[22] The spiritual welfare of the individual must not be jeopardized.[23]

When there is a confessor approved by the local ordinary in the house or if the religious is outside of the house for any reason whatsoever, he can, without the permission of the superior and unknown to him, confess to such a confessor,[24] and need not mention the fact to the superior.[25] The confessor is in no way obliged to ask the penitent if he has permission, or obtain this himself from the superior; or notify the latter; or question the religious as to his motive of approach, i. e., whether he comes for peace of conscience or not.[26]

The motive[27]—The religious should approach such a confessor for the peace of his conscience. These words do not imply that a special cause is necessary for the validity and liceity of such a confession so that if there were not some disquietude of conscience it would be unlawful. This can be deduced from the following reasons:

I. This is a privilege to religious and should be interpreted widely according to the axioms of law, *Quum beneficia principum sint interpretanda largissime*[28] and *Quum in beneficiis plenissima sit interpretatio*[29] and the general rule of law *odia restringi, et favores convenit ampliari.*[30]

II. Any confession is valid which is made seriously, for any serious confession truly tends to quiet the conscience.[31] The

22 Fanfani, *op. cit.* n. 127; Vermeersch, *loc. cit.;* CpR, (1922) III, p. 81.
23 Papi, *loc. cit.*
24 Fanfani, *op. cit.*, n. 127. cf. Vermeersch-Creusen, *loc. cit;* Cocchi, *op. cit.*, II, pars II, n. 36.
25 Creusen, *op. cit.* n. 89.
26 cf. Leitner, *op. cit.* p. 350.
27 cf. Treatment on Can. 522.
28 c. 16, X, *de privilegiis,* V, 40.
29 c. 22, X, *de privilegiis,* V. 33; cf. Wernz, *Jus Decretalium,* I, n. 161.
30 R. J., in VI°. Reg. 15.
31 Vermeersch-Creusen, *Epit.* I, n. 588; Fanfani, *De Jure Religiosorum,* n. 127, calls this opinion the more probable; Cocchi, *op. cit.*, II, pars II, n. 36. Creusen; *Religieux et Religieuses,* n. 89.

serious choice of a confessor is directed to a greater peace of conscience.[32]

III. The intention of the legislator is to promote peace of conscience and it is reasonable to presume that he would not make this peace of conscience a condition necessary for the validity of the confession[33] lest it give rise to scruples.[34] This is confirmed by the decree of Pius X, "In audientia,"[35] which made no mention of this condition.[36] It would, moreover, be very difficult in individual cases to judge whether the confession for the peace of conscience would be useful or not and instead of facilitating approach the consciences of the religious by the faculty of Canon 519 would be thrown into more and greater difficulties in contravention of the evident purpose of the legislator in granting this privilege.[37]

This confession would not only be valid but even licit according to the canon. This phrase must be taken in conjunction with the first words of the canon *firmis constitutionibus,* etc., and, therefore, confessions made in virtue of Canon 519 which do not violate the prescriptions of the constitutions in regard to confessions at definite times and to determined persons are not only valid but lawful.[38] The number of times that a religious may make use of this faculty is not determined by the Code, but simply and solely by his state of conscience.[39]

The confessor. This canon, as we have said being a privilege, should receive a wide interpretation. The law does not determine the branch of the clergy, whether religious or secular, nor the rite from which the confessor is to be chosen and therefore *ubi lex non distinquit nec nos distinguere debemus.*[40] The Code in Canon 519 directly and formally gives the faculty to

32 Vermeersch-Creusen, *ibid.*
33 Papi, *Religious in Church Law,* p. 51.
34 Vermeersch-Creusen, *loc. cit.*
35 *S. C.* De Rel. Aug. 5, 1913; AAS, V, 431; cf. Vermeersch, *Per.* VII, p. (24); n. 702, p. 173.
36 Chelodi, *Jus de Personis,* n. 256.
37 Fanfani, *op. cit.* n. 127, dubium, I.
38 Vermeersch-Creusen, *loc. cit.*
39 Augustine, *op. cit.,* III, p. 157.
40 Choupin, *L'Etat Religieux,* p. 214.

absolve religious men to all confessors, whether secular or religious, approved for confessions by the local Ordinary, according to Canons 877 and 879.[41]

The right to confess to priests of another rite for the peace of conscience was admitted before the Code [42] and is now contained in Canon 905. Thus religious can confess to priests of other rites which remain in union with the Holy See. Therefore, a Basilian monk could confess, for instance, in New York, to a secular or religious priest of the Latin rite if he is approved by the Archbishop of New York, and so also could an American Benedictine monk confess to a Greek-Ruthenian priest in Philadelphia if the latter is approved by the proper local Ordinary, the Greek-Ruthenian Bishop.[43]

Confessor Approved by the Local Ordinary. To exercise this faculty approbation by the local Ordinary is required and that alone suffices, no special approbation for religious being necessary.[44] Approbation implies not only recommendation but actual possession of faculties. Approval for confession and granting of faculties are one and the same in the Code [45] which requires only the presumed permission of the superior to exercise faculties granted by the local ordinary.[46]

The local ordinary, who can approve a confessor, may be (unless expressly excepted) besides the Pope, all those who rule or govern a diocese or territory equal to a diocese. Such are residential Bishops for their own territory, Abbots or Prelates Nullius, (i. e., having jurisdiction over some territory, but not

---

41 Cocchi, *op. cit.*, II, *pars* II, n. 36; Choupin, *op. cit.*, p. 215.

42 *S. C.* De Rel., *Roma et Aliarum*, May 3, 1914, AAS VI, 232; *An decretum sacrae Congregationis de Religiosis, die 5 Augusti 1913, comprehandat etiam confessiones quas religiosi ritus Latini faciunt apud confessarios ritus Orientalis et vicissim? Resp. Affirmative;* cf. Vermeersch, *Per.* VIII, n. 15; Chelodi, *op. cit.*, n. 256, p. 397 note 3; CpR, III, p. 80.

43 Cf. Can. 905, Can. 1; Leitner, *op. cit.* p. 350; Blat, III, *pars* 1, n. 234.

44 Choupin, *op. cit.*, p. 214.

45 Biederlack-Fuhrich, *op. cit.* n. 49.

46 Can. 874, § 1.

necessarily a diocese)[47] and their Vicar General; Administrators, Vicars and Prefects Apostolic and likewise Vicar Capitulars and Administrators during the vacancy of the see whether they are such under common law or according to approved constitutions.[48] This canon settles disputes which had arisen in regard to the words of the Decree of August 5, 1913, "*confessarios a locorum Ordinariis approbatis.*"[49] Some authors held that approbation was required of the ordinary of the place in which the confessions were to be heard. Others contended that the approbation of any local Ordinary whatsoever, was sufficient and therefore that a priest approved by any local Ordinary could hear the confessions of any male religious anywhere.[50] The present law, however, demands that the approbation come from the ordinary of the place in which the confessions are to be heard.[51]

This confessor need only be approved to hear the confessions of men and not all the faithful as is the common custom in our country.[52] In other countries it is not a rare thing that priests receive faculties for the confessions of men only, e. g., in Rome, and certain dioceses of Italy and Spain and, according to Augustine, even in our own State of Louisiana.[53] This canon speaks expressly of approbation by the ordinary. Since Cardinals, Canons Penitentiary and Pastors are not, strictly speaking, confessors approved by the ordinary but *ipso jure* enjoy ordinary jurisdiction in the forum of conscience, it might seem that they could not act in virtue of Can. 519. Cardinals, however, have, from the time of their promotion in consistory, the faculty of hearing confessions of all religious

---

47 Can. 198, § § 1, 2. Can. 199, § 1; Cf. Wernz-Vidal, *Jus Canonicum*, II, n. 367; Augustine, *op. cit.*, II, p. 173 ff; Choupin, *op. cit.*, p. 215.

48 Can. 432, § 3.

49 S. C. De Rel., AAS, V, 431; Vermeersch, *Per.*, VII, n. 702.

50 Vermeersch, *loc. cit.*, p. (25) ff.

51 Can. 874, § 1.

52 Cocchi, *op. cit.*, II pars II, n. 36.

53 Innocent XIII, Const. *Apostolici Ministerii*, May 23, 1723, § 19; cf. FJC, n. 280; Ballerini, *Opus, Theol. Mor.*, (ed. 1900), V, p. 296, n. 352, 3°; Augustine, III, p. 162; Creusen, *Religieux et Religieuses*, n. 95; Goyeneche, CpR II, (1921) p. 20; Bastien, *Directoire Canonique*, n. 360, note (2).

of both sexes and of absolving from all sins and censures except those most specially reserved to the Holy See and those connected with the revelation of the secret of the Holy Office.[54] They have not delegated jurisdiction from the local Ordinary of the actual place where this confession is heard, but they have ordinary jurisdiction by a special privilege. Therefore religious can confess to Cardinals at any time, even outside of the terms of Can. 519.

Canon penitentiaries and pastors, it is true, have ordinary jurisdiction *ipso jure* (Can. 401, § 1; 873, § 1,) nevertheless it is dependently upon the local Ordinary that both pastors and canon penitentiaries obtain and exercise their office. The right of nominating and instituting pastors, except in pontifical parishes, belongs to the local Ordinary,[55] even if it is a parish under the care of religious, the bishop must institute as pastor the religious priest presented by the religious superior.[56] The canon penitentiary is also be be appointed by the bishop, the local Ordinary.[57] Since this is a question of a privilege, *in favorabilibus* they can be truly said to be confessors approved by the local Ordinary for all the faithful coming to them.[58]

The same can be said for the pastor of a pontifical parish, who is instituted by the Pope, the supreme local Ordinary of the world.[59] In all convents, whether cloistered or not, confessions for peace of conscience can be made to visiting priests or others having approbation of the local Ordinary.

Priest with maritime faculties. Here again the question of approbation by the Ordinary of the place where the confession is to be heard, arises. Any approved priest, having rightly received faculties to hear confessions from either his own Ordinary (if it is a religious, the Ordinary of the place where his

54 Can. 239, § 1, 1°; *Ex audientia SSmi D. N. Pii PP X, Gratiae*, Dec. 20, 1911; cf. Vermeersch, *Per.*, VII, n. 737; Fanfani, *op. cit.* n. 127, c. ad dubium II.

55 Can. 455, § 1.

56 Can. 456.

57 Can. 399, § 1; cf. Blat., *op. cit.*, II, pars I, n. 439.

58 Fanfani, *op. cit.* n. 127, c, dubium II.

59 Can. 873, § 1.

house is located),[60] the Ordinary of the port from which the boat leaves or any intermediate port can hear the confessions of all male religious sailing with him and also those who, for any cause, come on board ship and even those who seek to confess to him, when he is on shore for some other reason. Male religious can be absolved by a priest with maritime faculties, who approach him for the peace of their conscience in virtue of Canon 519. This confessor can validly and licitly absolve all religious even from cases reserved by his own Ordinary, by the Ordinary of the penitent or by the Ordinary of the place, either where the sin was committed or in which the confessions are heard.[61] Exempt religious can also be absolved from all sins and censures reserved within the order.[62]

This canon revokes all contrary privileges. All rules, which restrain the liberty of the religious no longer have obligatory force even if at one time approved by the Holy See. Some contrary privileges were given in the past. Thus the Brothers of St. Francis de Paula were prohibited from confessing outside of their order by Julius II,[63] as were the Jesuits by Paul III.[64] Just as Pius V [65] would not permit the Dominicans, so also Urban VIII,[66] would not allow the Canons Regular of the Congregation of the Holy Cross in Portugal to confess to priests not of their order.

These religious were to be subject to their superiors in this matter. Pius X through the Sacred Congregation of Religious, August 15, 1913 however, admonished superiors that subjects could confess outside without getting their permission, and that

60 Blat, *op. cit.* III, *pars* I, n. 206.

61 Can. 883; Noldin, *De Sacramentis*, n. 343.

62 Can. 519.

63 Const. *Virtute conspicuos*, July 28, 1506; BRT, V, n. 13, § 22, p. 395.

64 Const. *Licet Debitum*, Nov. 19, 1549; BRT VI, n. 65, § 10, p. 395; this was confirmed by Leo XIII (Br. *Dolemus inter*, July 13, 1866; cf. Leo XIII, *Pontificis Maximi Acta*, VI, p. 120 ff).

65 Const. *Romani Pontificis*, July 21, 1571; BRT VII, n. 198, § 2, p. 295.

66 Const. *Romani Pontificis*, Sept. 10, 1625; BRT, XIII, n. 59, p. 396.

this must be observed despite contrary constitutions and privileges,[67] which were thereby revoked.

The Code likewise revokes all contrary privileges.

Powers of the confessor—He can absolve from sins and censures reserved in the institute, i. e., by a general law.[68] He can also absolve from censures "*latae sententiae*" inflicted by the superior and they can be considered as reserved to no one since the canon makes no distinction as to the way in which they are reserved.[69] A censure "*ab homine*" is reserved in the external forum and not by a general law but only in a particular case so that the confessor could not absolve from it in virtue of Canon 519.[70]

These principles apply to confessions of sins reserved by exempt religious superiors only. If it is a question of a non-exempt institute in which the local Ordinary has reserved a case the confessor cannot, in virtue of Canon 519, absolve a member of that institute, who has incurred the reservation, since the delegated jurisdiction he received from the local Ordinary has been restricted in regard to that case. The immediate and direct subject of reservation is the confessor whose jurisdiction and power it restricts.[71]

The same principles would apply to the confession of an exempt religious in virtue of Canon 519, if the same sin was reserved "ratione sui" both by the exempt religious superior and the local Ordinary of the place where the confession is made.

---

67 *Decr. S. C.* De Rel., Aug. 5, 1913; AAS, V, 43; "... *constitutionibus, ordinationibus apostolicis, privilegiis qualibet efficaciori forma concessis, aliisque contrariis quibuscumque, etiam speciali atque individua mentione dignis, minime obstantibus.*

68 Fanfani, *op. cit.*, n. 131.

69 cf. Bierderlack-Fuhrich, *op. cit.*, n. 48.

70 Fanfani, *op. cit.*, n. 131.

71 Can. 893 § 1-*Qui Ordinario jure possunt audiendi confessiones potestatem concedere aut ferre censuras, possunt quoque, excepto Vicario Capitulari et Vicario Generali sine mandato speciali, nonnullos casus ad suum avocare judicium, inferioribus absolvendi potestatem limitantes.*; cf. Arregui, *Summarium Theol. Mor.*, n. 607; Vermeersch-Creusen, *Epit. II*, n. 172; Blat. III, *pars* I, p. 255; Dargin, *Reserved Cases According to the Code of Canon Law*, p. 35; Noldin, *De Sacramentis*, n. 355; Tanquerey, *Theol. Mor.* I, n. 425; Augustine, *op. cit.*, IV, p. 391; *CpR.* (1922), III, p. 69-77; Genicot, *Theol. Mor.*, II, n. 337.

Such a confessor could not absolve, it seems, without special faculties[72] or without recourse to the local Ordinary. If they are to be absolved in virtue of jurisdiction received from the local Ordinary it seems that just as the limitation of the power of the confessor prevents him from absolving a "peregrinus" from a diocesan reservation,[73] it likewise prevents the absolution of a religious from a sin reserved both in the order and the diocese.[74]

Moreover if regulars were immune from the simple reservations of bishops, the conclusion would have to be drawn that they are bound only by pontifical reservations since by Canon 518, § 1 and 519 they can be absolved from reservations of the order. This seems to be foreign to the intention of the law. To make confession easy the Code wished to propose a common norm, to which both subjects and outsiders are to be subjected, by determining the origin of jurisdiction[75] for the confessions of all indiscriminately. Thus the main element to be considered in all cases of reservation is the place of confession and not the place or jurisdiction within which the sin was committed.[76]

Therefore male religious, whether exempt or non-exempt, who commit, either within the diocese or outside of it, a sin, even if it is not reserved within the order but in the diocese, cannot be absolved from that reservation in virtue of Canon 519.[77] Of course, the reservation of sins *ratione sui* ceases in cases of sickness which confine the penitent to the house or if the faculty has been refused or could not be requested without danger of grave injury to the penitent or violation of the seal.[78] For these and other censures outside of the order the confessor can absolve in more urgent cases according to Canon 2254 and in danger of death in virtue of Canon 2252.

---

72 Genicot, *loc. cit.*
73 *Pont. Com. ad C. I. C. Auth. Inter.*, Nov. 24, 1920, AAS XII, 364.
74 Cf. Vermeersch-Creusen, *loc. cit.;* Dargin, *loc. cit.*
75 Voltas, *CpR.* (1922), III, p. 76 ff.
76 Vermeersch-Creusen, *loc. cit.;* Dargin, *loc. cit.*
77 Voltas, *loc. cit.*; Creusen, *Religieux et Religieuses*, n. 89.
78 Can. 900 §§ 1, 2.

The faculty of absolving from reservations of local Ordinaries belongs *ipso jure,* (1) to the canon penitentiary;[79] (2) to pastors and those coming under that name (including quasi-pastors of quasi-parishes into which a vicariate or prefecture apostolic has been divided;[80] parochial vicars, if endowed with full parochial powers) during the time for the fulfilment of the paschal precept,[81] whether that be according to common law or extended by the Ordinaries. The confession need not be made for the fulfilment of the Easter duty;[82] (3) individual missionaries during the time they give missions to the people[83]

79 Can. 401, § 1; Can. 899, § 2.
80 Can. 216, §§ 2, 3; Can. 899 § 3.
81 Can. 451.
82 Vermeersch-Creusen, *Epit.* II, n. 180.
83 Can. 899, § 3.

APPENDIX

CONFESSORS OF SEMINARIANS.

Students for the secular priesthood in seminaries are not religious but they live in community and the code has made definite regulations for their confessors similar to those for religious.

ORDINARY CONFESSORS.

In every seminary there must be at least two ordinary confessors and a spiritual director, distinct from the rector of the seminary or college.[1] Since the spiritual director is wont to hear these confessions and is indeed generally the principal confessor, three confessors at least must be assigned. It is not necessary however that these three reside in the seminary or college.[2]

The Sacred Congregation for Seminaries and Universities at the command of Pius XI issued a decree to all local Ordinaries to the effect that a triennial report should be made to the Holy See in regard to their Seminaries. The question required to be answered, as to whether the spiritual directors who live in the seminary held any other office besides this[3] does not imply

---

1 Can. 1358.

2 Vermeersch-Creusen, *Epit.* II, n. 692.

3 *S. C. De Seminariis et Studiorum Universitatibus*, Decree *Quo uberiore*, Feb. 2, 1924; "*Utrum sit Magister Pietatis, seu Director Spiritualis, debita prudentia, doctrina, pietate ornatus, qui in seminario degat, nulloque alio officio implicetur (Can. 642, § 1 n. 2 § 2; 1358; 1360). An praeter ipsum adsint alii confessarii, sive ordinarii sive extraordinarii et praecepta Can. 1361, § 1-2. custodiantur,*" Cf. AAS XVII, 549, n. 10.

according to VERMEERSH-CREUSEN,[4] the suppression of the custom existing outside of Italy. Students by this custom choose professors as their own individual spiritual directors contrary to the Italian usage of one appointed spiritual director who can perform in the seminary itself no other office except that of master of religion in the minor seminary or any secondary school of the major seminary. The Congregation permits to those regions outside of Rome their own custom and merely requires the declaration in the report of the custom that is followed, which is permissible until Rome states otherwise.[5]

OTHER CONFESSORS.

Besides the ordinary confessors there should be appointed other confessors whom the students can freely approach.[6]

The freedom of approach is safeguarded by the fact that if these confessors live outside the seminary and a student desires to approach one of them, the rector shall call him without in any way asking the reason or showing signs of displeasure. If they live in the seminary the student can freely approach them, but always in accordance with the discipline of the house.[7] This should not become a custom or be done in a way detrimental to good order, e. g., by withdrawing without permission from the lecture room or study hall or common exercises. In exceptional cases however such a relaxation may be justified.[8]

The rule for religious communities that they may be given extraordinary confessors at least four times a year may also be applied here[9] but it is not obligatory.

QUALITIES OF CONFESSORS.

The spiritual director and the ordinary and extraordinary confessors should be only such priests as are distinguished not only for their learning but also for their virtues and prudence

4 *Epit.*, loc. cit.
5 Vermeersch-Creusen, *loc. cit.*
6 Can. 1301, § 1.
7 Can. 1361, § 2. cf. Blat, III, *pars* IV, n. 242.
8 Augustine, *op. cit.*, VI, p. 392; Blat, *loc. cit.*
9 Can. 566, § 2, 4°; Augustine, *op. cit.*, VI, p. 393.

so that they may be examplars to students in word and deed.[10] In matters of promotion to orders or expulsion of seminarians, even in very urgent cases which brook no delay, the vote of the spiritual director and the confessors is never to be asked and even consultation with them is forbidden.[11] Questioning about other matters is not prohibited, but abstinence from discussing his penitents is the better policy here even if his vote would be favorable. For if it is recognized that he favors his penitents, he will give occasion not only to vain adulation but even sacrilegious lies.[12]

The confessors are subject to the rector in all matters of discipline, studies and ordinary administration.[13] The rector of the seminary or college is forbidden to hear the confessions of his students living with him in the same house unless in particular cases they freely request it for some grave and urgent cause.[14] The principles governing the hearing of such confession are the same as those explained above for the confessions of novices by the novice master, where the definition of an urgent cause and particular cases is explained.[15] Since there is no peculiar jurisdiction required to absolve seminarians it is perfectly lawful for them when the occasion offers to go to other confessors.[16]

Appointment of Confessors.

This is to be made by the Bishop after consultation with the disciplinary and administrative seminary boards (from which the ordinary confessors are excluded as members) and after asking their advice.[17]

---

10 Can. 1361, § 1.
11 Can. 1361, § 3; cf. Augustine, *op. cit.*, p. 393. Blat, III, *pars* IV, n. 243.
12 Vermeersch-Creusen, *Epit.* II, n. 695.
13 Can. 1360, § 2.
14 Can. 891; Can. 1360, § 1.
15 Cf. chapter on Confessors of Novices, p.
16 Vermeersch-Creusen, *loc. cit.*
17 Can. 1359, §§ 1, 2, 4; cf. Augustine, *op. cit.*, VI, p. 390.

FREQUENCY OF CONFESSION.

Seminarians should go to confession at least once a week.[18] This can be urged in both major and minor seminaries but not in mixed colleges except for those candidates who manifest their intention of becoming clerics.[19] The canon states "Curent Episcopi" which shows that the obligation rests not upon the seminarians but the bishop to see that this rule is observed. The Ordinary may fulfill this obligation by questioning the rector in regard to this matter at the time of his visits and the latter must answer truthfully. Of course, knowledge received directly through confession can not be revealed by the confessors or the spiritual director, but the latter, having every opportunity, as Father Augustine says, to watch the students can without mentioning an individual make a statement as to the general observance of the rule.[20] Compulsion should not be used by the rector or spiritual director. Although the latter is to be always at the disposal of the seminarians to hear their confessions, liberty of conscience must be guaranteed them and no restriction imposed in regard to the choice of confessors. Since the canon lays down this rule for the weekly approach the rector and spiritual director could urge in public conferences the obligation of observing this rule and like religious superiors [21] could correct a seminarian for gross negligence. The penitent, if he does not desire to confess, should at least present himself to the confessor to receive his blessing.

---

18 Can. 1367, 2°.
19 Vermeersch-Creusen, *Epit.* II, n. 701.
20 Augustine, *op. cit.*, VI, p. 405 ff.
21 Can. 595, § 1, 3°.

PART II

CONFESSORS OF FEMALE RELIGIOUS

CHAPTER VII.

THE ORIGIN AND DEVELOPMENT OF THE LAW.

I. In Rules of Religious Orders.

The stages of legislative progress on this matter are much better defined than those of male religious due to the fact that, although the religious women are sometimes subject to regulars, the attendance of a priest for confession would require special legislation in religious institutes and local and general councils. The confessor of male religious in their own houses might be assumed as a matter of course but the cloister of females required special regulations.[1]

At the inception of female monasticism one can hardly expect to find anything definite except, perhaps, the fact that the nuns did confess to a priest.

Pachomius.

This originator of the cenobitical life for monks also has attributed to him a rule for the nuns of his time, who lived in communities under his system and of whom his sister was superioress. This rule is not authentic, yet its translation by St. Jerome may contain some of his principles, for it was written during the century in which he lived, i. e., the fourth.[2] In this rule of Pachomius are the words "Seniores qui monasterio virginium delegati sunt."[3] Whether these *seniores* were priests and heard the confessions of these nuns, cannot, with

1 Schaaf, *The Cloister*, p. 30, 31.
2 St. Benedict of Aniane, *Codex Regularum*, MPL, CIII, 116.
3 *De Disciplina Puellarum*, LXXXII. Gazaeus, *Cassiani Opera Omnia*, p. 816.

certainty, be determined. LADEUZE merely says that these monks were to instruct them in Scripture and perform the divine offices and other necessary services for the nuns.[4] Gazaeus goes even further and says there must have been spiritual confessors or fathers living in the neighborhood by whom the nuns were instructed and directed. These were commonly called confessors (qui vulgo confessarii vocantur).[5]

St. Basil. (Born about 316).

His rule for nuns states that, if the priest thinks it fit, it would be advisable that when a sister confesses, the abbess should be present at the time he imposes the penance for the emendation of the sinner.[6] He speaks openly of confession to the priest as something distinctive, for "culpa" confession of nuns was made to their mother superior. The priest had it at his discretion to impose the penance through the abbess for the good government of the community. There was evidently one priest appointed in charge of the Basilian monasteries of nuns, one of whose functions was the hearing of the nuns' confessions. This is the first appearance of the ordinary confessor.

St. Augustine.

About the year of 423 A. D. St. Augustine of Hippo, Africa, wrote his two hundred and ninth (now 211th) letter containing his so-called rule for nuns. He speaks in this of public accusation of self or of others rather than of sacramental confessions and the superioress as well as the priest had the right to impose the penance.[7] No argument can be drawn from this rule as to whether the priest heard sacramental confessions apart from this public, "culpa" confession.

---

4 Ladeuze P., *Cenobitisme Pakhomien*, p. 303, note (6); Cf. Schaaf, *op. cit.* p. 14.

5 Gazaeus, *op. cit.*, p. 824.

6 St. Benedict of Aniane, *Codex Regularum*, cap. 199, MPL CIII, 847; Clarke, (*St. Basil the Great*, p. 97), implies that these might be only senior brothers.

7 St. Augustine; *Epistola*, CCXI; MPL, XXXIII, 962.

St. Caesarius of Arles, 470-542, A. D.

His rule makes mention only of the admission of the priest, deacon and subdeacon and a few lectors of proven character for the celebration of Mass and other divine services.[8] It is not clear whether these divine services include confessions heard by the priest.

Cistercians.

There were no other evidences of the religious confessor in the subsequent rules for women until the confirmation of the already existent practice of having a sort of ordinary confessor in the rule for Cistercian nuns. This rule was written by the abbot Blessed Aelredus (Ethelredus) of the Cistercian abbey of Rivesbey, England. He did not impose the appointment of an ordinary confessor as of absolute obligation but strongly advised it. Where it was possible, an elderly priest of good moral character was to be provided for every large monastery or church. The nuns were to speak to him rarely, except concerning confessional matters or for their edification. From him they were to receive counsel in doubt and consolation in tribulations.[9]

Order of Fontevrault.

The rule of the order founded by Blessed Robert de Arbrissel, was written about 1116 or 1117. The Order was composed of both monks and nuns and the abbess was supreme in all temporal matters. There was, however, a confessor general, under whom the priests functioned in spiritual matters. All the nuns from the abbess down had to confess. Even the

---

8 Caesarius Arelat., *Sermo ad Sanctimoniales,* Cap. 33; MPL LXVII, Cf. Schaaf, *The Cloister,* p. 20.

9 *Regula sive Institutio Inclusarum, B. Aelredi; "Ergo si fieri potest provideatur in magno monasterio vel ecclesia presbyter aliquis senex, maturus moribus, cui raro nisi de confessione et animae aedificatione loquatur; a quo consilium accipiat in dubiis, in tribulationibus consolationem;"* Holsten, *Codex Regularum,* I, p. 422; cf. Heimbucher, *Die Orden und Kongregationen,* I, 417 ff; Weber, *Cath. Encycl.* VI, 130 ff.

sick under this system had to be brought into chapel to make their confessions.[10]

Arguing from the fact that the priests were under a confessor general, it might conclude that there were many who heard these confessions.

Gilbertines.

The year of 1139 brings to light the rule of St. Gilbert of England. Under this rule the existence of an ordinary confessor is assured. Provision was to be made for a discreet priest, who was to go to the different houses of the nuns to hear their confessions at what is termed the "confessional windows."[11] This confessor is evidently of the same order, for that was the common practice in such cases.

The Poor Clares.

St. Francis attracted Clare by his example of evangelical poverty. It does not seem that St. Francis composed a definite rule for St. Clare.[12] The rule of St. Clare was approved by Pope Innocent IV in 1253. The sisters with the permission of the abbess were to confess at least twelve times a year.[13]

Constitutions of St. Bridget.

St. Bridget founded the Monastery of Nuns and a house of brothers of the order of St. Salvator[14] in the year of 1363.

This rule, approved by Urban VI in 1379, was peculiar inasmuch as there were allowed only thirteen priests. Here we notice the first appearance of the election of confessors. The election was to be unanimous. Probably this was due to that

---

10 *Regulae Sanctimonialium Fontis Ebraldi, Vetusta Statuta*, n. 16. MPL, CLXII, 1086; Lea, "*A History of Auricular Confession*," I, 201, n. 16.

11 *Regulae Ordinis Sempringensis; Capitula de Monialibus; "Provideatur sacerdos discretus . . . qui circumeat Domos nostros sanctimonialium et suscepturus ad fenestram confessiones . . . In Domo ubi confitebitur assideant duae discretae, remotae a fenestra, ut videant, qualiter se habuerit, quae confitetur.*" cf. Holsten, *op. cit.*, II, 476.

12 Schaaf—*The Cloister*, p. 27.

13 Innocent IV, Const. *Solet annuere*, Aug. 9, 1253, ch. III; BRT, III, n. CXXXIII, p. 573.

14 Boniface IX, const. *Ab origine*, Oct. 7, 1391; BRT, IV, C. VII, p. 620.

principle which Boniface VIII had already given in his Liber Sextus, that whatever affected all should be approved by all.[15]

So the abbess would select as confessor of all that one of the thirteen priests, who was chosen by the community. The bishop would constitute and confirm him as confessor general with full faculties to bind and loosen, correct and reform and all the brothers and sisters and even the abbesses were to obey him in everything.[16] All the sisters, priests and brothers were to confess to the confessor general at least three times a year. Since the consciences of all must be cleansed many time a year by confession, the confessor general could choose as many of the other twelve as he wished to hear these confessions. These confessors were to be prepared to hear confessions at all times.[17]

The points to be noticed in this rule are that (1) there was a confessor general, who was to hear the confessions of all, similar to our modern ordinary confessor. (2) He was to be appointed to that office only after election by the entire community. (3) He became the superior. (4) He could appoint additional confessors.

These mark big strides in the legislation of religious institutes in the direction of leniency.

This order and its rule was approved again in 1391 by Boniface IX.[18]

Papal Privileges.

Sixtus IV, 1476, noted for the privileges he granted to the different orders of religious, extended to the sisters of Blessed Mary of Mt. Carmel, the right to choose a suitable confessor, with the consent of their superiors. He, once during life and also at the time of death, having heard their confession, could grant full remission of all sins and give the apostolic indulgence.[19]

---

15 *Quod omnes tangit debet ab omnibus approbari.* R. J. in VI°, Reg. 29.

16 *Regula Sancti Salvatoris seu Constitutiones Sanctae Birgittae Viduae*, ch. XII; cf. Holsten, *op. cit.*, III, p. 112.

17 *ibidem.* ch. xiii; Holsten, III, p. 112.

18 Boniface IX, const. *Ab origine.* Oct. 7, 1391; BRT, IV, C. VII, p. 620.

19 Sixtus IV, Const. *Dum attenta,* Nov. 28, 1476, BRT. V, C. XV, p. 245.

Leo X granted another privilege to the nuns of Blessed Mary Magdalene in his bull "*Salvator noster,*" of May 19, 1520, giving very extensive faculties to their confessors. These confessors, if suitable and acceptable to the superiors of the society, had to be provided for these nuns. They could absolve all the nuns from all sins, crimes and excesses no matter how grave and enormous, even if reserved to the Apostolic See. This could be done as often as there was need, provided a suitable penance was imposed.[20]

This was quite an advance over previous legislation, for it gave the nuns the right to use this privilege as often as necessary unlike that of Sixtus IV, which was to be used only once during life and once before death.

After the Council of Trent, these rules need be considered no further, for they would but incorporate its precepts, since no new rule could be used without papal approval.

Article II.

Pre-Tridentine Local Conciliar Legislation.

Council of Aix-la-Chapelle, 816.[21]

The Councils of the Church did not treat of this matter definitely and it was no doubt due to abuses that the Council of Aix-la-Chapelle, held during the reign of Pope Stephen IV

---

20 Leo X; Bull "*Salvator noster,*" May 19, 1520; BRT. V, C. XLIII, p. 746, § 8.

21 The Council of Toledo held in 398 or 400 contains a prescription which has been taken by some authors as referring to the confessor of the nuns of those times (cf. Lea, *A History of Auricular Confession and Indulgences,* I, p. 179). The words of Chapter VI of the Council are these: "Item neque puella Dei aut familiaritatem habet cum confessore, aut cum quolibet laico sanguinis alieni." (cf. Mansi, III, 999; Harduin, III, 998.)

Other authorities such as Du Cange (*Glossarium ad Scriptores Mediae et Infimae Latinitatis, II,* col. 952) interpret this word "confessore" as meaning a chanter. This seems to be the better view especially since the word is used in that sense in chapter IX of the Council. Moreover, the whole Council treats of the different offices in the Church, i. e., the diaconate, sub-diaconate, etc. It is logical, then, to consider this term as applying to the chanter and

and Emperor Louis II, in 816 formulated prescriptions for the confessor of nuns. The nuns had the obligation of the cloister and the priests were to go there to hear their confessions. The priest that heard their confessions was the one attached to the neighboring church. It cannot be ascertained whether there were many or only one priest who had the office of hearing these confessions, as the council speaks only of the manner in which they were to be made, i. e., before the altar and in the sight of witnesses. The sick could be heard in their houses, but the priest had to bring a deacon and subdeacon with him, who, in this case, acted as the witnesses. The purpose of this was that the priest might have proof that he conducted his office in the right way.[22]

Council of Paris, 829.

The words of the Council of Aix-la-Chapelle, were substantially reproduced in the decree of the Sixth Council of Paris of 829. The monks and canons were permitted by the Council to hear the confessions of nuns and canonesses, but the monks were not allowed to enter monasteries to hear nuns' confessions.[23] The capitularies of the French kings had incorporated the rulings of the Council of Paris in August, 837.[24]

Council of Paris, 1212.

Shortly before the Council of Paris in the year of 1210, Innocent III was forced to condemn an abuse which had arisen in the dioceses of Burgois and Palencia, which had come to his notice of the abbesses of these dioceses, hearing the confessions of their nuns.[25]

---

22 *Conc. Aquisgranense an. 816*—Liber II, cap. XXIII, XXVII; Mansi, XIV, col. 276.

23 *Concilium Parisiense* VI; Hefele, IV, p. 64; Mansi, XIV, 565; Harduin, IV, 1323.

24 *Capitularia Regum Francorum,* Cap. XIX, Mansi XIIII B, C. 1141.

25 Letter to the Bishops of the dioceses of Burgois and Palencia, III, Dec. 11, 1210, "Quum igitur id absonum sit paritor et absurdum, (*nec a nobis aliquatenus sustinendum*) *discretioni vestrae per apostolica scripta* mandamus, quatenus, ne id de cetero fiat, *auctoritate* curetis *apostolica* firmiter inhibere, quia, licet beatissima virgo Maria dignior et excellentior fuerit Apostolis universis, non tamen illi, sed istis Dominus claves regni coelorum commisit. c. 4, X, *de Sententia Exc.* V, 38.

This condemnation, no doubt, led the Council of Paris convened by Cardinal Robert Courzon, a famous teacher of the University of Paris and legate to France,[26] to condemn likewise the abominable practice of abbesses and chaplains of prohibiting their nuns to confess to others than themselves. The council prescribed that the diocesan bishops provide them with a discreet and honest confessor of a suitable age lest the blood of these nuns might be required of them on the day of the strict judgment.[27] In these very strong words repeated in 1214 by the Council of Rouen,[28] there can be seen the hatred of the Church for any such abuses which render the Sacrament of Penance odious to nuns. The importance of suitable confessors to assure liberty of conscience, was firmly established by this council.

Fourth Lateran Council. 1215.

This council only treats indirectly the confessor of nuns inasmuch as it prescribes annual confession for all who have attained the use of reason.[29] Between this council and that of Trent, there was no further development of the law in regard to the confessor of women religious.

Article III.

From the Council of Trent to the Constitution "Pastoralis Curae."

Just as the regular prelates preserved the exclusive right of hearing the confessions of their male subjects, either themselves or through their delegate, so they also observed the same practice in regard to the nuns subject to them.[30] It was to give more freedom of conscience to the nuns that the Council of Trent published its decree on the confessors of nuns on De-

26 Hefele, *op. cit.*, V, p. 857.

27 *Concilium Parisiense*, Anno (1212); Ch. VII; Hefele, *op. cit.*, V, p. 869.

28 *Concilium Rotomagense;* Statuta, pars 3, cap. 37; cf. Mansi XXII, col. 912.

29 *Concilium Lateranense* IV, an. 1215, Cap. XXI; Mansi, XII, 1008; Denzinger, *Enchiridion Symbolorum*, n. 437; c. 12, X, *De Poenitentiis*, V, 38.

30 Vermeersch, *Periodica*, V, p. (4).

cember 3, 1563.[31] This law, which from its very wording applied only to nuns, granted them:

(1) An ordinary confessor, whose duty it was to hear all the confessions of the nuns.

(2) An extraordinary confessor, who was to go to the convent for the same purpose two or three times a year.

The bishops did not wait long to enforce the decree of Trent. The Council of Salzburg in 1569[32] insisted upon its observance, while the Council of Florence in 1573[33] specified two times at least, i. e., before the Assumption and after Ash Wednesday, as the periods, during which the extraordinary confessor should be given besides other time approved by the bishop.

The question that caused most trouble after the Council of Trent was the approbation necessary to hear the confessions of women religious. In confessional discipline at this time, there existed a distinction between approbation and jurisdiction. Approbation was defined as the authentic judgment or declaration of suitability and sufficiency of a priest to hear confessions. The conferring of jurisdiction, on the other hand, was an act of the will by which the superior granted such a priest power over his subjects to hear their confessions. Thus

31 Session, XXV, *de regularibus*, c. 10 *"Attendant diligenter episcopi et ceteri superiores monasteriorum sanctimonialium, ut in constitutionibus earum admoniantur sanctimoniales, ut saltem semel singulis mensibus confessionem peccatorum faciant, et sacrosanctam Eucharistiam suscipiant, ut eo salutari praesidio muniant ut omnes oppugnationes daemonis fortiter superandas. Praeter ordinarium autem confessorem alius extraordinarius ab episcopo et aliis superioribus bis aut ter in anno offeratur, qui omnes confessiones audire debeat. Quod vero sanctissimum Christi corpus intra chorum, vel septa monasterii, et non in publica ecclesia, conservetur: prohibet sancta synodus, non obstante quocumque indulto aut privilegio."* cf. Ehses, *Concilium Tridentinum* Tom. 9, pars. 6 Actorum, Page 1082.

32 *Concilium Salisburgense*, March 14, 1569, Ch. V; Mansi, XXXVI, col. 243.

33 *Concilium Floriense*, an. 1573; Rubric LII, Ch. VIII; Mansi XXXV a, col. 795.

it is clearly evident that the conferring of jurisdiction necessarily presupposed the approbation.[34]

The Council of Trent did not change the discipline on the approbation and appointment of confessors of nuns. Therefore, confessors of nuns, subject to local Ordinaries, were approved by the latter, while confessors of nuns, subject to regulars, received their approbation from the regular Prelates of that institute as the Ordinaries of these nuns.[35] These superiors also granted the jurisdiction to hear the confessions of these nuns.[36] But Gregory XV, led by the desire of having the sacrament administered by worthy and upright priests, enacted uniform legislation in this matter.[37] Before the Council of Trent, by pontifical privileges,[38] regulars had jurisdiction to hear lay people, but the Council of Trent required that these be approved by the bishops.[39]

Gregory XV also demanded for nuns the same right. Their confessor, even if he was an exempt regular, was to be adjudged suitable by the local Ordinary and approved by him. This held even for the ordinary and extraordinary confessor of nuns subject to regulars. This approbation was to be given gratis.[40] The regular superiors retained the right of presentation of the confessors for the nuns subject to them, to the Bishop to receive

---

34 Ferraris, *Bibliotheca Prompta*, v. Approbatio, Art. I, n. 1-5, p. 663; Cf. Bouix, *Tractatus De Jure Regularium*, pars V, Cap. III, q. 1, p. 213 ff.

35 Pellizarius *Tractatio de Monialibus* Cap. X, Section III, Sub-section I, n. 163; Pius V. (Const. "*Ea est officii,*" July 3, 1568, BRT VII, n. XCIX, p. 681.) in the reformation of the rules of the 3rd Order of Penance of St. Francis states that approbation of confessors is to be given by the general or provincial. Monasteries of exempt nuns subject to the Holy See were ruled by bishops in spiritual but not in temporal matters; Chokier, *Tractatus de Jurisdictione Ordinarii in Exemptos*, p. 259.

36 Pius V, Const. *Romanii Pontificis* July 21, 1571, BRT vol. VII, n. CXCVIII, p. 931; Cf. Vermeersch, *De Religiosis*, II, n. 204, also *Periodica*, V, p. (2).

37 Const. *Inscrutabili*, Feb. 5, 1622, intro.; FJC, n. 197.

38 Leo X, Const. *Dum Intra*, Dec. 17, 1516, FJC, n. 72, § 6, 7; C. 2, III, *de Sepulturis*, 7, in Clem.

39 Gregory XV, Const. *Inscrutabili*, *loc. cit.*, § 1, 2, 3, 4.

40 Gregory XV, *loc. cit.*, § 5.

his approbation.[41] Regular superiors elected or appointed before the publication of this constitution "*Inscrutabili*" of Gregory XV, could hear the confessions of nuns subject to them without episcopal approbation if the nuns freely requested them to do so. But superiors elected, appointed, or whose office terminated legitimately after its publication, could not be confirmed for another time to hear confessions of nuns, unless judged and approved by the diocesan bishop.[42] Such approbation was required even for confessors of nuns subject to cardinals.[43]

Disregard of this decree gave rise to abuses to remove which Clement X reaffirmed the prescriptions of Gregory XV. He stated that general approbation for the confessions of the faithful was never to be considered as approbation for nuns subject to the approving bishop. Special approbation was required. He also limited the jurisdiction of the confessor to the monastery to which he was appointed. Likewise a confessor approved by the bishop to hear confessions of nuns on one occasion, could not, when his appointment ceased, hear these confessions without new approbation.[44]

Innocent XIII in 1723 reasserted the necessity of episcopal approbation for regular confessors of nuns subject to their rule. He required that the permission of their superiors be preceded by an examination before the diocesan bishop, to be followed by the approbation of the latter. Moreover, he revoked all contrary and even immemorable customs.[45]

His successor, Benedict XIII, reaffirmed this necessity of episcopal approbation.[46] But in his constitution "Pastoralis Officii," he granted the superiors general and even provincials

---

41 Pellizarius, *loc. cit.*, n. 165; Bouix, *op. cit.*, pars 5, q. XXIII, p. 262.

42 Cf. Ferraris, *op. cit.*, v. Approbatio art. III, n. 2, 3, p. 695. S. C. Conc. to the Abbot General of the Vallambrosians, Nov. 23, 1637; Ferraris, loc. cit., n. 4.

43 Giraldus, *Expositio Juris Pontificii*, III, p. 971.

44 Clement X, Const. *Superna*, June 21, 1670; FJC, n. 246, § 4.

45 Innocent XIII, Const. *Apostolici Ministerii*, May 23, 1723, § 20, 21. FJC, n. 280.

46 Benedict XIII, Const. *In Supremo*, Sept. 23, 1724; § 17; FJC, n. 283; const. *Pastoralis Officii*, March 27, 1726. § 8, FJC, n. 292.

of any regular order of Spain the privilege or indult of validly and licitly hearing the confessions of nuns subject to them without diocesan episcopal approbation.[47]

Based on this, there arose the opinion that all religious superiors could act in virtue of this constitution. This constitution, however, as can be seen, granted an indult, a privilege, which could not be extended beyond the limits of the territory for which it was granted.[48] Greater difficulty in regard to the universal observance of the laws on approbation was caused when Urban VIII, March 3, 1625, suspended the execution of the constitution Inscrutabili in the kingdoms of Portugal and Spain, until he or his successors should decide otherwise.[49] This suspension was revoked by Clement X in his Constitution *Superna*, which was a universal law promulgated to remove doubts and contentions that had arisen in regard to the *Inscrutabili*. This constitution of Clement X was reaffirmed by the Congregation of the Council. Despite this revocation of the suspension, some regulars of these kingdoms and especially the Cistercians, continued to resist and oppose the execution of the constitution *Inscrutabili* and the decrees of the Congregation of the Council. They contended that they were not expressly mentioned in these constitutions as their privileges would require, if they were to be revoked.[50] This led Clement XII in his Constitution "Admonet Nos," August 11, 1735, to bind all regulars of these kingdoms, including every order, society and congregation to the observance of these constitutions and decrees under pain of ecclesiastical punishments contained in the constitution of Gregory XV and Clement X.[51] A few

---

47 *Pastoralis Officii*, ibid.; Cf. Giraldus, *Expositio*, J. P., III, p. 748, 970. Confessors of the nuns of the Annunciation and those called Barbarinae of the City of Rome were exempted from this law being approved by the Cardinal protectors since they were entirely subject to the latter's jurisdiction in regard to spiritual and temporal affairs. Brief of Alexander VII, May 6, 1663, Clement IX, Jan. 16, 1668; Cf. Giraldus, *op. cit.*, p. 971.

48 Cf. Ferraris, *loc. cit.*, n. 4, 15, 16. note (1); Cf. Bouix, *op. cit.*, q. XXIII, p. 257.

49 Cf. Clem. XII, Const. *Admonet Nos*, Aug. 11, 1735; FJC, n. 297, § 1.

50 Clement XII, ibid. § 2.

51 Clement XII, ibid. § 3.

years after his accession to the See of Peter as successor to Clement XII, Benedict XIV confirmed the existing discipline on this matter. He stressed the examination necessary for the approbation of confessors of nuns in his Constitution, "*Ad Militantis,*" March 30, 1742.[52] The next year he imposed this discipline upon the Greek Melchite confessors of the Basilian nuns of the Monastery of Kesruano subject to the Abbot General of the Congregation of St. John of Soairo.[53]

ARTICLE IV.

FROM THE CONSTITUTION "PASTORALIS CURAE" TO THE DECREE "QUAMADMODUM."

Benedict XIV in subsequent constitutions "*Pastoralis Curae,*" of August 5, 1748,[54] and "*Quamvis Justo,*" of April 30, 1749,[55] urged again the observance of these rules.

Clement XIII,[56] on December 11, 1758, made matters clearer by confirming a decision of the Congregation of the Council to the effect that regular confessors, to obtain the faculty of hearing nuns' confessions, were to personally present themselves to the bishop. The testimony of their superiors as to their sufficiency and suitability sent to the bishop, would not suffice.

This legislation, so far treated, was made specifically for nuns and only for their confessions was special approbation required. But very often jurisdiction for confessions of other religious women, who were not nuns, was given by bishops to certain priests exclusively.[57]

For religious of simple vows, the confessors were to observe the statutes of the bishops of individual dioceses. The bishops, however, were wont to reserve to themselves the special approbation for professed of simple vows,[58] as is evident from the letters of approbation and the synodal statutes of many dio-

52 § 19, 20; FJC, n. 326.
53 Encycl. Lit. *Demandatum,* Dec. 24, 1743; FJC, 388, § 23, 24.
54 § 9, FJC. 388.
55 § 13, FJC. 398.
56 Const. *Inter Multiplices,* § 5; Fontes, 449.
57 Biederlack-Fuhrich, *op. cit.*, n. 49, p. 91.
58 Gury, *Compendium Theol. Mor.*, II, n. 568, p. 260; Aertnys, *Theol. Mor.*, Lib. VI, n. 233, p. 149.

ceses.[59] Gradually, this custom was introduced into the Church, which Leo XIII in his constitution *Conditae a Christo,* of Dec. 8, 1900, approved.[60] This was formulated very clearly by the Congregation of Religious in Article VI of the Decree *Cum de Sacramentalibus,* of Feb., 1913,[61] and is contained in Canons 876 and 525.

The constitution, *Pastoralis Curae,* published by Benedict XIV on August 5, 1748, is of the greatest importance, for it is an interpretation of the Council of Trent and a concise statement of all previous papal legislation. It also approved many decrees of the Congregation of the Council.[62]

The prelates of monasteries were wont to appoint one confessor for a period of three years. This had often caused great anguish and affliction of soul to nuns living in cloister. Through shame and other causes, some were prevented from revealing the hidden things of their consciences. Thus they were led to detract from the integrity of confession and cast themselves into the abyss of eternal damnation.[63] That this is not rarely happened, Benedict XIV knew from the matters treated by the apostolic Penitentiary, from his experiences as a bishop and from cases brought to him at the chair of Peter. As a result Benedict XIV stated that he did not wish to revoke the law of one confessor of nuns to a monastery as given in the Council of Trent. On the other hand, he would not allow every nun

---

59 *Statuta Dioecesis Novaroensis,* (. . . *in Synodo Dioecesana tertia* . . . 1878), n. 63, p. 51; *Synodus Dioecesana Manchesteriensis* I (1886), *Statuta,* n. 118, p. 29; *Synodus Dioecesana Neo-Eboracensis V,* (1886), n. 158, p. 40; *Synodus Dioecesana Albanensis IV* (1887), *Statuta* n. 75, p. 13 (ter), "*Ad valide absolvendas religiosas, illis exceptis quae justa de causa extra Monasterium suum versantur, specialis a Nobis requiritur facultas;*" *Synodus Dioecesana Albanensis V* (1890), n. 88, p. 34; ibid. VI (1895), n. 87, p. 35; cf. *Acta et Decreta I Concilii Plenarii Australasiae* (1885), n. 91, p. 33; ibid. *II Concilii* (1895), n. 94, p. 36; cf. Hizette, *op. cit.,* p. 106, Appendix II for the synods of Belgium.

60 Pt. I, § 11, Pt. II, § 8; cf. Col. S. C. P. F. (1907), n. 2097.

61 Art. VI. AAS, V, p. 62.

62 Vermeersch, *Periodica,* V, p. (4).

63 Const. *Pastoralis Curae,* § 1, FJC, n. 388; Cf. Choupin, L'Etat Religieux p. 205, 206.

to choose her own confessor, but by casuistry he attempted to give remedies for particular cases that might arise.[64] For this purpose he outlined the laws for the extraordinary confessor. His prescriptions were (1) That bishops and regular prelates had to give, in conformity with the Council of Trent, an extraordinary confessor two or three times a year to those monasteries of nuns respectively subject to them. The council made this decision because some nuns could not make an integral and beneficial confession to their ordinary confessor.[65] (2) He interpreted the Council of Trent as not imposing an obligation upon the superioresses, professed, novices and girls being educated in a monastery, of confessing on these occasions to the extraordinary confessor. They were only required to present themselves before him at least, to receive advice if they did not care to confess. The purpose of this was to prevent comparisons and suspicions which otherwise would arise as to the necessity for going of those who appeared before the extraordinary confessor.[66] (3) The choice and appointment of the extraordinary confessor was left to the same person who could appoint the ordinary confessor. Therefore, a bishop should give the extraordinary confessor to nuns subject to him while the regular prelate was to do the same for his nuns. If the bishop neglected this, the Cardinal Penitentiary could, upon request, appoint a confessor approved by the Ordinary of the place with all faculties. The failure of the regular prelate to appoint an extraordinary confessor for his own nuns, could be supplied by the appointment made by the local Ordinary.[67] (4) Sick nuns could request of their respective superior, whether the bishop or the regular prelate, the appointment of a particular confessor and upon failure to receive their request, could apply to the Cardinal Penitentiary.[68] (5) Bishops and regular prelates had the obligation of appointing a confessor, outside of

64 ibidem, § 1; cf. Vermeersch, *Periodica,* V, p. (5).

65 Const. *Pastoralis Curae,* ibidem, § 2.

66 ibidem, § 3.

67 ibidem, § 4.

68 ibidem, § 5.

those regularly appointed, for those nuns refusing to confess to the ordinary confessor of the community. This confessor was to be one approved for the confessions of nuns. If the priest, to whom the nun desired to confess, was not approved, then the Ordinary had the obligation of approving him at least for one confession or as many times as he judged prudent and expedient. Failure of the regular superior to comply with such a request granted to a nun the right of recourse to the Cardinal Penitentiary. The latter could appoint one already approved for the confession of nuns, either of another order or a secular.[69]

(6) Even for their peace of mind and greater progress in the spiritual life nuns could request a particular confessor already approved. Although these requests were not to be granted rashly neither could they be rejected without cause. The superiors appointing were to make their decision according to the following considerations: (1) if there was no reason for suspicion, (2) if the confessor had not only the legitimate approbation of the Ordinary, but, moreover, common testimony to his good character. When these conditions were satisfactorily fulfilled, there was no reason why an individual nun should not receive a special confessor. Benedict closes this part of his constitution with the exhortation to bishops and superiors to grant this confessor when asked.[70]

(7) Benedict demanded in the extraordinary confessor, whether of a community or an individual, the following qualities: (a) that his character be known by his integrity of morals and prudence, which is generally assured by maturity of years; (b) that he be approved for nuns' confessions by the Ordinary. This approbation was necessary even to hear the confessions of nuns subject to regulars or when the confessor was granted by the Cardinal Penitentiary.[71] (8) For the community confessors Benedict made certain regulations.

69 ibidem, § 6.
70 ibidem, § 7, 8.
71 ibidem, § 9.

For nuns subject to the bishop, the ordinary confessor was to be a secular and while the extraordinary was also to be of that branch of the clergy. Nevertheless, the custom of appointing a regular to this office through the lack of suitable seculars could be tolerated. The ordinary confessor of nuns subject to regulars, was to be of their own order. Although regulars had the right to appoint an extraordinary confessor of another order, there was no obligation to do so. Neglect upon the part of the regular superior to appoint an extraordinary confessor, gave the bishop the right to designate a suitable secular or regular of another order to hear the confessions of those nuns subject to regulars.[72] In monasteries of nuns subject to regulars, the extraordinary confessor had to be given once a year from the secular clergy or another order. Otherwise the bishop could supply this defect.[73] The frequency with which the regular prelate was obliged to grant an extraordinary confessor to communities over which he had charge, was determined as two or three times a year.[74] Benedict prohibited the ordinary confessor from placing any obstacle in the way of the extraordinary confessor in the performance of his office. The ordinary confessor was also forbidden to hear the confessions of any of those within the monastery or pious house, while the extraordinary confessor was performing his office. On the other hand, the extraordinary confessor was forbidden under pain of incurring the punishments laid down by Benedict XIV's predecessors to return to the monastery after fulfilling his office and to talk to the nuns.[75]

The common law up till that time did not explicitly treat of institutes of sisters or women of simple vows, nor did it impose upon them the law of the unity of confessors. They were subject in this matter to the will of the bishops. The latter, however, had the practice of appointing only one ordinary confessor.[76] Benedict XIV realized that the same conditions which

72 ibidem, § 10.
73 ibidem, § 11, 12.
74 ibidem, § 13, 14, 15.
75 ibidem, § 17, 18.
76 Vermeersch, Periodica V, p. (4); Choupin, op cit., p. 206.

existed in communities of cloistered women, would also arise in any community of religious women whatsoever. He, therefore, exhorted the bishops to observe the same form of discipline in regard to the extraordinary confessor for those religious who are not bound by the laws of the cloister, yet who live in community. He desired these regulations to be extended to conservatories of women or girls, for which only one ordinary minister of the Sacrament of Penance was appointed by the superiors.[77]

The question arose as to whether these words had force of law. The affirmative seemed the more probable, but even in this event the words of the decree referred only to the appointment of the extraordinary confessor in a community that had only one ordinary minister of the Sacrament of Penance. Where the community had two or three ordinary confessors, the above constitution certainly could not be interpreted as directly affecting them.[78]

In the constitution *Quamvis Justo* edited the year following on April 30th, 1749, by the same Pontiff, he interprets this paragraph of the constitution mentioned above. This constitution was directed to the "English Ladies," women of simple vows, who were subject to the local Ordinaries in regard to the appointment of confessors. Their confessors were to be chosen from the suitable secular or regular clergy. Benedict expressed the hope that the Bishops would, in this regard, keep in mind and observe those things which he had set down in his constitution "Pastoralis Curae" to be observed in the apopintment of confessors of non-cloistered women living in community.[79] The expression "set down to be observed" is a rigorous term of law and denotes not a counsel but an obligation. Hence the con-

---

77 Ibid. § 3.

78 Curran, Confessors and Confessions of Religious Women of Simple Vows, p. 18.

79 Const. *Quamvis justo*, April 30, 1749; FJC n. 398, § 13.

stitution "Pastoralis Curae" seems to have had force of law for congregations of simple vows having only one ordinary confessor.[80]

That this law for ordinary confessors was extended to religious congregations of women of simple vows, is evident from the response given by the Congregation of Bishops and Regulars to the Bishop of Trent. This reply placed women of solemn and simple vows on the same footing and the bishop was given faculties to reappoint confessors for a second or third term on the condition that the special rules for reappointment were observed.[81] The only rules given up till that time had been those laid down in the constitution "Pastoralis Curae." Therefore, the regulations of this constitution in regard to the ordinary confessor were extended to congregations of religious women of simple vows.[82]

There were many other responses of the Roman congregations which show that the prescriptions of Benedict XIV also applied to communities of women of simple vows.[83]

But the discipline was not exactly the same, for some exceptions were allowed to the regulations set for women professing solemn vows, for instance; (1) a regular priest could be ordinary confessor to women of simple vows;[84] (2) any priest hearing confessions in a public church, though not approved for women religious, could absolve school sisters, who lived in community outside of the cloister, and who received the sacraments and attended the divine services in the parish church;[85] (3) disobedience to the law in regard to triennial

---

80 Curran, *op. cit.*, p. 20.

81 S. C. EE et RR, *Tridentina.* Jan. 29, 1847. Ad. 3; cf., Bizzarri, p. 116; Vermeersch, *De Religiosis*, II, n. 226.

82 Curran, op. cit., p. 22.

83 S. C. EE et RR, Apr. 22, 1872; Col. S. C. P. F. ed. 1893, n. 433. S. C. EE et RR, June 20, 1875; Col. S. C. P. F. (ed. 1907), n. 1446; Cf. Vermeersch, *op. cit.*, n. 229.

84 Benedict XIV, Const. *Quamvis Justo*, Apr. 30, 1749, § 14; FJC, n. 388.

85 S. C. EE et RR, Apr. 22, 1872, ad. 3; Col. S. C. P. F. (ed. 1893), n. 433.

change of confessor rendered confessions heard and absolutions given illicit[86] but not invalid as in the case of nuns of solemn vows.[87]

Article V.

From the Decree "Quemadmodum" to the Code of Canon Law.

The greatest effect of the decree Quemadmodum published Dec. 17, 1890, was to introduce greater uniformity and certainty although it did not change the existing discipline in the matter of the confessors of religious women.[88] The prologue of the decree gives the cause for its promulgation which is the re-statement once more of the same trouble which has led to developments of law in this matter up to the present. The abuse which caused this decree, was the fact that superiors made their subjects manifest their consciences to them, denied them an extraordinary confessor and prohibited them from receiving Communion. Therefore, Leo XIII, through the Congregation of Bishops and Regulars, published this decree. It was directed to all lay institutes not only of women of solemn and simple vows, but even to those institutes to which the members were bound only by a promise.[89]

The decree did not lay down a new law on the confessor of religious women but only affirmed the existence of the old law of Benedict XIV and that it retained its full force for all religious women, whether of solemn or simple vows. All old laws and customs remained in force, except in those points which were contrary to this decree in regard to the manifestation of conscience and the reception of Communion. Contrary customs, which, even if immemorable, were abrogated by this decree.[90] Thus religious women of simple vows were placed on equal footing in regard to confessors with those of solemn vows.[91]

---

[86] S. C. EE et RR, June 20, 1875, ad. 3; Col. S. C. P. F. (1907), n. 1446.

[87] S. C. EE et RR, March 4, 1591; *in Ragusina*, Oct. 2, 1626, and March 27, 1647; cf. Ferraris, *op. cit.*, v. *Monialis*, Art. V, n. 19; p. 1099; Cf. Bouix, *Tractatus de Jure Regularium*, p. 334, n. 8°, (ed. 1883); Curran, *op. cit.*, p. 26.

[88] Cf. Curran, op. cit., p. 28.

[89] S. C. EE et RR—Decree, *Quemadmodum*, Dec. 17, 1890, intro. Col. S. C. P. F. (1907), n. 1745.

[90] Ibidem, intro. and § 4.

The same Pope Leo XIII in 1900 issued his constitution *Conditae a Christo,*[92] in which he contented himself with the insistence that the constitution *Pastoralis Curae* and the decree, *Quemadmodum,* must be observed.[93]

But the laws up to the present on the confessors of religious women since they were given at different times and for different places, necessarily lacked unity. Doubts could arise as to whether they applied to all orders, whether those of solemn or simple vows or whether they could be extended to communities having no vows at all, but living a life in conformity to religious rule. The tendency of the latter laws treated above was towards conformity of discipline. Where the law did not explicitly state for what religious it was made, the bishop had the power to treat them all alike. Even after this there was still room for doubt. As a result, the Congregation on Religious Affairs co-ordinated these laws and published them in concise form in the decree *Cum de Sacramentalibus.*[94] The changes adopted gave greater freedom on most points than even the most liberal of the older laws. This decree bound all bishops, regular prelates, religious and confessors. It may be summarized as follows: (1) The unity of the confessor for a community is retained. The number of nuns, however, or any other just cause, warranted appointment of a second or even several ordinary confessors.[95] (2) The maximum term of office of the ordinary confessor was three years. There was an intermediate lapse of one year before reappoinment,[96] except when there were no other qualified confessors or when the majority of the religious, by secret ballot, requested his reappointment. In these cases the Bishop or Ordinary could reappoint the same confessors immediately. Religious who had no vote

91 Curran, *op. cit.,* p. 29.
92 S. C. EE et RR, Dec. 8, 1900, Col. S. C. P. F. (1907), n. 2097.
93 ibidem, pt. I, § XI; pt. II, § VIII; Cf. Curran, op. cit., p. 29.
94 S. C. De Religiosis, Decree of Feb. 3, 1913, AAS, V, 62, intro. Cf. O'Donnell, Ir. Ecc. Rec. (Fifth Series, Vol. I, 1913), p. 419.
95 AAS, ibidem, n. 1.
96 ibidem. n. 9.

in other matters, had the right of a voice in this decision. The dissenting minority had to be provided for otherwise. There was no longer the necessity of appealing to Rome for dispensation or of a two-third majority for this reappointment.[97] (3) There is no change in regard to the law of the extraordinary confessor, except that he was to come "*pluries*" instead of "*bis aut ter*" during the year. Every religious was obliged to present herself at least to receive his blessing.[98] Trent had required that he hear all confessions.[99] This decree insisted upon the supplementary confessor of the decree "Quemadmodum," to whom the religious could easily apply in individual cases. It made what was formerly an exhortation now a command.[100] (5) The decree approved of the special confessor for the sake of peace of mind and greater progress in the way of God. This confessor was to be easily granted by the Ordinary. The latter, without interfering with the liberty of conscience, was at the same time to take precautions against abuses and remove them if they should arise.[101] (6) The old rule was retained that when the convent was subject to the bishop he was to make the appointment of ordinary and extraordinary confessors. If the convent was subject to a regular superior the latter had the right of presentation of the confessor to the Ordinary from whom the necessary approbation was to be received.[102] (7) The same qualities were required in the confessors as formerly. They could be chosen from the regular or secular clergy, provided they had no authority over the nuns in the external forum. The age was set at forty years as the general rule for the ordinary confessor. For sufficient reason the Ordinary could select younger men qualified in other respects. All interference by the confessor in the internal or external government of the

97 AAS, ibidem, n. 2; O'Donnell, op. cit., p. 420.

98 AAS, ibidem, n. 3; Pastoralis Curae § 3. FJC, 388.

99 Sess. XXV, de Reg. c. 10: Ehses, *Concilium Tridentinum*, Tom. 9, pars. 6, Actorum, p. 1082.

100 AAS, ibidem, n. 4; O'Donnell, op. cit., p. 421.

101 AAS, ibidem, n. 5.

102 AAS, ibidem, n. 6.

community was forbidden.[103] (8) The religious superioress, when legitimately requested by a sister for a supplementary confessor, could not directly, or indirectly ask her motive for such a request, or in any way show displeasure. For the first violation of this prohibition the superioress was to be admonished by the Ordinary. Upon repetition of the offense the Congregation for Religious Affairs was to be consulted and, according to their decision, the Ordinary was to remove her from office.[104]

This law differed from the Decree of 1890, only in regard to the penalties prescribed.[105] (9) To prevent shame in going to confession, the religious were not to speak to one another about confessions of other sisters nor to upbraid those asking for special confessors. Violation of this precept merited punishment by the superioress or the Ordinary.[106] This was a new regulation.[107] The religious were not to permit human motives to be the sole cause for asking for special confessors. This request was to be made for their spiritual good and greater progress in virtue.[108] This was just a restatement of the law of 1890. (10) When outside of the convent religious could confess in any church or oratory, whether public or semi-public, and to any confessor generally approved for the faithful. Inquiries and objections to the use of this privilege by the superioress, were prohibited. The religious, on the other hand, were in no way bound to report to their superioresses, when they confessed outside of the convent.[109] (11) A religious seriously ill, even though not in danger of death, had the right of requesting any approved confessor. For the duration of this sickness she could confess to him as often as she desired.[110] This was a new concession inasmuch as a simply approved confessor could absolve gravely sick religious even outside of the

103 AAS, ibidem, n. 7-10.
104 AAS, ibidem, n. 11.
105 O'Donnell, Ir. Ecc. Rec. (Fifth Series, Vol. I, 1913), p. 422.
106 AAS, ibidem, n. 12.
107 O'Donnell, ibidem.
108 AAS, ibidem, n. 13.
109 AAS, ibidem, n. 14.
110 AAS, ibidem, n. 15.

danger of death. Finally, this decree was to be added to all rules and constitutions of religious communities and publicly read in the vernacular once a year in the chapter of the religious. This decree was to bind notwithstanding anything to the contrary, even though worthy of special and individual mention.[111]

Thus in this decree pre-Code legislation reached its climax. This decree had been practically incorporated in the present code together with subsequent interpretation of it.[112]

Introduction to Canonical Treatment.

Evidently Holy Mother, the Church demands of these confessors all the qualities necessary in all ordained priests to whose care she commits the administration of the Sacrament of Penance. Before hearing confession, there is necessary suitable knowledge, while in the act of confession there is the obligation of teaching and advising, of questioning and of absolving the penitent, unless the latter is indisposed. After confession the confessor is bound most strictly to observe the seal of sacramental secrecy and also to correct the defects committed in confession. These obligations naturally arise from the offices that are incumbent upon the minister of the sacrament of Penance, i. e., the office of *physician*, by which he should cure the diseases of the soul and prescribe remedies to prevent relapse; the office of *teacher*, by virtue of which he imparts to the penitent necessary knowledge; and the office of *judge* of the sins and dispositions of the penitent with the concomitant obligation of reconciling him to God by absolution.[1] But besides these, there is necessary special jurisdic-

---

111 O'Donnell, loc. cit.

112 S. C. De Rel., Sept. 2, 1913. *Mechlinen;* cf. Vermeersch, *Periodica,* VII, n. 745; S. C. De Rel. June 1, 1917; AAS, IX, p. 276; Vermeersch, *op. cit.,* VIII, n. 119; Choupin, L'Etat Religieux, p. 208.

1 Noldin, *De Sacramentis,* n. 381; cf. Azpilcueta, *Enchiridion sive Manuale Confessariorum et Poenitentium,* cap. IV, p. 103 ff.

tion, whether ordinary or delegated over the penitent.[2] The confessor of women religious, moreover, whether he be a secular or a religious priest and no matter of what rank or dignity, is to be endowed with that peculiar jurisdiction for the hearing of the confessions of these religious, without which he cannot validly and licitly perform that office.[3] No special jurisdiction, however, is required for the confessions of postulants or societies of pious women.[4] The legislation on the confessor of female religious was gathered together and clarified by the decree *Cum de Sacramentalibus* of the Congregation for Religious, which has formed the basis of our present legislation. The Code in Canon 520-527 treats of the ordinary, extraordinary and supplementary confessors appointed to communities and the special confessors of an individual religious, of the sick and those to whom they go for the peace of their conscience. The code defines the rights and obligations in this regard of the religious, the confessor, the superioress and the local Ordinary. Many things, questionable in the past, have been cleared up, while in those which remain unchanged an interpretation in the light of the old law, will have to be used.

The following chapters deal with an exposition of the legislation on this point. It is to be well noted that these Canons apply to all female religious and their novices,[5] regardless of exemption or solemnity of vows and also to women of pious societies living in common but without public vows.[6]

---

2 Can. 872.
3 Can. 876, § 1.
4 cf. Genicot, *Theol. Mor.* (ed. 1922), n. 339, note 2.
5 Can. 566, § 1.
6 Can. 675.

CHAPTER VIII.

SPECIAL JURISDICTION REQUIRED FOR THE CONFESSIONS OF RELIGIOUS WOMEN.

It was not until the constitution *Inscrutabili* of Gregory XV that all confessors of nuns had to be approved for this office by the local Ordinary,[1] but from that time on, although the regular superiors still granted the jurisdiction for the nuns subject to them, this approbation was required for the validity of the absolution.[2]

This remained the constant discipline for nuns and was extended very often in particular cases by bishops to confessors of other religious, not nuns, by giving exclusive jurisdiction over them to certain priests. This custom was approved by Leo XIII in his constitution *Conditae a Christ,* December 8, 1900.[3] Approbation had become almost synonymous with jurisdiction, for when a priest was approved, he generally received by the same act jurisdiction to hear these confessions, and in reality there was only a theoretical distinction. Approbation as distinct from jurisdiction has fallen into desuetude and the Code presents them today as synonymous and without distinction.[4]

CANON 876.

§ 1. Revocata qualibet contraria particulari lege seu privilegio, sacerdotes tum saeculares tum religiosi, cuiusvis gradus aut officii, ad confessiones quarumcumque religiosarum ac novitiarum valide et licite recipiendas peculiari iurisdictione indigent, salvo praescripto Can. 239, § 1, n. 1, 522, 523.

1. Gregory XV, Const. *Inscrutabili,* Feb. 5, 1622; FJC n. 199.
2. Bouix, *De Jure Regularium,* II, p. 262.
3. Pt. I, § 11; pt. II, § 8; Col. S. C. P. F. (ed. 1907), n. 2097.
4. Biederlack-Fuhrich, *De Religiosis,* n. 50; Vermeersch-Creusen, *Epit.* II; n. 143.

Special Jurisdiction Required for the Confessors of Religious Women

All priests both secular and religious, regardless of rank or office, with the exception of Cardinals (Can. 239, § 1, 1°) and the confessor chosen for the peace of conscience (C. 522) and also the confessor of the sick (C. 523) need this special jurisdiction in order to validly and licitly hear the confessions of female religious and their novices. The law is absolute and exceptions cannot be made, e. g., for the fact that a regular confessor is of the same order as the penitent or even for the episcopal dignity. Therefore, the custom of bishops hearing confessions of religious in the diocese of another Ordinary, without the faculties from the latter, is absolutely wrong and such confessions would be invalid. Bishops have not the same privilege as Cardinals in this regard. Moreover, they cannot presume faculties, for valid jurisdiction must be given expressly in writing or by word of mouth.[5] Neither would the office of director of the whole institute or the mother house, nor that of regular superior, nor even that of general suffice to hear the confessions of nuns subject to them without special jurisdiction from the local Ordinary. Such confessions would be invalid.[6] Neither can pastors hear confessions of nuns if they have not special jurisdiction.[7] Immemorable customs or privileges conceded directly or indirectly by the Holy See would not suffice to permit this in any case.[8] These priests not only need the approbation of the Ordinary, but also delegated jurisdiction from him, since, as we have said, the distinction between approbation and delegated jurisdiction, no longer exists under the Code.[9] The source of approbation and delegated jurisdiction in all cases of confessions of religious women under the code is the same person, the local Ordinary. The rules stated by Clement X in his constitution *Superna*[10] are still in force. These rules are: (1) that confessors generally approved for

5 Can. 879 § 1; cf. Creusen, *Religieux et Religieuses*, n. 90.
6 S. C. Conc. Nov. 23, 1637; cf. Ferraris, v. *Approbatio*, III, n. 3, 4, p. 695.
7 Vermeersch-Creusen, *Epit.* II, n. 145.
8 Creusen, *loc. cit.;* Can. 4; Can. 876 § 1, contains an express clause of revocation.
9 Biederlack-Fuhrich, *op. cit.*, n. 50; Vermeersch-Creusen, *Epit.* II, n. 143.
10 June 2, 1670; § 4, FJC, n. 246.

the faithful, are never considered as approved for confessions of nuns; (2) that assignment to one community does not give the faculty to validly hear the nuns of another convent; (3) that the confessor appointed only for single occasions[11] cannot hear the confessions of religious women at other times. If the Ordinary, in granting faculties, does not explicitly state that the confessor appointed may hear the confessions of all religious women on all occasions, he is restricted in the exercise of his faculties to the convent to which he is appointed.[12]

Special jurisdiction means, as Augustine states, that the Ordinary expressly states in granting faculties "*etiam ad confessiones religiosarum ac novitiarum*" or some similar form. Of course, the very appointment of a priest as the confessor of religious implies this grant of jurisdiction necessary for the performance of the office, even though by mistake this is not expressly stated in the written or oral appointment. This is not opposed to Canon 879, § 1, because the appointment as such of the confessor, includes jurisdiction.[13]

Since this canon distinguishes between religious and novices these words must be taken disjunctively. Therefore, a priest expressly appointed as confessor of the professed religious only, could not, in virtue of that appoinment, hear the confessions of the novices, since they are not religious properly so-called.[14] For the same reason, the confessor who has been appointed only for novices could not hear the confessions of the professed. Canon 566, § 1, states that novices are to be provided with confessors in the same way as religious, i. e., an ordinary and extraordinary confessor, etc. This does not imply that the confessor of the novices and the professed could not be one and the same person. That he has faculties for the professed and novices will be certain when he is appointed "for the commu-

---

11 Augustine, IV, p. 267; Father Augustine here seems to confuse the approbation of the time of Clement X with the modern idea of jurisdiction. This identity did not exist at the time this constitution was published.

12 Augustine, *loc. cit.*

13 Augustine, *op. cit.*, p. 269.

14 Can. 488, 7°.

nity." Then, according to Canon 514, § 1, he can hear the confessions of all composing the community, i. e., the professed, novices, postulants, servants, students, guests and the sick, staying there day and night. The wording of the faculties must be considered to determine the extent of his jurisdiction.

This peculiar jurisdiction is necessary for validity and liceity. This is a trace of the old law which required even approbation for validity.[15]

The Local Ordinary Grants This Jurisdiction.

The term Local Ordinary includes all those mentioned in Canon 198, § 1, i. e., the Pope for the whole Church, and for their own territories, Residential Bishops, Abbots, and Prelates Nullius, and the Vicar Generals of these, Administrators, Vicars and Prefects Apostolic. This also includes all the "ad interim" successors of the above mentioned, either by prescription of law or constitution. No other religious superiors, however, are included.[16]

The Effect of This Law.

Canon 876, § 1, revokes every contrary particular law or privilege. Such a particular law existed in Spain and Portugal in virtue of the suspension of enforcement of the constitution *Inscrutabili* of Gregory XV in these countries by Urban VIII, on March 3, 1625.[17]

This suspension was revoked by Clement X in his constitution *Superna*.[18] Benedict XIII, on March 27, 1726,[19] granted to superior generals and provincials of all orders in Spain the privilege or indult of validly hearing, without episcopal approbation, the confessions of nuns subject to themselves.[20] All such privileges are now avoided by the Code.

15 S. C. Conc. Nov. 23, 1637; cf. Ferraris v. *Approbatio*, III, n. 3, p. 695.

16 Can. 198, §§ 1, 2.

17 Cf. Clement XII, Const. *Admonet nos*, Aug. 11, 1735, § 1; FJC, n. 279; Benedict XIV, *De Synodo Diocesana*, IX, 15, 9; Augustine, IV, p. 268.

18 Cf. Clement, ibid.

19 Const. *Pastoralis officii*, § 8; FJC, n. 292.

20 It is due to an oversight then that Father Augustine, O. S. B. (*Commentary on Canon Law*, IV, 268), states, "we know of no privilege granted after the aforesaid constitution of Gregory XV" (i. e. *Inscrutabili*, Feb. 6, 1622).

CHAPTER IX.

CHOICE AND DELEGATION OF CONFESSORS.

CANON 876.

§ 2. Hanc iurisdictionem confert loci Ordinarius, ubi religiosarum domus sita est, ad normam Can. 525.

This is in conformity with the prescriptions of Canon 198 and 873, which prescribe that only local Ordinaries have ordinary jurisdiction over territories and that regular superiors, unless they are at the same time local Ordinaries, have only personal jurisdiction over their own immediate subjects.

CANON 525.

Si religiosarum domus Sedi Apostolicae immediate subiecta sit vel Ordinario loci, hic eligit sacerdotes a confessionibus tum ordinarios tum extraordinarios; si Superiori regulari, hic confessarios Ordinario praesentat, cuius est eosdem pro audiendis illarum monialium confessionibus approbare et Superioris negligentiam, si opus sit, supplere.

Religious Houses Subject to the Holy See Directly or to the Local Ordinary.

Appointments. The decree of the Congregation of Religious of 1913,[1] distinguished between houses subject to the local Ordinary and those subject to the regular superior. It did not, however, mention the method of procedure to be followed for those houses subject directly to the Holy See, but over which the Bishop had the same jurisdiction as delegate of the Holy See.

Canonists, however, applied the same principles to them

[1] N. VII.—AAS V, p. 63; 2nd Eng. Trans. ibid, p. 247.

as are now embodied in the Code, appealing to the anterior legislation of Benedict XIV, developed in the constitution "Pastoralis Curae."[2]

This required that both ordinary and extraordinary confessors be approved by the local Ordinary, since that was the law of the Apostolic Constitutions, even for those appointed by their respective regular superiors, for the nuns subject to them and even those confessors granted by the Cardinal Penitentiary. This legislation was approved by Leo XIII in the decree *Quemadmodum* of 1890[3] and the constitution *Conditae a Christo* of 1900,[4] and again in the Normae of 1901 of the Sacred Congregation of Bishops and Regulars (art. 141). On all hypotheses, then, it was the local Ordinary alone who could choose such confessors and give jurisdiction to them.[5]

The present Code very plainly states this same principle as the law. The local Ordinary of the place where the confessions are to be heard, is to choose and appoint the confessors both for houses subject to the Holy See directly or to himself. He can do this even for houses subject only by indult or exception to himself.[6] In this country all religious communities of women are subject to the local Ordinary who makes the appointments.[7] Of nuns subject to Regulars, there can hardly be any question in the United States. The religious of France and Belgium are also subject to their local ordinaries, except the Sisters of Charity of St. Vincent de Paul, who are subject to the Superior General of the Lazarists.[8]

---

2 Aug. 5, 1748, §§ 6, 9; FJC, n. 388.
3 S. C. EE et RR, Dec. 17, 1890; n. 4; Col. S. C. P. F. (ed. 1907), n. 1745.
4 Dec. 8, 1900, pt. 1, n. 11; Col. S. C. P. F. (ed. 1907), n. 2097.
5 Hizzette, *Confessions des Religieuses*, p. 43.
6 Blat, II, pars II, n. 588.
7 Cf. *II Conc. Baltimorense*, tit. VIII, n. 419; *III Conc. Baltimorense*, Tit. VII, *de Regularibus*, n. 93; cf. Bizzarri, p. 735 ff.; Col. S. C. P. F. (ed. 1907) n. 1263.
8 Decree of Leo XIII, July 15, 1882; cf. Hizzette, *op. cit.*, p. 43; S. C. EE et RR, Apr. 15, 1891; Vermeersch, *De Rel.* II, n. 231.

Houses Subject to Regular Superiors.

The decree *Cum de Sacramentalibus*[9] and the Code both give to the regular superior the right of presenting to the local Ordinary, the confessor for his own nuns. The superior, however, cannot give him faculties to hear confessions. This is evident from the words of the Decree of 1913 "*si vero Superiori regulari, hic Confessarios Ordinario praesentat, cujus est iisdem audiendi confessiones potestatem concedere,*" while the Code states "*hanc jurisdictionem confert loci Ordinarius.*" The Ordinary can reject the priest presented, but the superior retains the right to present another. The Ordinary should not habitually grant faculties to priests not presented by their proper superiors.[10] Therefore, the Ordinary could occasionally appoint, by way of exception, e. g., when the priest presented was not suitable, a priest not properly presented without violating the law. Even if he did this habitually the delegation would be valid. The exercise of these faculties would be unlawful without at least the presumed permission of the superior. The Code further requires that when confessors are presented by their proper superiors, they should not be denied jurisdiction without a just cause,[11] unless they are found unsuitable by examination.[12]

It is to be noted that in the first part of the canon, the words used are "*religiosarum domus,*" referring to houses subject to the Holy See or the Local Ordinary, while in the last clause they are "*illarum monialium.*" Blat[13] claims that these words of the last clause refer only to nuns properly so-called because only they can be subject to regulars. But it seems that the same can be said of any order or congregation of sisters of simple vows subjected by privilege to a certain order or congregation, unless the privilege expressly states the contrary.[14] To

---

9 S. C. De Rel. Feb. 3, 1913; n. VII; AAS V, p. 63.
10 Can. 874. § 2.
11 Can. 874. § 2.
12 Can. 877.
13 *Commentarium in Textum* C. I. C., II, *pars* II, n. 588.
14 Fanfani, *op. cit.,* n. 138.

determine this it is necessary to consult and to examine the documents from the Holy See and their constitutions, etc.[15]

The Confessors to Be Appointed.

It is the local Ordinary who is to appoint the ordinary and extraordinary confessor of a community and also the special confessors in virtue of 520, § 2 and 521, § 2.[16] Father Papi states that, where there is a question of the four classes of confessors mentioned in Canons 520 and 521, they are all chosen by the Ordinary of the place except in the cases of communities subject to regulars. If he means by this that the regular superior can present the ordinary and extraordinary confessor of the community properly so-called, i. e., to whom all the religious must at certain times present themselves, and no others, that statement is correct. It cannot, however, be admitted that the regular superior has the right of choosing the confessor for the peace of conscience or greater advancement in the religious life given as a special ordinary confessor to an individual religious under Canon 520, § 2, for the canon explicitly states "*Ordinarius facile concedat.*" In this case it is not necessary to have the presentation of the superior. This is evident from the fact that the canon permits the religious to choose any confessor she desires. Neither must the regular superior present nor can he claim the right to present the supplementary confessors of Canon 521, § 2, for the canon gives that right to the local Ordinary alone in the following words: "*Ordinarii locorum . . . aliquot sacerdotes pro singulis domibus designent.*" The decree *Cum de Sacramentalibus* contains the same prescriptions in regard to these points.[17]

Superioresses will be entirely within the law in expressing their desires to the Local Ordinary in regard to the choice of confessors. That is particularly the case if such a community desires to have an extraordinary confessor of a determined reli-

15 Bastien, *op. cit.*, n. 362, note (2).

16 Papi, *op. cit.*, p. 61; Blat, II *pars* II, n. 588—refers this to supplementary confessors only.

17 S. C. de Rel. Decree *Cum de Sacramentalibus*, Feb. 3, 1913, n. 1-7; AAS. V, p. 62 ff.

gious institute. The superioress should be sure of the legitimate consent of the religious interested. She can then request the local Ordinary for the necessary powers for him. Needless to say that the Ordinary in such a case is always to safeguard his complete liberty of action,[18] for he is to judge as to the sufficiency of the reasons and make his decision accordingly. The superioress cannot impose upon the confessor her directions. Neither can she advise the confessor as to what penances to give or to bring pressure to bear on the consciences of postulants, who are concealing obstacles opposing their admission, etc. But in certain cases the confessor will be obliged to declare in confession to postulants and novices that they either should reveal certain obstacles, which hinder their profession, or leave the convent.[19]

Neglect by Regular Superior.

The local Ordinary has the right to supply this deficiency by appointing ordinary and extraordinary confessors for nuns subject to regulars. This dates back to the time of Benedict XIV, who made regulations to this effect in regard to the extraordinary confessor of the community. The bishop could supply this defect; (1) if regular superiors failed to give their nuns an extraordinary confessor two or three times a year;[20] (2) in that case the bishop was free to appoint any suitable priest and not necessarily from the order to which the nuns were subject, but another order or the secular clergy.[21]

At least once a year this extraordinary was to be chosen from the secular clergy or another regular order. After failure of the superiors to grant this confessor, the bishop could supply the defect as above.[22] Now the Code extends to the granting of both ordinary and extraordinary confessors.

18 Creusen, *Religieux et Religieuses, op. cit.*, n. 98.
19 Bastien, *Directoire Canonique*, n. 355 and p. 222, note 2.
20 Const. *Pastoralis Curae* Aug. 5, 1748, § 4; FJC, n. 388.
21 ibid, § 12.
22 ibid, § 12.

CHAPTER X.

THE ORDINARY COMMUNITY CONFESSOR.

The ordinary confessor was a necessary part of community life, but never became the subject of general and universal church legislation until the Council of Trent.[1] This council commanded bishops and other superiors of monasteries of nuns to incorporate in their constitutions the admonition that the nuns should go to confession monthly. For this purpose an ordinary confessor was to be appointed. This law, of course, applied only to nuns of solemn vows. This prescription was reaffirmed by Benedict XIV in his famous constitution *Pastoralis Curae,* August 5, 1748.[2] This diseipline was not extended to all women of simple vows until the constitution *Conditae a Christo,* of December 8, 1900.[3]

CANON 520.

§ 1. Singulis religiosarum domibus unus dumtaxat detur confessarius ordinarius, qui sacramentales confessiones universae communitatis excipiat, nisi propter magnum ipsarum numerum vel aliam iustam causam sit opus altero vel pluribus.

An ordinary confessor should be given to individual houses of female religious, of any institute whatsoever;[4] whether of pontifical or diocesan right; whether (1) living in papal or episcopal cloister; whether nuns of solemn vows (in the United States, only those of the Visitation Order of the convents at Georgetown, D. C.; Mobile, Ala.; St. Louis, Mo. and Baltimore,

---

1 *Sessio XXV, De Regularibus,* c. 10, cf. Mansi, 33, p. 176; Ehses, *Concilium Tridentinum,* t. 9, p. 1082.

2 FJC n. 388, § 1.

3 Pt. 2, n. 8; Col. S. C. P. F. (ed. 1907), n. 2089.

4 Can. 488, 5°; *In canonibus qui sequuntur, veniunt nomine: Domus religiosae, domus alicujus religionis in genere.*

Md.)[5] or sisters of simple vows or those whose vows by their institute are solemn but in certain places, by prescription of the Holy See, are simple. By using the generic term *female religious* the Code makes no distinction.[6]

The word used by the legislator *detur* is the imperative form of the present subjunctive mood implying an obligation both on the community of asking for an ordinary confessor and especially on the local Ordinary, to give such a confessor.[7] This is clear, of course, if it is a *formal house,*[8] or one canonically constituted, where there are six resident professed religious women.

Question—Must an ordinary confessor be given houses in which there are less than six resident professed religious?

Before the Code an answer was given by the Congregation for Religious to the Bishop of Linz,[9] to the effect that there was no obligation of appointing a confessor for communities of less than six, at least if they could not go to a church to frequent the sacrament there after the manner of the faithful.

Does this reply still have force after the code?

First Opinion—BRANDYS,[10] BIEDERLACK-FUHRICH,[11] STADT-

---

5 S. C. EE et RR, Sept. 30, 1864, *Americana Votorum, Bizzarri,* p. 735 ff; Col. S. C. P. F. (ed. 1907), n. 1263. cf. Smith, *Notes on the II Plenary Council of Baltimore,* p. 329, 330.

6 Can. 488, 7°; *Religiosorum, qui vota noncuparunt in aliqua religione; . . . . sororum, religiosae votorum simplicium; monialium, religiosae votorum solemnium aut, nisi ex rei natura vel ex contextu sermonis aliud constet, religiosae quarum vota ex instituto sunt solemnia, sed pro aliquibus locis ex Apostolicae Sedis praescripto sunt simplicia;*
Can. 490—*Quae de religiosis statuuntur, etsi masculino vocabulo expressa, valent etiam pari jure de mulieribus, nisi ex contextu sermonis vel ex rei natura aliud constet. cf. Fanfani, De Jure Religiosorum,* n. 134 (ed. 1925).

7 Fanfani, *loc. cit.*

8 Can. 488, 5°.—*domus formatae, in qua sex saltem religiosi professi degunt.*

9 S. C. De Rel. July 3, 1916; ad 3; *Obligationem non adesse nominandi confessarium ordinarium pro sororibus, si earum communitas sex saltem sororum numerum non attingat; cf. AKKR,* t. 97, p. 85; cf. *Vermeersch-Creusen, Epit.* I, n. 591.

10 *Kirchliches Rechtsbuch,* p. 153.

11 *De Religiosis,* p. 87.

MULLER,[12] and GROSSMAN,[13] infer that this response had from that time on force for the whole world. VERMEERSCH-CREUSEN[14] grant probability to this opinion (A) since this canon does not contain the words "etiam in domibus formatis" used in other places in the Code to settle doubts as in Canon 597, § 1, in regard to the observance of the cloister; and (B) because the decrees on Canon 520 after the Code, and which will be treated later, were not promulgated officially, i. e., in the *Acta Apostolicae Sedis.* Other arguments submitted in favor of this opinion are: (1) that this is a doubtful law and in virtue of Canon 6, 2° should be interpreted in accordance with the old law.[15] (2) This reply to the Bishop of Linz was a declarative interpretation of the decree of 1913 and needed no promulgation.[16] (3) The reply has not been revoked because Canon 4 requires for the revocation of privileges and indults granted before the Code an express clause of revocation. Such a clause is not contained in the Code.[17]

Second Opinion. The better opinion contends that this reply no longer has force since the Code. The reasons submitted in proof thereof are the following:

1.—There is no parity in reasoning between Canon 520, § 1, and the case of Canon 597, § 1, because the cloister, being a thing by its nature limited to space, would have to be clearly defined in the canon speaking of its extent and observation. Moreover, the Code uses the words "*religiosa domus,*" which are equivalent to the expression *qualibet domus.*[18]

2.—If this response was an authentic interpretation of the law of 1913, in order that it might retain its force after the

12 *Das Neue Ordensrecht,* p. 18.
13 *L. Q. S.,* 73, p. 156-157.
14 *Epit.* I, n. 591.
15 Shäfer, *Ordensrecht,* p. 112.
16 Grossam, *LQS,* 73, p. 157.
17 Rausch, *LQS,* 74, p. 630, ff.
18 Chelodi, *Jus de Personis,* n. 257.

Code, it should have been promulgated, according to Canon 17, § 2, before May 19, 1918, and the official *Acta Apostolicae Sedis.*[19]

Since it was at least to explain the doubts submitted, Leitner considers it as a restrictive interpretation of the decree of 1913. Since it was never published authentically, it never had universal force before the Code,[20] i. e., it was not part of the common law.[21]

3.—This reply has been explicitly revoked, because Canon 876, § 1, which using the words *Revocata qualibet contraria particulari lege seu privilegio,* requires special jurisdiction for the reception of the confessions of women religious and their novices.[22]

4.—This is not a doubtful law and appeal, therefore need not be made to Canon 6, 2°, which states that canons repeating the old law in its entirety should be interpreted in the light of the old law, or to Canon 15, whereby irritating and inhabilitating laws do not urge in doubt of law. Appeal to these canons would be necessary only if the reply to the Bishop of Linz had been authentically promulgated, either before or after the Code. In fact, since the Code, there have been two responses to the contrary on this specific point. Therefore, this law is not, by any means, doubtful in the light of the pre-Code response of Linz.

5.—The doubt caused by this reply of 1916, led the Archbishop of Prague to ask the Pontifical Commission for the Authentic Interpretation of the Code if this reply was still in force or whether Canon 520 must be followed and a confessor appointed for every house, although the number of religious

---

19 cf. Leitner, *Handbuch des Katholischen Kirchenrechts* (Dritte Lieferung, 1922), p. 353; Chelodi, *loc. cit.;* can. 17, § 2—*Interpretatio authentica, per modum legis exhibita, eandem vim habet ac lex ipsa; et si verba legis in se certa declaret tantum promulgatione non eget et valet retrorsum; si legem coarctet vel extendat aut dubium explicet, non retrotrahitur et debet promulgari.*

20 Chelodi, loc. cit.

21 Prümmer, *Manuale J. C.* n. 190, note (2).

22 Leitner, *op. cit.*, p. 353; Chelodi, *op cit.* n. 257, note (3).

did not exceed six. The commission replied[23] that the prescriptions of Canon 520 must be followed. This was reaffirmed in another reply of the Commission.[24] It is true that these latter two responses were not promulgated officially as Vermeersch-Creusen states,[25] but neither was the reply to the Bishop of Linz, which was an answer to a particular question and not of much value after the Code. Therefore, these responses of 1920 take precedence over the pre-Code reply. After the Code it seems that even for small communities of less than six professed resident religious there must be a regularly appointed ordinary confessor, especially since the Code does not distinguish in the canon between formal and non-formal houses.[26] "Ubi lex non-distinguit, nec nos distinguere debemus."

6.—Vermeersch states that these decisions refer only to confessors who hear confessions in the house itself. Therefore, if the religious can frequent the sacraments in the parish church, there is no need to appoint an ordinary confessor.[27] But this seems to be against the intention of the Code, which, as Creusen says,[28] is that a confessor be appointed for every community for that very purpose of avoiding frequentation of the parish church by the religious women for the reception of

---

23 *I. Archiepiscopus Pragensis sequens dubium proposuit:* Die 3 Julii 1913. *Religiosorum Ordinario Licenensi respondit ad 3 um: Obligationem non adesse nominandi confessarium ordinarium pro sororibus, si eorum communitas sex saltem sororum numerum non attingat. Can.* 520 *CJC praescribit vero hodie ut singulis religiosarum domibus detur confessarius ordinarius. Utrum responsio die 3 Julii data hucusque valet vel agendum est juxta Can.* 520 *et pro unaquaque domo religiosarum, etsi numerus sex in eadem domo non excedit, confessarius ordinarius deputandus est? R. Serventur praescriptiones* Can. 520 CJC; S. C. De Rel.; Jan. 10, 1920; cf. *AKKR*, t. 100, p. 47; Hilling, *CJC Interpretatio*, p. 37.

24 *Episcopus Osnabrugensis die 2 Dec.* 1920 *sequentia dubia proposuit:* 1°. *Utrum stricta obligatio singulis religiosarum domibus seu respective unicuique communitati dandi confessarium tam ordinarium quam extraordinarium urgeat etiam quoad domos religiosas, in quibus minus quam sex religiosae professae degunt an solummodo quoad domos formatas?* Can. 520, § 1, et 521, § 1, R.—*Provisum in canonibus* 520 et 521 etc.; Hilling, *op. cit.* p. 37.

25 *Epit.* I, n. 591.

26 Creusen, *Religieux et Religieuses*, n. 92; Bastien, *Directoire Canonique*, n. 355.

27 Vermeersch-Creusen, *Epit.* I, n. 591.

28 *Religieux et Religieuses*, n. 92.

the sacraments. The principle, however, as deduced from the canon, is that it only applies to religious or other pious persons living in community under a rule and a superior, provided they have a chapel or some other place in which they can confess habitually. The norm for judging deems to be the fact that they have an oratory or not in which to confess. If they have not, it would not be necessary to appoint an ordinary confessor for them. Therefore, those religious occupied in towns or cities with teaching, etc., and without an oratory, are no more obliged to have an ordinary confessor than other women who live in community, e. g., homes, being subject to common law. School sisters were for this reason expressly exempted from this law in the past by the Congregation of Bishops and Regulars[29]

The pastor or any other priest, who happens to be in the parish, if approved for the faithful, needs no further approval or delegation of jurisdiction, for he is not considered as the ordinary confessor of the community.[30] There is nothing to prevent the Chaplain of a community from being their ordinary confessor.[31] Whether without necessity this would be expedient, is left to the prudent judgment of the Ordinary.[32] Cardinals can be ordinary confessors of a community without delegation. (Can. 239, § 1, 1°).

---

29 *S. C. EE et RR, Apr. 22, 1872, ad 3; in Atrabatin; . . . Porro illae Sorores, communiter sed extra clausuram degentes, non habent sacellum privatum, sed ecclesiam parochialem sicut caeteri frequentant, ibidem Missae et caeteris officiis adsistentes, sacramenta tum Poenitentiae tum Eucharistiae recipientes; illae insuper Sorores saepius de parochia in aliam transeunt secundum Superiorissae generalis voluntatem. Porro, num in hisce circumstantiis applicanda sit juris dispositio circa triennalem confessariorum mutationem . . . ? Resp. ad 3; Sorores de quibus agitur posse peragere extra piam propriam domum sacramentalem Confessionem penes apud quemcumque confessarium ab Ordinario approbatum.;* Col. S. C. P. F., (ed. 1907) n. 1384; cf. Genicot, *Th. M.*, (ed. 1909) II, n. 339; Bastien, *op. cit.*, n. 355: cf. Grossam, L. Q. S. 73, p. 157.

30 S. C. P. F. Feb. 20, 1877; Col. S. C. P. F., (ed. 1893) n. (437).

31 Fanfani, *op. cit.* n. 40.

32 Goyeneche, CpR V, p. 31,

Article II.

The Unity of the Confessor.

Unus dumtaxat detur confessarius.

I. The General Rule.

The unity of confessor is prescribed by these words for each community, consisting of professed religious, novices and others staying there over night from sundown as servants, students and guests.[33] This was contained in the Council of Trent,[34] and made the general rule by Benedict XIV.[35]

The reason for having only one ordinary confessor in a community, is for unity of direction. The latter is the gauge of good order and discipline, since divergence of ideas in spiritual direction easily engenders discord.[36] Every confessor has his own methods of leading souls, and each confessor feels differently towards the same soul, one trying to urge it and another to moderate it.[37] Some confessors, members of religious orders, even had the practice of trying to lead their nun penitents to the customs and usages of their own order. Thus they sowed

---

33 Can. 514, § 1; cf. S. C. EE et RR, *Decr. Tridentina*, Jan. 29, 1847. ad 1; Bizzarri, *op. cit.* p. 116; Vermeersch, *De Rel.*, II, n. 226.

34 Sess. XXV, c. 10, *De Regularibus;* Mansi, 33, p. 176; *Ehses, Counc. Trid.*, 9, p. 1082.

35 Const. *Pastoralis Curae*, Aug. 5, 1748, § 1; FJC, n. 388; *S. C. EE et RR, Quemadmodum*, Dec. 17, 1890, ad 4; *Col. S. C. P. F.* (ed. 1907) n. 1745; *Normae*, June 28, 1901, Art. 140; *S. C. De Rel.* Decree *Cum de Sacramentalibus*, Feb. 3, 1913, AAS V, 62; Boudinhon, C. C.; 36, p. 269; Bucceroni, *Casus Conscientiae*, II, p. 182.

36 Choupin, *Recents Decrets du Saint Siege concernant les Religieux et Religieuses*, p. 30; also *Nature et Obligations de l'Etat Religieux*, p. 200; Bastien, *Directoire Canonique*, (ed. 1923), n. 355; Boudinhon, *CC.* 36, p. 269; Curran, *Confessors and Confessions of Religious Women of Simple Vows* p. 36 ff. Leitner, *Handbuch*, p. 354; Brandys, *Kirchliches Rechtsbuch*, p. 153; Biederlack-Fuhrich, *De Religiosis*, p. 87; Schäfer, *Ordensrecht*, p. 111.

37 Joder, AKKR, 79, p. 464.

the seeds of discontent, causing grave detriment to the spiritual progress of all. This was forbidden by the Congregation of Bishops and Regulars.[38]

Exceptions.

I—The law of one confessor applies to convents of nuns, communities of sisters, novitiates[39] and communities of religious women of pious societies living in community but without public vows,[40] It does not bind boarders and servants or inmates of orphanages, old ladies' homes, hospitals, etc., and those in the house for the sake of education.[41] This was explicitly decided for colleges of girls by the Congregation of Bishops and Regulars.[42]

II.—Because of a great number of religious more confessors can be granted to a community.[43]

The number required is not determined by the Code,[44] but a community numbering more than fifty religious can be considered as warranting another confessor. Less than twenty or even twenty-five would hardly suffice.[45]

III.—Other just causes for appointing more confessors are not mentioned by the Code. The Congregation of the Council, January 27, 1748, first permitted the Canons of Rimini to appoint a vice-confessor in cases of absence or sickness of the ordinary confessor of nuns. The latter, of course, needed the approbation of the Bishop.[46] Other causes would be the re-

38 S. C. EE et RR, Dec. 3, 1767, *to a Dominican Cloister of Buenos Ayres; cf Analecta Juris Pontificii, I,* 30, col. 1291; quoted in AKKR, 78, p. 685; 79, p. 464.

39 Can. 566, § 1.

40 Can. 675.

41 Can. 514, § 1.

42 S. C. EE et RR, *in Mazzara,* Dec. 7, 1906, ad 7; cf. Vermeersch, *Per.* III, n. 172; *Il Monitore Ecclesiastico,* XVIII, p. 529 ff; Mothon, *Traite de la Confession Sacramentelle,* p. 8.

43 S. C. EE et RR, in Mazzara, *loc. cit.*

44 Leitner, *Handbuch, (Dritte Lieferung)* p. 354, places it at 100 or more. The same in Brandys, *Rechtsbuch,* p. 153; Schäfer *Ordensrecht,* p. 111.

45 Fanfani, *De Jure Religiosorum,* n. 134.

46 S. C. Conc. *in Ariminen,* ad 11, 12; AKKR, 79, p. 466; Cf. Augustine, *A Commentary on Canon Law,* p. 158.

pugnance of the sisters to confess to the ordinary confessor;[47] the presence of persons speaking different languages; or different communities in the same house, e. g., novitiate, normal school for the professed, etc.;[48] if the majority of the religious have voted to retain the ordinary confessor and yet those dissenting, must be provided for according to Canon 526;[49] if there would be the necessity of confirming the same man in office too often.[50] These would be sufficient reasons to appoint more than one ordinary confessor. It must be remembered that the decision as to the sufficiency of the reasons is left to the bishop who is to approve the confessor.[51] The just cause should not be too severely estimated, since reappointment for such reasons was tolerated under the old law.[52] The bishop can, to avoid confusion, assign to each of the confessors, one category or a certain number of religious,[53] so that he is ordinary confessor of only one part of the community.[54] Chelodi thinks this is the intention of the law.[55] But there is nothing to prohibit, and in fact, it is to be desired that these confessors receive cumulative jurisdiction over all the religious of the house.[56] The superioress should be notified if the jurisdiction of each confessor is limited to a particular part or extended to the whole community.[57] If the jurisdiction is given without restriction or distinction, then any religious of the community

---

47 Benedict XIV, *Const. Pastoralis Curae*, § 1 ff; Aug. 5, 1748; FJC. n. 388; S. C. EE et RR, Normae (1901), art. 140; S. C. *De Rel "Cum de Sacramentalibus,"* n. 1, AAS, V, 62.

48 Boudinhon, *op. cit.* p. 274; *Creusen Religieux et Religieuses*, n. 92; Sabetti, *Comp. Th. M.*, n. 778; Vermeersch, *Per.* IX, p. (12); Leitner, *Handbuch* (Dritte Lieferung) p. 354; Brandys, *Rechtsbuch*, p. 153.

49 Bastien, *Directoire Canonique*, n. 355.

50 Vermeersch, Per. IX, p. 12.

51 Fanfani, *De Jure Rel.*, n. 134; Cocchi, *Commentarium in* C. I. C., II, pars II, n. 39.

52 S. C. EE et RR *in Turritana* Feb. 1753; Bizzarri, p. 374; cf. Vermeersch, *Per.* IX, p. (12) Choupin, *op. cit.*, p. 222; Papi, *Religious in Church Law*, p. 52.

53 Bastien, *op. cit.*, n. 355.

54 Vermeersch-Creusen, *Epit.* I, n. 591.

55 *Jus de Personis*, n. 257.

56 Vermeersch, *Per.* IX, p. (12); Papi, *op. cit.*, p. 51; Choupin, ***Nature, etc.*** *l'Etat Religieux*, p. 222.

57 Creusen, *Religieux et Religieuses*, n. 92.

is perfectly justified in going to any one of these confessors unless the rules or constitutions prescribe otherwise.

The same priest can be ordinary confessor for more than one community,[58] nor is there any legal prohibition that he be extraordinary confessor of another community.[59]

But in these cases a new approbation is required for each convent, unless he is given general faculties for all nuns of the diocese or a particular order.

Duty of the Ordinary Confessor.

The ordinary confessor is to hear the confessions of the community. In its widest embrace the community includes at the most those enumerated in Canon 514, § 1, i. e., the servants, students, sick and guests staying there day and night.[60] It may happen that a confessor of religious will not have diocesan faculties for the faithful, e. g., a priest from another diocese to whom are given the faculties to hear the confessions of religious women only. If he has faculties only for the one community to which he is appointed, he has no right to hear the confessions of another community, even of the same order.[61] Neither could he hear the confessions of outsiders or religious of the same order, but of another community coming to him,[62] unless their approach was made in virtue of Canon 522 for their peace of conscience. On the other hand, if they are there day and night, they become the guests mentioned in Canon 514, § 1, and he can absolve them in virtue of Canon 520 as the ordinary confessor of the community. If the bishop had granted, as

---

58 S. C. EE et RR. Sept. 1, 1905; Reply to the Bishop of Havana, ad 1 et 4; ASS XXVIII, p. 148; cf. Vermeersch, *Per.* II, n. 93.

59 Vermeersch, *Per.* I, p. 472; Curran, *Confessors and Confessions of Religious Women of Simple Vows*, p. 38.

60 For full explanation of those included in Canon 514, § 1 cf. treatise on Can. 518, p. 1.

61 Clement X, *Const. Superna*, June 21, 1670; § 4; FJC, n. 246; Innocent XIII, *Const. Apostolici Ministerii*, May 23, 1723; FJC, n. 280, § 19; S. C. EE et RR, *Decr. Tridentina*, ad 1; Bizzarri, *Loc. cit.*; Aertnys, Th. M., II (ed. 1906), n. 234; Marc, *Institutiones Morales*, (Ed. 1885) II, n. 1764.

62 S. C. EE et RR. *Tridentina*, Jan. 28, 1847 ad 1; Bizzarri, p. 116.

some bishops do,[63] to the confessor of one convent, approbation for all convents of the same religious order or for all religious women, he could, on the first presumption, hear the confessions of all religious of the order who come to him and on the second hypothesis all religious women within the diocese without distinction.

The ordinary confessor can, moreover, hear the sisters of his community if they are outside of the convent lawfully.[64] He can do this only within the limits of the territory of the local Ordinary, who delegated him, for delegated jurisdiction cannot be used outside of these limits.[65]

In regard to the absolution of reserved sins and censures incurred by the religious under his charge, his faculties are exactly the same as for the faithful in general.[66] Consequently, he cannot absolve from these without particular mention of that power by the bishop. Being ordinary confessor gives him no special jurisdiction in these matters.[67]

The ordinary confessor is bound to go to the convent to hear the confessions of the community at least once a week and give them the opportunity to fulfill their obligation of weekly confession according to Canon 595, § 1, 3°, and their constitutions. He can always insist upon a fair consideration in this matter, but he should arrange for a time to perform this office, which will be convenient to the community. He is to go to the community also whenever he is reasonably called for the purpose of hearing confessions.[68]

The religious, on the other hand, must receive the confessors appointed for them.[69]

---

63 *Decreta Synodi Hartfordensis* IV (Connecticut 1887) n. 96; *ibid. Synodus* II, n. 35; *Confessarius autem pro uno monialium conventu approbatus, censetur approbatus pro omnibus ejusdem ordinis conventibus in nostra dioecesi existentibus, ibique, Rectore quidem non inscio, confessiones licite audire potest.*

64 S. C. EE et RR, *Tridentina*, Jan. 29, 1847 ad 2; Bizzarri, p. 116.

65 Can. 873, § §1, 2.

66 Vermeersch, *Per.* I, p. 280.

67 Curran, op. cit., p. 16.

68 S. C. EE et RR, Vallisoletana, Apr. 4, 1704; Bizzarri, p. 287, ad. 5.

69 S. C. EE et RR, Vallisoletana, (reproposed), March 12, 1705; Bizzarri, p. 288.

THE ADMINISTRATION OF THE LAST SACRAMENTS.

CANON 514.

§ 1. In omni religione clericali ius et officium Superioribus est per se vel per alium aegrotis professis, novitiis, aliisve in religiosa domo diu noctuque degentibus causa famulatus aut educationis aut hospitii aut infirmae valetudinis, Eucharisticum Viaticum et extremam unctionem ministrandi.

§ 2. In monialium domo idem ius et officium habet ordinarius confessarius vel qui eius vices gerit.

In houses of nuns it is the ordinary confessor who has the right and duty of ministering the last sacraments of Viaticum and Extreme Unction, or the one who takes his place. For that purpose they can enter the cloister.[70] This refers properly only to convents of nuns of solemn vows, or those equal to solemn vows, i. e., those whose vows by their institute are solemn but in certain places by prescription of the Holy See are simple.[71]

This canon, then, does not apply to houses of sisters.[72]

Therefore, the ordinary confessor and his substitute have the right and obligation of administering the last sacraments not only to the professed but even novices, postulants[73] and others, staying there day and night. In the latter class would be included female servants, students, guests and patients[74] who are to be attended by the confessor and not the parish priests in whose parish the convent is situated. Male patients and guests, however, would not be included because of the cloister.[75]

The vice-gerent of the ordinary confessor has this right in the absence of the latter. This term "vice-gerent" applies pri-

---

70 Can. 600, § 3°.
71 Can. 488, 7°.; cf. Augustine III, p. 145.
72 Fanfani, *De Jure Rel.*, n. 416.
73 Fanfani, *op. cit.*, n. 201, *dubium* II.
74 For those who are included cf. treatment on Canon 518.
75 Augustine, *op. cit.* III, p. 144; Fanfani, *loc. cit.*

marily to the substitute for the ordinary confessor who has been appointed by the local Ordinary but not exclusively to him as Father Papi claims.[76] These words *vices gerit* apply equally to all confessors of religious women, except the one in Canon 522,[77] and all those who substitute for him not only in the office of hearing confession but even in any of the other functions attached to his office. Therefore, it could be the chaplain in the absence of the appointed substitute or any priest whatsoever in the absence of all others and in a case of necessity.[78]

The confessor is the one to assist the dying religious, just as the pastor for his parishioners.[79] In communities of sisters the pastor of the place has this right and duty of administering the last sacraments and assisting the dying or the chaplain whom the Ordinary has made equal to the pastor,[80] as is done in Belgium.[81]

The Ordinary can, for a just and grave reason, exempt totally or partially religious families and pious houses, which are in parochial territory and not exempt *a jure* from the care of the pastor.[82] If this is done, the pastor should be notified by the Ordinary and he cannot interfere in the administration of the last Sacraments by the chaplain.[83] Salesian Sisters, engaged in education before the Code, asked exemption, but it was considered inexpedient.[84] More probably, the sisters in seminaries are exempt from the jurisdiction of the pastor and dependent

---

76 *Religious in Church Law*, p. 146.

77 cf. treatment on canon 522.

78 Can. 844, § 2; 938, § 2; Creusen, *Religieux et Religieuses*, n. 120; Fanfani, *op. cit.*, n. 416.

79 S. C. De Rel. Feb. 6, 1924; AAS XVI, p. 96-101.

80 Can. 514, § 3—*In alia religione laicali hoc jus et officium spectat ad parochum loci vel ad cappellanum quem Ordinarius parocho suffecerit ad norman can.* 464, § 2; Bastien, *op. cit.* n. 290.

81 Creusen, *op. cit.* n. 120.

82 Can. 462, § 2; Vermeersch-Creusen, *Epit.* II, n. 581.

83 Augustine III, p. 145.

84 S. C. EE et RR, Apr. 19, 1844; Bizzarri, p. 497. cf. Augustine III, p. 145.

upon the rector of the seminary in these matters.[85] They can be considered as a part of the family of the seminary.[86]

Dwelling of Ordinary Confessor.

The cloister discipline of the old law, required that the confessor live in a house separated from the monastery of the nuns.[87] But this was mitigated by the *Normae* of 1901[88] and the *Dei Providentia*,[89] issued in 1906 by the Congregation of Bishops and Regulars for congregations of simple vows. The only requirement being that the entrance to the dwelling of the confessor be a separate one from that of the house of the sisters and that between the convent and the confessor's dwelling there must be no communication passage.[90]

Salary of Ordinary Confessor.

The bishop should assign the ordinary confessor of each convent or community of religious an annual salary, sufficient to support him in a befitting manner. The amount to be given should be determined from the customs of the place and the resources of the community.[91] This canonical rule is, of course, founded on the presumption that the office of ordinary confessor requires so much attention that it would not permit him to assume any other office no matter of how little importance.[92]

Such a condition will seldom occur in our country. In the

---

85 Can. 1368.

86 Fanfani, *op. cit.*, n. 417.

87 S. C. EE et RR, *in Arimen*, Jan. 22, 1576; Aug. 19, 1578; Jan. 2, 1579; Jan. 22, 1593; *in Bononien*, May 3, 1593; *in Januen*, Nov. 14, 1603; *in Mantuana*, Nov. 22, 1604; cf. Ferraris, *Bibliotheca Prompta*, V. Moniales, V, n. 68, p. 1109; Alexander VII, Const. *Felice*. Oct. 20, 1664, § 7; FJC, n. 240.

88 S. C. EE et RR, June 28; art. 178.

89 S. C. EE et RR, July 16, 1906; cf. Vermeersch, *Per.*, II, n. 133.

90 Mothon, *Traite de la Confession Sacramentelle*, p. 18 ff; Bastien, *Directoire Canonique*, n. 370.

91 S. C. EE et RR, Nov. 29, 1659; Ferraris, op. cit., v. *Moniales* V, n. 70; Barbosa, *Jus Ecclesiasticum Universum*, (ed. London, 1718) t. I, p. 661, n. 139; Pellizarius, *Tractatio De Monialibus*, Ch. X, n. 176, ed. Venice, 1651, p. 440).

92 Mothon, *loc. cit.*

United States the confessors are generally priests engaged in other duties, who go to hear the confessions of religious only at stated intervals.

The salary must not be paid in food, clothing, furniture or presents of any kind, but only in money. This rule is to be observed for all confessors, whether of the secular or religious clergy.[93] The giving of presents to the confessor by the religious, whether in their own name or that of the community and even with the consent of the superioress, was condemned.[94]

These rules were made for nuns of solemn vows. They can be applied, moreover, to all modern institutes of women religious or to communities of women without vows and even to oblates, provided the same motives demand their application.[95]

Article III.

Term of Office of the Ordinary Confessor.

The Council of Trent prescribed that an ordinary confessor be given to nuns,[96] but did not determine in any way the duration of his office. It was the Congregation of Bishops and Regulars[97] that for the first time on March 4, 1591,[98] restricted his office to the period of three years. This was done to remove an abuse which had grown up in the town of Como of the ordinary confessor, holding this office for life. The three-year term was thereafter, the constant norm, as is evident from the consistent replies of this congregation, which claimed for this term the

---

93 S. C. EE et RR, *in una Bononien*, June 19, 1601; *in Januen.*, Jan. 28, 1603; *Recanaten*, Apr. 19, 1624; cf. Ferraris, *loc. cit.*, n. 71, 72; Pignatelli, *Consultationes Canonicae*, VII, con. 85, n. 20; Pellizarius, *loc. cit.*, n. 176; Bizzarri, p. 387; An J. P., Serie IX, col. 570.

94 Clement VIII, Const. *Religiosae Congregationes*, July 19, 1594, FJC, n. 178; Urban VIII, Const. *Nuper a Congregatione*, Oct. 16, 1640; FJC, n. 178; Alexander VII, Const. *Sacrosancti*, Jan. 18, 1658; FJC, n. 235, § 2.

95 Mothon, *op. cit.* p. 20; also *Etat Religieux*, art. 190, p. 282 ff.

96 *Sess. XXV.*, *De Regularibus et Monialibus*, c. 10; cf. Ehses, *Concilium Tridentinum*, IX, p. 1082.

97 AKKR, 79, p. 467.

98 S. C. EE et RR, *in Comen.;* Cf. Bizzarri, p. 12.

approval of Gregory XIV[99] in its decrees.[100] Those who heard confessions of nuns after the termination of the three years without permission of the congregation, were to be declared suspended from the office of hearing confessions.[101]

This prescription held at first only for nuns of solemn vows and was later extended to women of simple vows,[102] whether of papal approval or not. It applied to all institutes for the communities of which an ordinary confessor had been appointed since abuses in this matter could as easily arise for them as for nuns of solemn vows. The difference between communities of nuns and those of simple vows was that when the latter were without a cloister there was no obligation on the bishop to appoint an ordinary confessor. The members of such communities could confess to any approved priest. When, however, the bishop did appoint one, the same difficulties arose.[103]

With the enormous increase of institutes bearing the name of conservatories of women and virgins in the 17th century, this triennial rule was applied to their confessors.[104] Moreover, the continued and rapid multiplication of communities of simple vows required frequent approvals of this rule by the Congregation of Bishops and Regulars.[105]

Finally this rule was given also to societies of women living in community, having an ordinary confessor.[106] The only relief from this law was by dispensation to reaffirm for a term or two.[107]

---

99 S. C. EE et RR, *Veronen*, Feb. 15, 1593; Bizzarri, *loc. cit.;* Boudinhon, CC, 36, p. 270.

100 S. C. EE et RR, *Neapolitana*, Nov. 26, 1602; Bizzarri, p. 13; *Mechlinen*, March 10, 1634; ibid, p. 24; Sept. 2, 1617, Col. S. C. P. F. (Ed. 1893) n. 427. AKKR 100, p. 468; *In Ragusina* Oct. 2, 1626; March 27, 1647 and elsewhere, cf. Ferraris, v. *Moniales*, V, p. 1099 ff.

101 Ferraris, *loc. cit.*

102 Battandier, *Guide Canonique*, (ed. 1923) n. 250.

103 Joder, *Beichtvateramt in Frauenklöstern;* AKKR, 79, 469.

104 S. C. EE et RR, March 18, 1649, July 25, 1655; Joder, AKKR 79, 470.

105 S. C. EE et RR, To Bishop of Brescia, June 1815, *Analecta Juris Pontificii*, L. 30; 1829, ibid; March 16, 1840; ibid; Jan. 16, 1864, ibid, series 9,894; cf. Joder, AKKR, 47, p. 470.

106 S. C. EE et RR, *Oregonopolitana*, Col. S. C. P. F. (ed. 1907), n. 1446, ad 2.

107 S. C. EE et RR, *Tridentina*, Jan. 20, 1847, ad 3; Bizzarri, p. 116.

In 1865 it was demanded that this be added to the rules.[108] This law was reiterated by the decree "Quemadmodum" of Leo XIII in 1890,[109] and in the decree "Cum de Sacramentalibus," Feb. 3, 1913, edited by the same congregation,[110] in which all past legislation on this matter was summed up and is practically presented in the same way by the Code.

CANON 526.

Religiosarum confessarius ordinarius suum munus ne exerceat ultra triennium; Ordinarius tamen eum ad secundum, imo etiam ad tertium triennium confirmare potest, si vel ob sacerdotum ad hoc officium idoneorum penuriam aliter providere nequeat, vel maior religiosarum pars, earum quoque quae in aliis negotiis ius non habent ferendi suffragium, in eiusdem confessarii confirmationem, per secreta suffragia, convenerit; dissentientibus tamen, si velint, aliter providendum est.

Communities in Which This Law Binds

The application of this law gives some difficulty for although the word *religiosarum* is used without distinction there are some communities not bound to the observance of this law. The prescription of the triennial change of the ordinary confessor applies not only to nuns having solemn vows, but also to sisters of simple vows,[111] and even school sisters or hospital sisters, if they live in community and have a definite confessor.[112]

It is certain that the larger institutes having their own

---

108 S. C. EE et RR, Aug. 5, 1865, An. JP series 9, p. 893; ad 7; June 16, 1876, *to the Nuns of the Abandoned Poor*, AKKR, 79, p. 471; Battandier, *op. cit.*, n. 250.

109 S. C. EE et RR, Dec. 17, 1890, ad 4; col. S. C. P. F. (ed. 1907), n. 1745.

110 AAS V, 62, n. 2.

111 S. C. EE et RR, June 1815, An. JP, lib. 30; 1829 ibid; 1841 ibid; 1864, ibid; 1865 ad 7, An. JP, series 9, 893; 1876 June, AKKR, 97, p. 471; cf. Battandier, *Guide Canonique*, n. 250.

112 S. C. Prop. Fide, *to the Vicar of Egypt*, Feb. 20, 1877; Col. S. C. P. F. (Ed. 1893), n. 437; AKKR, 79, p. 471.

chapel and confessor are bound absolutely by this rule[113] regardless of the fact that the religious are transferred frequently from one house to another, such as sisters of Charity serving in hospitals[114] or educating the youth.[115]

The frequent transfer of the personnel of an institute does not prohibit the observance of the three-year law by all houses.[116]

In those institutes in which the sisters confess in their own chapel, although Mass is said not by the confessor but by another priest if the former is the one to whom they must all confess he is the ordinary confessor and can only perform this office for three years. The three-year law holds only for the ordinary confessor who goes to the convent, conservatory or any other place in which a number of women lead a community life, for the purpose of hearing their confessions.[117]

In some parishes there may be two or three school sisters, who live in community outside of the cloister, but have not their own chapel. If an ordinary confessor has not been appointed for them they can frequent the parish church for Mass and reception of the Sacraments of Penance and Eucharist. To the confessor of these sisters, even if he be the only priest in the parish, i. e., the pastor, the three-year law is not to be applied. These sisters can confess outside of their house to any confessor approved by the local ordinary.[118]

Shorter Terms.

Another difficulty arises in regard to the constitutions of a community prescribing a shorter term than the code, e. g., the term of office of the ordinary confessor of the Dominican

---

113 Joder, AKKR, ibid.

114 S. C. EE et RR, *Tridentina*, ad 3; Jan. 27, 1847; Bizzarri, p. 116.

115 S. C. EE et RR, *Oregonopolitana*, ad 2; June 20, 1875; Col. S. C. P. F. (ed. 1907), n. 1446.

116 Joder, AKKR, 79, 472.

117 S. C. EE et RR, To Archbishop of Oregon City, July 20, 1887; Col. S. C. P. F. (Ed. 1893), n. 436; (ed. 1907), n. 1384. AKKR, 79, 472.

118 S. C. EE et RR, to Archbishop of Oregon, Apr. 22, 1872, ad 3; Col. S. C. P. F. (ed. 1893), n. 433; (ed. 1907) n. 1384.

sisters is two years.[119] But the Code only prohibits terms of office which are longer than three years and not those which are less. Therefore these constitutions, whether they have papal or only episcopal approbation are not abrogated by the present code since they are not opposed to it[120] as is evident from Canons 520, 525, § 2 and 526, which treat of the term of office of the ordinary confessor, and contain no clause abrogating shorter terms. Since the purpose of the Code is to limit an excessive length of time in office and not to restrict the terms as such, and even gives the bishop the right in certain circumstances to reappoint for a total of nine years continued service, it seems that on the same grounds the ordinary confessor could serve nine successive years of lesser terms as prescribed by the constitutions.[121]

Cessation of Office

The office of the ordinary confessor ceases according to the prescription of Canon 34, § 3, 2°, on the beginning of the recurring day upon which it began.

Therefore, the ordinary confessor's term ceases at the beginning of the day of the same date upon which he received his faculties to act as ordinary confessor three years before.[122]

Questions.

I. The question then arises as to the validity and liceity of confessions heard and absolutions given by the ordinary confessor after the three-year term is ended and without further

119 *Constitutiones Fratrum S. Ordinis Praedicatorum* (Paris 1886), Dist. II, c. III, n. 730, "*Confessarii monialium . . . ultra biennium in officio suo non perdurent.*" cf. Lucidi, *De Visitatione SS. Liminum,* II, n. 148, p. 187; Shäfer, *Ordensrecht,* p. 119; Leitner, *Handbuch,* p. 361.

120 Can. 489. *Regulae et particulares constitutiones singularium religionum, canonibus hujus Codicis non contrariae, vim suam servant; quae vero eisdem opponuntur, abrogatae sunt.*

121 cf. Curran, *Confessors and Confessions of Religious Women of Simple Vows,* p. 42.

122 Brandys, *Kirchliches Rechtsbuch,* p. 161; Fanfani, *op. cit.,* n. 134.

approbation. The Congregation of Bishops and Regulars declared such confessions to be valid but the exercise of this ministry illicit.[123]

Confessors Exempt from This Law.

This law does not apply: I, to the extraordinary confessor of the community;[124] II, to the supplementary confessors of the community (Can. 521, § 2), for the canon refers explicitly to the ordinary confessor only; III, to the special ordinary confessor given to an individual religious (Can. 520, § 2), whether given to one or many religious, for his office lasts as long as the spiritual necessity or utility of the religious requires;[125] IV, to the pastor or priest to whom the religious of their own choice confess habitually in a church;[126] V, to the confessors of female novices if they have their own distinct confessor for the term of noviceship would be two years at the most,[127] so that the same priest would not be the ordinary confessor for the same persons for a full three-year term;[128] VI, to confessors of girls in conservatories or women in homes.[129]

Reappointment to the Same Office.

The religious under the old law had to receive for the first term the confessor appointed for them by their superiors.[130]

---

123 S. C. EE et RR, June 20, 1875, ad 3, *Oregonopolitana;* Cf. Col. S. C. P. F. (ed. 1893), n. 436; (ed. 1907) n. 1446: cf. Aug. 24, 1868, AKKR, 79, p. 476.

124 Shäfer, *Ordensrecht*, p. 120; Cocchi, II pars II n. 46.

125 S. C. de Rel. Apr. 22, 1917; Vermeersch, *Per.* VIII, n. 119, p. 229, 230 (*Annotationes*) cf. Brandys, *Rechtsbuch*, p. 162.

126 S. C. EE et RR, *Majarien et Civitatis Plebis*, Dec. 7, 1906, ad 5; Vermeersch, *Per.* I, n. 172; ibid. III, n. 652; Choupin, *Recents Decrets*, p. 43.

127 Can. 555, 566; Leitner, *Handbuch* p. 119; One cannot agree with Dr. W. Grosam (L.Q.S. 73, p. 317) that they should be bound to this law. The main purpose of the law is not as he says that a confessor might not get a fast hold on the community and its traditions, etc., but that these religious have variety of confessors. This is sufficiently obtained by the fact that they must leave the novitiate after two years at the most.

128 Vermeersch-Creusen, *Epit.* I, n. 591.

129 S. C. EE et RR, Dec. 7, 1906; Vermeersch, *Per.* III, n. 172; cf. Bastien, *op. cit.*, n. 366, as was explicitly decided before the Code.

130 S. C. EE et RR, *Vallisoletana*, March 12, 1705 (re-proposed case of Apr. 4, 1705) Bizzarri, p. 288.

Later they could, for sufficient reason, i. e., discord or dislike for the one appointed, etc., present their reasons to the Congregation of Bishops and Regulars which would remove him directly. To guard this freedom the power was withdrawn from the bishops of appointing a confessor for longer than three years. Approval for the second term was reserved to the Congregation of Bishops and Regulars and for the third to the Pope himself.[131] These indults of reappointment were generally given to bishops for only one occasion and seldom for a full year and always with the express command that the rules of the Congregation of Bishops and Regulars were to be followed.[132] The condition for re-appointment under indult was that for the second term the consent of two-thirds of the religious in secret ballot was required. For the third term unanimous consent was demanded.[133]

This discipline was greatly mitigated by the decree of the Congregation for Religious of Feb. 3, 1913, "Cum De Sacramentalibus,"[134] which gave to the bishop the right to reappoint for a second and third successive term without an indult. This is also the law of the Code.

Sufficient Cause for Reappointment.

They are comprised in the following two, each of which is sufficient reason of itself and their concomitant existence is not required.[135]

I. *If there is a dearth of suitable priests for the office* and the bishop cannot otherwise provide for the need, reappointment

131 S. C. EE et RR, Jan. 16, 1864; Aug. 1865, ad 7, *to the Sisters of Christian Charity;* quoted by Joder, AKKR, 79, p. 471; cf. An. JP, lib. 80, 81.

132 Joder, *loc. cit.*

133 Bizzarri, p. 13, footnote 1.

134 S. C. De Rel.; AAS V, 52, ad 2.

135 Mothon, *Traite de la Confession Sacramentelle,* p. 14; Choupin, *L'Etat Religieux* p. 235; Brandys, *Rechtsbuch* p. 162.

can be made in such conditions, even if the religious do not request his maintenance in office. The previous vote of the religious is not required.[136] The words of the decree "Cum De Sacramentalibus" *rursus eligi ut ordinarius*[137] seemed to some to imply that the vote of community was necessary for the reappointment even in cases of dearth of suitable priests,[138] but the Code has settled this by using the words *rursus deputari* and *confirmari* and also by the correlative *vel, vel,* clauses of Canons 524 and 526, § 2, showing plainly that either reason suffices. Therefore election by the community is not necessary where there is a lack of suitable priests.

The bishop is not authorized to reappoint for this reason unless there is physical or moral impossibility of supplying the lack of priests in any other way than by the continuing the same confessor in office.[139]

This may occur even when the bishop has many priests at his disposal if they lack the requirements necessary for the confessor of religious women.[140]

II. *When the majority of the religious request the confessor's retention.* This concession was first given by the decree "Cum de Sacramentalibus."[141] Thus, the former requirements of an indult together with the two-third vote for the second, and the unanimous vote for the third appointment were done away with. Now all that is required is the vote of the absolute majority, i. e., one more than half the number of those voting, and not a relative majority, i. e., a plurality of votes, since it is a question here of only voting "yes" or "no."[142] The right of voting is extended in this matter not only to those who in

136 Mothon, *loc. cit.;* Choupin, *loc. cit.*
137 Art. 11; AAS V, p. 63.
138 Vermeersch, *Per. VII,* p. 92.
139 *Nouvelle Revue Theologique,* 1913, p. 128; quoted by Choupin, *loc. cit.;* p. 236.
140 Cf. chapter on—*Qualities of Confessors*; Curran, *op. cit.,* p. 43; Bastien, *op. cit.* n. 366; Cocchi, II *pars* II n. 46.
141 AAS V, 52.
142 cf. Can. 101, § 1. Mothon, *op. cit.* p. 15; Choupin, *L'Etat Religieux,* p. 246; Bastien, *Directoire Canonique,* n. 366,

other affairs have the right of suffrage but all others who are affected by it as individuals "*Quod omnes tangit, debet ab omnibus approbari,*"[143] Reg. 29, RJ in VI.° This includes besides nuns of solemn vows; those religious of institutes of solemn vows who have only simple vows; not only the professed but lay sisters;[144] and according to some even novices.[145]

It is true that novices are included if they have no confessor of their own and confess to the ordinary confessor of the professed. If on the other hand they have their own distinct confessor since they can hardly come under the name of religious, they are not, it seems, included by the canon.[146] In congregations in which the religious are being constantly changed from one house to another the right of suffrage belongs to those who are actually living in the house when the third year of the confessor's term is completed.[147]

The vote is to be determined by secret ballot [148] upon which it is not necessary to place a signature or the motive for voting. Those who can not write can give their vote orally or signify their approval with an X or some similar sign.[149] To eliminate all these difficulties the common custom of using a white ball to signify assent and a black one for rejection is by far the better system.[150] The dissenting minority must be provided for in some other way. If they consent spontaneously to accept the ordinary confessor again the difficulty ceases. If on the other hand they persist in their desire to have another confessor, the local Ordinary must make sufficient provision for them. It is to be noted however that it is the bishop who appoints the confessor and despite the vote he has the right to

143 Can. 101, § 2; Blat. II, pars II, n. 589.
144 Blat, *loc. cit.;* Shäfer, *Ordensrecht,* p. 119.
145 Choupin, *loc. cit.*
146 Vermeersch-Creusen, *Epit. I,* n. 591; Bastien, *loc. cit.*
147 S. C. EE et RR, Apr. 22, 1872, ad 2; Col. S. C. P. F. (ed. 1893), n. 433; AKKR, 79, p. 480.
148 The method of procedure is described in Canon 171.
149 Choupin, *op. cit.,* p. 236 ff.
150 Brandys, *Rechtsbuch,* p. 162.

appoint him or not as he sees fit. The vote makes the reappointment possible but not obligatory.[151]

Appointment for a fourth consecutive term, even if the sisters desire it and the bishop thinks it necessary, can not be made without dispensation or indult from the Congregation of Religious. Such an indult was required by the old law for the second and third term.[152] Such an indult was granted September 2, 1913, to the bishops of Belgium. By virtue of this indult they could for five years confirm the ordinary confessors of sisters for the length of time which seemed suitable to them. The vote of the sisters in this case was necessary.[153] These bishops were required on the other hand to preserve all other conditions necessary for the liberty of conscience of the religious. On November 23, 1922, quinquennial faculties were given to the diocese of Tours [154] to continue the confessor in office but the vote of the religious was required. The Congregation of Religious also gave to American Bishops the faculty to confirm for a fourth and fifth term, with the consent of the religious provided the minority do not object. This can be determined by another ballot. If they still object, the bishop must give them another confessor.[155] These episcopal faculties hold only for five years, from one quinquennial report to another.

B. *Reappointment after a Lapse of a Year.*

Before the code the legislator wishing to assure a certain variety of confessors for a community formulated practical di-

---

151 Boudinhon, C. C., 36, p. 273; Brandys, *op. cit.*, p. 162.

152 Benedict XIV, Const. *Pastoralis Curae*, Aug. 5, 1748, § 1; FJC, n. 388; S. C. EE et RR, June 27, 1815; An. JP, lib. 30; Jan. 16, 1864, An. JP, series, 9, p. 894; Aug. 5, 1865, ad 7; June 16, 1876; all quoted by Joder, AKKR, 79, p. 470. ff.; cf. Shäfer, *Ordensrecht*, p. 120; Brandys, *loc. cit.;* Cocchi, II, *pars* II, 46; Fanfani, *op. cit.* n. 134.

153 Vermeersch, *Per. VII*, n. 745.

154 Creusen, *Religieux et Religieuses*, n. 99.

155 Hilling, *Supplementum*, p. 48.

rections in its reply to the Bishop of Mazzara, Sicily.[156] This reply stated that there must be an interval of a complete year from the termination of the office of ordinary confessor before he could become extraordinary confessor for the same community except in the case of dearth of priests. Nor could he remain as the particular ordinary confessor of those nuns who did not want to go to the other confessor,[157] except the nun was in danger of death, or she refused to confess to the other confessor, or if she asked for him for the peace of her conscience or greater progress in the spiritual life.[158]

The decree "Cum de Sacramentalibus" in the eleventh article presented the same law as is now reproduced verbatim in Can. 526, 524, § 2.

CANON 524.

§ 2. Confessarius ordinarius non potest renuntiari extraordinarius nec, praeter casus in Can. 526 recensitos, rursus deputari ordinarius in eadem communitate, nisi post annum ab expleto munere; extraordinarius vero immediate ut ordinarius renuntiari potest.

If the reasons considered above of dearth of priests or the request of the sisters do not exist then the ordinary confessor can only be reappointed to the same office or to that of extraordinary confessor in the same community after the lapse of a year from the completion of his office. But there is nothing to pre-

---

156 S. C. EE et RR, *Majarien et Civitatis Plebis*, Dec. 7, 1906;
2. *Puo un confessore ordinario, spirato il triennio, mandarsi dal Vescovo nella stessa Communita religiosa come straordinario bis vel ter in anno a norma del Tridentino?* (*Sess. XXV, c. 10, De Regularibus*).
Resp. ad 2.—Negative antequam annus ab exspiratione triennii elapsus fuerit, excepto casu quo ob penuriam confessariorum Ordinarius aliter procedere nequeat; Vermeersch, *Per.* III, n. 172; Boudinhon, C C, 36, 339.

157 Ibid; Q.3; *Puo tollerarsi che un confessore ordinario, spirato il triennio, resti confessore abituale, ossia straordinario particulari di talune monache, perche esse non vogliono confessarsi con altri?*
Resp. ad 3—*Negative exceptis casibus de quibus in primo dubio.* (i. e. the case specified in the constitution "Pastoralis Curae," of Benedict XIV.)

158 Benedict XIV, Const. *Pastoralis Curae*, Aug. 5, 1748; FJC, n. 388.

vent his becoming ordinary confessor of another community immediately afterwards.[159]

The full year is to be determined from the prescriptions of Canon 34. Therefore, since the beginning of the year of interval coincides with the beginning of the day, e. g., if his faculties ceased on the 30th of April, 1926, then the time is completed at the beginning of the day of the same number of the succeeding year,[160] i. e., April 30, 1927. When the year of interval is complete he may be reappointed by the Bishop at any time, e. g., if the ordinary or extraordinary confessor should die, and no indult would be required.[161] After the year of interval there is no longer any restriction as to the number of times that he can be reappointed provided the conditions necessary for this exist at the end of each successive term. There is nothing in the law to render this procedure illicit, and it is left to the conscience and prudence of the Ordinary.[162]

It is advisable, however, that this should be avoided if possible, for it seems to be at least against the spirit if not the words of the law.

The Code has settled the disputes existing before it as to the meaning of the word *extraordinary* of the decree "Cum de Sacramentalibus." All admitted that he could not become the extraordinary community confessor of the Ember weeks. Hizette,[163] basing his opinion on the reply to the third question of the Bishop of Mazara quoted above, claimed that he could not become the particular habitual ordinary confessor of those who did not wish to address the confessor except in the cases mentioned by Benedict XIV. He could, however, be appointed supplementary confessor due to lack of priests. Most authors, on the contrary, held, as did Boudinhon [164] and Vermeersch,[165] that only that priest is the "ex officio" extraordinary confessor,

159 Brandys, *Rechtsbuch*, p. 161; Fanfani, *op. cit.*, n. 134.
160 Can. 34, § 3, 2°.
161 Vermeersch, *Per.* VII, p. 93.
162 Curran, *Confessors and Confessions of Religious Women of Simple Vows*, p. 45.
163 *Confessions des Religieuses*, p. 53, note (1).
164 *Canoniste Contemporain*, 36, p. 339 ff.
165 *Periodica*, VII, p. 92.

who is appointed as such for the whole community. Therefore this prohibition did not prevent the ordinary confessor becoming the supplementary confessor of the community or the particular ordinary confessor of an individual religious. The latter opinion is the one that seems to be accepted by the present law. There is only one confessor who is called in the Code "extraordinary" and he is the confessor obligatory for the community four times a year.[166] Therefore the ordinary confessor can under the present Code become the supplementary confessor of Canon 521, § 2 or the special ordinary confessor requested by a religious (Can. 520, § 2), immediately upon the completion of his term.[167] The prohibition to go to the convent[168] and hearing confessions while the extraordinary is functioning no longer obliges. The ordinary confessor should, however, avoid this lest in any way he diminish the liberty of approach to the extraordinary confessor.[169]

If, however, the local Ordinary has appointed the extraordinary confessor for a fixed time[170] he can receive immediate appointment as the ordinary confessor of the same community at the cessation of this appointment. This was permissible also under the law of 1913.[171]

---

166 Can. 521, § 1.
167 Brandys, *op. cit.*, p. 163.
168 S. C. EE et RR, *Bononien*, Jan. 1749, ad 1; Bizzarri, p. 31.
169 Aertnys-Damen, *Theologia Moralis*, t. II, n. 373.
170 Bastien, *op. cit.*, n. 364.
171 S. C. De Rel. decree "Cum De Sacramentalibus," Feb. 3, 1913, n. 11; AAS V, p. 63.

CHAPTER XI.

THE EXTRAORDINARY COMMUNITY CONFESSOR.

Some nuns had refused at times to confess to the ordinary confessor granted to them by the Council of Trent and the extraordinary confessor was given to them to safeguard the integrity and the right and profitable usage of this sacrament.[1]

This confessor even when appointed by regular superiors for nuns subject to them had to be approved by the bishop.[2] By the prescription of the Council of Trent this confessor was necessary only for convents of nuns but Benedict XIV exhorted all the bishops of the church to extend this privilege to all nuns not living in cloister but in community, to all conservatories and colleges for women and girls since the same things were to be avoided there as among cloister nuns.[3] He himself prescribed it for the "English Ladies" of simple vows.[4] This exhortation was made a prescription in many cases by the Congregation of Bishops and Regulars[5] and confirmed for all religious even of simple vows by the decree "Quemadmodum" of Leo XIII, by his constitution "Conditae a Christo,"[7] and the decree

---

1 Benedict XIV, Const. *Pastoralis Curae,* Aug. 5, 1748, § 2; FJC n. 388.
2 ibid, §§ 4, 10.
3 ibid, § 3; FJC, *loc. cit.*
4 Ben. XIV. Const. *Quamvis justo,* Apr. 30, 1749, §§ 13, 14; FJC, n. 398.
5 May 9, 1860; June 6, 1860; July 23, 1860; Sept. 27, 1861; cf. Bizzarri, p. 780, 782, 786, 794; Feb. 24, 1863, An. JP, Series 9, c. 272; May 17, 1865, ibid. c. 891, ibid, 1021; March 22, 1862, ibid. lib. 71, c. 633; cf. AKKR, 79, p. 714. Cf. Pius IX Ep. Encyc., *Cum Nuper,* Jan. 20, 1858; FJC, n. 523, § 3.
6 S. C. EE et RR, Dec. 17, 1890, n. 4; S. C. P. F. (ed. 1907), n. 1745.
7 Leo XIII, Const. *Conditae a Christo,* Dec. 8, 1900; pt. 2, n. 8; Col. S. C. P. F. (ed. 1907), n. 2097.

"Cum Sacramentalibus" issued by the Congregation of Religious in 1913.[8] It is offered by our present Code in the following words:

CANON 521.

§ 1. Unicuique religiosarum communitati detur confessarius extraordinarius qui quater saltem in anno ad domum religiosam accedat et cui omnes religiosae se sistere debent, saltem benedictionem recepturae.

I. *An Extraordinary Confessor.*

From the canon the general rule is evident that there should only be one extraordinary confessor for each community. Moreover the same canon, § 2, prescribes supplementary confessors most likely to obviate difficulties which would arise if there is only one extraordinary. But as in the case of the ordinary confessor exceptions may be allowed and the bishop or superior would not exceed his right in appointing several extraordinary confessors if there was a great number of religious or some other just motive,[9] as mentioned under Canon 520, § 1. This is not explicitly stated in the law but it seems only just that it should be so for it is analagous to the case of the ordinary confessor. Moreover Canon 520 is much stricter containing the prohibition (*unus dumtaxat detur confessarius*) of more than one ordinary confessor, except when the number of the religious in the community or some other just cause demands the appointment of more than one. Canon 521, § 1, however, simply states *detur confessarius extraordinarius* without any prohibition to appoint more than one. If the Code explicitly permits it in these circumstances under a canon that contains an express prohibition *a pari* at least more than one extraordinary confessor can be given to communities under the same conditions.

From the wording of the canon it seems to be the mind of the legislator that the same priest should be sent four times

---

8 S. C. EE et RR, Feb. 3, 1913, n. 3; AAS V, 62.

9 Boudinhon, C C, 36, p. 275; Curran, *Confessors and Confessions of Religious Women of Simple Vows*, p. 57.

during the year, so that the religious would have a sufficiently stable and continuous direction. But if suitable priests are lacking, it does not seem repugnant to the law that now one and then another is sent as extraordinary confessor on one of these occasions.[10]

The canon uses the word *detur,* the imperative form of the present subjunctive implying an obligation upon the bishop who is to give such a confessor to the community.[11]

II. *Every community of religious women*—is to receive an extraordinary confessor. This canon uses the words *unicuique religiosarum communitati* while Canon 520, § 1, speaking of the ordinary confessor says *Singulis religiosarum domibus.* The difference in wording does not imply a difference in meaning, for a community could hardly exist as such without a house in the sense of these canons. Neither could there be a religious house in the juridical sense without the element of personality present, otherwise it would just be religious property.[12] Moreover, the word community can not be taken in the sense sometimes used in English as applying to the whole institute. Therefore, these two phrases are synonymous in meaning and an extraordinary confessor would have to be appointed to every house for which an ordinary confessor is required. It follows also just as an ordinary confessor must be appointed even for houses which are not formal[13] so also an extraordinary must be appointed for houses of less than six members. This is evident from the whole purpose of the extraordinary confessor in its juridical history which was to afford relief from habitual confession to the ordinary confessor. The fact of the appointment of the

---

10 Vermeersch-Creusen, *Epit.* I, n. 593; Fanfani, *De Jure Religiosorum,* n. 135.

11 Cf. Treatment upon Can. 520, § 1, Fanfani, *op. cit.,* n. 134.

12 Can. 488, 5°. *Domus religiosae, domus alicujus religionis in genere; domus regularis, domus ordinis; domus formatae, domus religiosa in qua sex saltem religiosi professi degunt, quorum, si agatur de religione clericali, quatuor saltem sint sacerdotes;* Cf. Can. 531, ff. which treat of the administration of goods.

13 Cf. Explanation of Can. 520, § 1; Brandys, *Kirchliches Rechtsbuch,* p. 154.

ordinary confessor demands as its complement the appointment of the extraordinary confessor for these two offices are correlative.

III. *Number of Visits.*

The Council of Trent only required the extraordinary confessor to go to the convent twice a year.[14] This was confirmed by the subsequent Pontiffs who wrote on this point including Benedict XIV [15] and continued until the time of the decree of the "Cum de Sacramentalibus" of 1913 of the Congregation for Religious [16] substituted the word *pluries*. This, however, was very indefinite and authors appealing to the rule of law that plurality is contained in the number 2, *pluralis locutio duorum numero est contenta*,[17] interpreted the law as requiring at the most two visits to hear confessions.[18] It was no doubt to remove this difficulty and show that the intention of the Church is to a greater frequency of approach, that four visits are required by this canon which give a sort of stability to his direction.[19] The four intervals need not be equal. He should go about once every three months, but a difference of a week or two is not of importance. The "quater temps" or ember weeks, marking the change of the seasons, have become by a laudable custom the times generally observed for the approach of the extraordinary confessor. This is however in no way prescribed and nothing prevents the presentation of the extraordinary confessor at other times, e. g., during retreats.[20] *The*

---

14 *Sess. XXV, De Regularibus*, c. 10; Ehses, *Concilium Tridentinum*, t. 9, 1082; Cf. Hizette, *Confessions des Religieuses*, p. 32, note (1).

15 Const. *Pastoralis Curae* § 4; FJC, n. 388.

16 S. C. EE et RR, *Cum de Sacramentalibus*, Feb. 3, 1913, n. 3; *Pluries in anno, unicuique religiosae communitati, detur confessarius extraordinarius ad quem omnes religiosae accedant oportet, saltem ut benedictionem accipiant;* ASS V, 62; 2nd. *Eng. Trans.* ibid. p. 246; Vermeersch, *Per.* VII, n. 652; Hizette, *Confessions des Religieuses*, p. 32.

17 RJ in VI°, Reg. 40.

18 Boudinhon, C C., 36, p. 275; Curran, *op. cit.* p. 57.

19 Vermeersch-Creusen, *Epit.* I, n. 593.

20 Fanfani, *op. cit.*, n. 135; Bastien, *Directoire Canonique*, n. 357; Creusen, *Religieux et Religieuses*, n. 94; Choupin, *L'Etat Religieux*, p. 225; Hizette, *op. cit.* p. 33; Brandys, *Rechtsbuch*, p. 154; Mothon, *Etat Religieux*, p. 235.

question arises—Can the extraordinary confessor go to the convent more than four times a year to discharge his functions?

FANFANI,[21] SHAFER [22] and VERMEERSCH-CREUSEN take the view that he can not of his own free will,[23] for whether that would be opportune is left to the judgment as well as the consent of the bishop. If such were the case, he would become like the ordinary confessor. The extraordinary confessors of the religious houses are forbidden to go more than four times to hear the confessions of the community.[24] The contrary view sponsored by AERTNYS-DAMEN,[25] PAPI,[26] GENICOT,[27] KINANE,[28] MOTHON[29] and BATTANDIER [30] is the better in proof of which the following reasons are submitted:

I—The words used are *qui quater saltem in anno accedat.* Now the words of any law must be understood according to their proper signification in the text and context.[31]

According to common usage this word *saltem* has the meaning of "at least, or at the least, or the minimum." [32] It evidently implies here that the minimum number of times that the extraordinary confessor is to visit the convent for the purpose of hearing confessions is four times a year but that he may do so

---

21 *De Jure Religiosorum*, n. 135, dubium, II.
22 *Ordensrecht*, p. 114.
23 Vermeersch-Creusen, *Epit.* I, n. 592.
24 Creusen, *Religieux et Religieuses*, n. 94.
25 *Theol. Mor.*, II, n. 374.
26 *The Government of Religious Communities*, p. 134.
27 *Theol. Mor.* II, n. 341.
28 *Ir. Ecc. Rec.*, Dec. 1923, XXII, 640 ff.
29 *Etat Religieux*, p. 235, note 28. He requires the demand of the community.
30 *Guide Canonique*, n. 254.
31 Can. 18, *Leges ecclesiasticae intelligendae sunt secundum propriam verborum significationem in textu et contextu consideratam;*
32 Facciolati, *Totius Latinitatis Lexicon* Vol. II, p. 468, who proves that the contention of some etymologists, that this word had the meaning in certain places of the English word *only*, is wrong, since it should be reduced in all cases to mean the minimum; Cf. Andrews, *Latin-English Lexicon.* p. 1349; Walde, *Lateinisches Etymologisches Wörterbuch*, p. 673.

more frequently.[33] If *four* was the maximum number of times that he should approach them, either the word *saltem* should have been omitted entirely for it is unnecessary and misleading [34] or a restrictive phrase such as *ne pluries quam quater,* should have been inserted to show the exact meaning.

II. Canon 18 demands that in interpreting the law if it be doubtful, that besides the words of the law parallel places in the Code should be consulted. The word *saltem* is used in the same way in which it has just been interpreted in various places in the Code.[35]

III. Following the third method of Canon 18 it is evident that this was the mind of the legislator. Before the Code, as explained above, there was a dispute in regard to the interpretation of the word *pluries,* which some, following the rule of law "pluralis locutio in numero duorum est contenta," considered

---

33 Kinane, *loc. cit.;* Battandier, *Guide Canonique,* n. 254; In proof of this contention that the word *saltem* does not exclude a greater number than the one, which it is modifying, are offered the very clear words of *Barbosa,* who gives the precise canonical meaning and force of the word as understood in law.
"*Adjecta dispositioni numerali non excludit majorem numerum, quam fuerit expressum, ut si dicatur quod debeant esse tres canonici saltem, possunt adesse quatuor, quia non restringitur dispositio . . . . De sui enim natura non excludit . . . . Est implicativa, non autem limitativa;*" *Tractatus Varii, Dictiones Usufrequent., Dictio,* CCCLV, n. 2, 4, 5, p. 782 (1660).

34 Kinanee, *loc. cit.*

35 Thus Can. 906, speaking of the obligation of annual confession, states that all those having attained the use of reason are bound to confess all their sins *saltem semel in anno.* Surely no one would prohibit them because of the word *saltem* from confessing more often. Canon 126 states that secular priests should make a retreat *tertio saltem quoque anno.* Yet the interpretation of these words as restricting a priest to one retreat every three years could not be sustained, since it is against the approved custom of a yearly retreat. The same holds for the junior clergy examinations mentioned in Canon 130 *examen singulis annis saltem per integrum triennium* yet many bishops require that their priests undergo these examinations for five years e. g. in the Archdiocese of New York. Religious superiors are told in Canon 595, § 3 to see to it that their subjects go to confession *semel saltem in hebdomada.* We could not, on any grounds, exclude them from more frequent approach to this sacrament. Bishops and religious superiors on the other hand are to see to it that their priests celebrate Mass *saltem singulis diebus dominicis aliisque festis de praecepto divinis operentur* (Can. 805) while that they celebrate more often is a thing to be desired and no restriction could be placed upon it, because of that word *saltem.*

to imply two visits as sufficient. The legislator used the word *saltem* to settle this dispute requiring at least four visits and thereby approving the custom existing before the Code of having him go four times a year at the ember weeks.[36]

It may be objected that if more than four visits are permitted, where can a limit be set? It is evident that the extraordinary confessor may not go so frequently as to become almost an ordinary confessor, for the Council of Trent permitted it two or three times, the "Normae" of 1901 [37] even more often[38] while the decree "Cum de Sacramentalibus" extended this to include several visits "pluries." [39]

These must form the norm and since the exceptional needs of the community, e. g., the community desired the extraordinary at the time of retreats taking place outside of Ember weeks,[40] would hardly demand it more frequently, KINANE is justified in placing the number about six or seven times.[41] It is true that the Ordinary can limit the number of times the extraordinary confessor can go[42] for he alone can delegate jurisdiction for the confessions of religious women.[43] But if the Ordinary has appointed him without any restriction of this kind as extraordinary confessor in regard to the number of times he is to visit the convent to hear confessions, without any further authority he can hear confessions more than four times. If he heard beyond the times permitted by Canon 520, § 1, or the rule of the Ordinary, provided he had not been told that his jurisdiction ceased after a certain number of visits, in virtue of the jurisdiction received by his very appointment, the confessions are valid although his

---

36 Curran, *op. cit.* p. 57.

37 art. 143.

38 Hizette, op. cit., p. 32.

39 n. 3, AAS V, 62; cf. preceding page.

40 Schäfer, *Ordensrecht*, p. 113.

41 Kinane, *Ir. Ecc. Rec., loc. cit.*; Creusen (*op. cit.* n. 94), states that the religious superioresses of the diocese of Bruges, Belgium, can, without further authorization, invite him to hear the confessions of the religious if the ordinary confessor is incapable of fulfilling his office. He is not by this fact dispensed from his visit during the Ember week of September.

42 Can. 878, § 1 states "*Jurisdictio delegata aut licentia audiendarum confessionum concedi potest certis quibusdam circumscripta finibus.*"

43 Can. 876, § 1.

action is unlawful. This is evident from the fact that the extraordinary confessor is in a different position from those confessors whose jurisdiction is derived from law and limited by all the conditions of law.[44]

If he should go two or three times more of his own accord to hear the confessions of the community it seems from the wordinf of the canon, that all the religious should present themselves to him.

IV. *All the religious must present themselves* to the extraordinary confessor.

The old law required that all dwelling in the monastery, both nuns and secular women,[45] who were there as students, guests, sick or servants, etc., present themselves to the extraordinary confessor. Refusal to do so by the nuns was to be punished by their superioresses, while girl students making the same refusal were to be expelled.[46] This obligation was restricted by the decree "Cum de Sacramentalibus" to religious properly so-called.[47]

This restriction is adopted by the present canon. Therefore, the obligation of presentation of self to the extraordinary confessor only binds religious properly so-called, i. e., nuns with solemn vows or sisters with simple vows,[48] and novices must also present themselves since they are to have an extraordinary confessor [49] although not necessarily distinct from the extraordinary confessor of the professed. The same reasons that urge for the observance of this law by the professed hold also for the novice.

Pious societies of women living in community even without vows [50] are also bound to the observance of this law since the

44 Kinane, *loc. cit.;* Biederlack-Fuhrich, *De Religiosis,* n. 49.
45 Benedict XIV, Const. *Pastoralis Curae,* § 3; FJC, n. 388.
46 Decree of Clement XI, S. C. EE et RR, Dec. 12, 1708; given to the monasteries of Rome by the Cardinal Vicar of Rome; cf. Bizzarri, p. 293; Ferraris, v. Monialis, V, n. 37, p. 1103; Cf. Benedict XIV, *Pastoralis Curae* loc. cit.; *Normae* S. C. EE et RR (1901), art. 143.
47 S. C. EE et RR, Feb. 13, 1913, n. 4; AAS V, 62; 2nd Eng. Trans. ibid., p. 266.
48 Can. 488, 7°.
49 Can. 566, § 1.
50 Can. 675.

Code prescribes the same discipline for them. Girl students in colleges [51] were explicitly exempted from this law by the Congregation of Bishops and Regulars before the Code.

"At least to receive his blessing." It is not prescribed that the individual religious make a sacramental confession to the extraordinary confessor. This dates from the time of Benedict XIV who interpreted the words of the Council of Trent [52] "Qui omnium confessiones audire debeat" as not implying an obligation to make sacramental confession if they did not so desire, but only of presenting themselves to receive salutary advice. This was prudently decided so that all the religious could without shame present themselves to the extraordinary confessor, and to prevent the suspicion that might arise if certain nuns went to him and others did not. The reason for approach of the former might have become a matter of discussion among the others.[53] Another purpose for this was to prevent accusation of neglect upon the part of the superiors in their duty of offering religious an opportunity of quieting their consciences.

CANON 524.

§ 2. . . . in eadem communitate . . . extraordinarius vero immediate ut ordinarius renuntiari potest.

This was first introduced by the decree, "Cum de Sacramentalibus." [54] There exists no rule for limiting the time of service of the extraordinary confessor in the same community or which imposes any renewal. This seems to be the reason why the Congregation authorized the extraordinary confessor to become ordinary confessor without interruption.[55]

The law is so lenient for the ordinary confessor because, although the religious are bound to present themselves to him,

---

51 S. C. EE et RR, *Majarien et Civitatis Plebis*, Dec. 7, 1906, ad 7; ASS, XL, p. 54; Vermeersch, *Per.* III, n. 172.

52 *Sess. XXV, De Regularibus*, c. 10; Ehses, Concilium Tridentinum, t. 9, 1082.

53 Benedict XIV, Const. *Pastoralis Curae*, Aug. 5, 1748; § 3; FJC, n. 388. Fanfani, *De Jure Religiosorum*, n. 135; Hizette, *Confessions des Religieuses*, p. 33. Cocchi, II, *Pars* II, n. 39. Biederlack-Fuhrich, *De Religiosis*. n. 49; Genicot, *Theol. Mor.* II, n. 341.

54 Art. XI, AAS, V, 63.

55 Boudinhon, CC, 36, p. 340.

they are not bound to make a sacramental confession and can simply ask his blessing. Circumstances may, however, be such that the passage from extraordinary to ordinary will not be without inconvenience.[56] The Ordinary should watch out that the sisters be not limited for many years to two priests. This can easily happen, when, except for the interval required by law after the term of the ordinary confessor, the office of ordinary and extraordinary is interchanged between two priests. This is undesirable unless the exceptional qualities of the confessors make their very stability in office pleasing to all.[57] That the extraordinary confessor was not bound by the three-year term[58] was the rule before the Code. Since the Code does not prohibit this it can be retained as the principle now.[59]

It is to be noted that the jurisdiction of the extraordinary confessor in regard to the members of the community extends as far and no further than that of the ordinary confessor,[60] unless expressly stated to the contrary.

---

56 Battandier, *Guide Canonique*, n. 264.

57 Vermeersch-Creusen, *Epit.* I, n. 592.

58 S. C. EE et RR, *Majarien et Civitatis Plebis*, Dec. 7, 1906; Vermeersch, Per. III, n. 172.

59 Fanfani, *op. cit.*, n. 135; Bastien, *op. cit.* n. 357.

60 Curran, *op. cit.* p. 57.

CHAPTER XII.

QUALITIES OF THE ORDINARY AND EXTRAORDINARY CONFESSOR.

Under the old law, as promulgated by Benedict XIV, all priests were not eligible for the office of confessor. Nuns subject to regulars were to be provided by the regular superior with an ordinary confessor of their own order. Although regular superiors could, they were not obliged to grant the extraordinary confessor from another order or the secular clergy more than once a year.[1] For nuns subject to the bishop the rule was that their ordinary confessor was to be a secular priest. The exclusion of regulars as ordinary confessors of such religious was extended to religious of simple vows.[2] Although the extraordinary confessors of nuns subject to the bishop were to be seculars, Benedict sanctioned the custom, due to a lack of suitable priests in the various dioceses, of appointing a regular to this office.[3]

These prescriptions remained in force until the decree "Cum de Sacramentalibus."[4]

The only exclusion retained by the decree was that of priests having authority over the religious in the external forum. The principal motive for this innovation came from the Bishops who could not otherwise observe the law of the three-year renewal of the ordinary confessor due to the dearth of suitable priests. In multiplying the ordinary confessors the Holy See wished to

1 Benedict XIV, Const. *Pastoralis Curae*, Aug. 5, 1748, §§ 10, 11; FJC n. 388.

2 S. C. EE et RR, Sept. 1, 1905 ad IV; ASS XXVIII, 48; Col. S. C. P. F. (ed. 1907), n. 2219; Vermeersch, *Per.* II, n. 93, *annotatio*, p. 42; cf. Hizette, *Confessions des Religieuses*, p. 47.

3 Benedict XIV, *loc. cit.*

4 n. 7; AAS V, 63.

suppress as soon as possible the reason or pretext alleged.[5] The Code has the same prescription making no distinction between the regular and secular clergy.

CANON 524.

§ 1. In munus confessarii religiosarum et ordinarii et extraordinarii deputentur sacerdotes, sive e clero saeculari, sive religiosi de Superiorum licentia, morum integritate ac prudentia praestantes; sint insuper annos nati quadraginta, nisi iusta causa, iudicio Ordinarii, aliud exigat, nullam potestatem in easdem religiosas in foro externo habentes.

I. Eligible Priests.

A. *All priests, whether secular or religious are eligible.*

Seculars being subject to the bishop directly can be appointed to these offices without further question. It it is a question of religious women belonging to some religious order, it is not prescribed but is often advisable that a religious of the same order be assigned as confessor, that he might more easily direct the religious women in the spirit and observances of the order.[6] Religious priests however require the permission of their superiors because the constitutions of certain orders will not allow their priests to be ordinary confessors of religious women, e. g., Jesuits,[7] except in the absence of every other priest as was the case in the missions.[8] These prescriptions should be followed, for the superior may have special reasons for not approving the choice.[9] If the bishop should appoint one without at least presumed permission of the superior, this omission would not affect the validity of the confession but only the lawfulness of the absolution. All that is required for validity is the special approbation by the bishop for the hearing of the confessions of

---

5 Hizette, *op. cit.*, p. 48.
6 Fanfani, *loc. cit.*, n. 140.
7 Can. 874, § 1; op. cit., p. 48.
8 Creusen, *Religieux et Religieuses*, n. 98.
9 Bastien, *Directoire Canonique*, n. 363.

the religious women.[10] Although the bishop acts wrongly in not consulting the superior the faculties would be valid despite his objection.

B. *Exceptions.*

Those having power over the religious women in the external forum can not receive these incumbencies. This is a confirmation of the legislation in force in the past which tends more and more to mark a separation between the external and internal forum. Its purpose is to prevent superiors, as confessors of the religious, from using or abusing knowledge acquired in the penitential forum by the exercise of their jurisdiction in the external forum. Such actions or even suspicion or fear would break down the confidence of the religious in the sacrament of penance.[11]

This would include those having dominative power or the power of jurisdiction.[12]

I. *In the Secular Clergy.* They are: (1) The bishop,[13] (2) the vicar general,[14] for it is not a good thing that they have power over the same persons in the forum of conscience and the juridical forum also, lest the former be rendered hateful and thus prevent integral confessions; (3) the delegate or visitor of the bishop for every house or institute since he can be called an ecclesiastical superior for the sisters whom he visits:[15] (4) other persons having diocesan administration such as school directors, superintendents, examiners, inspectors, or supervisors of hospitals, etc.,[16] who can give orders to the religious,[17] and

---

10 Can. 876, § 1.
11 Hizette, *op. cit.*, p. 49.
12 Blat, II, *pars* II, n. 587.
13 S. C. EE et RR, *to the Bishop of Parma*, 1780; An. JP, lib. 30, col. 1283; cf. Joder, AKKR, t. 79, p. 453; 1889, cf. Hizette, *op. cit.* 49.
14 S. C. EE et RR, *in Sorana*, July 23, 1537; *in Mutinen*, Feb. 3, 1597; Ferraris, v. *Monialis*, V, n. 24, p. 1100; Lucidi, *De Visitat. SS. LL.*, II, 189; March 17, 1893, cf. Joder, AKKR, t. 79, p. 453; Hizette, *loc. cit.*, Boudinhon, CC, 36, p. 335; Bastien, *op. cit.*, n. 363; Vermeersch-Creusen, *Epit.* I, n. 591; Cocchi, II, *pars* II, n. 44; Lanslots, *Handbook of Canon Law*, p. 157.
15 Boudinhon, *op. cit.*, p. 336; Hizette, *op. cit.*, p. 49.
16 Vermeersch-Creusen, *Epit.* n. 591; Fanfani, *De Jure Religiosorum*, n. 140; Papi, *Religious in Church Law*, p. 60; Leitner, *Handbuch (Dritte Lieferung)*, p. 361.
17 Leitner, op. cit., p. 261.

(5) even the pastor, who directs his own school, for the nuns teaching in his school or for others if his parish duties would suffer thereby.[18] In places where sisters teach in parish schools living away from their convent the pastor should not be appointed as their confessor. Although he is not strictly speaking their superior, nevertheless he has great authority in the Catholic school and conflicts between him and the superioress can easily arise. Moreover, the obligation of the seal may prevent his taking action against things which his office would demand. If the ordinary can not appoint a more suitable one as ordinary confessor he should allow the sisters to freely approach any confessor in any parish church. Allowance must be made for an ordinary who has a just cause for ordaining matter differently.[19]

The chaplain, however, can also be the confessor. There is nothing to prevent this unless some other authority is superadded. The catechist in schools and educational institutions under the direction of religious women or teachers, specialists in certain branches of study, or procurator or econome, etc., are offices which in themselves confer no power over the religious.[20]

II. *In the Regular Clergy.* Ineligible are superiors having authority immediately over the convent, which include practically the provincial and superior of the house[21] but not the Vicar of the Convent[22] unless he is at the same time superior of the house. Otherwise he is the substitute for the superior only during very short periods of the latter's absence.

---

18 S. C. EE et RR, *in Una Venetiarum*, July 26, 1594; *in Parmensi*, March 7, 1652; *in Raurinensi*, Aug. 2, 1562; and often elsewhere; Ferraris, o. c. V. *Monialis*, V, n. 25; *Venetiarum*, March 17, 1592; cf. Bizzarri, p. 332; *Rossanen*, July 7, 1780, id., p. 394. cf. Cocchi, II, pars II, n. 44; Bastien, l. c.

19 Vermeersch-Creusen, *Epit.* I, n. 591; Schäfer, *Ordensrecht*, p. 119.

20 Leitner, *op. cit.*, p. 361.

21 Hizette, *loc. cit.*, Boudinhon, *loc. cit.;* Aertnys-Damen, *Theol. Mor.* II, n. 375 (ed. 1920).

22 Fanfani, *loc. cit.*, includes him.

C. *Personal Qualities.*

These requirements are even found shortly after the Council of Trent. Trent in many replies that were given in regard to the ordinary and extraordinary confessor of the religious.

A. Integrity of Morals and Prudence. The qualities are necessary by reason of his ministry for if he is to conduct such fervent souls to higher perfection he should be an example to them.[23] The bishop need be only morally certain that these qualities exist, but one judged suitable by his[24] superiors, whether secular or religious, to exercise this ministry for religious women need not worry. He must be content in the judgment of his superiors that he has the integrity and prudence required.[25]

More prudence is necessary in confessors of religious than of the ordinary faithful. (1) Because religious perfection can hardly be obtained without an instructor. (2) Women are naturally less prudent and therefore in the spiritual life are exposed to various and dangerous illusions, which ordinarily they can not dispel without the direction of a prudent and discreet confessor or spiritual director. (3) They easily desist from things which they have begun well unless strengthened by more efficacious persuasions and excited to greater things, which help only the confessor can give to religious women. (4) They are by nature timorous, and therefore can be easily kept from revealing their troubles of soul, unless they have an experienced spiritual physician, who can with the greatest tact discover these infirmities and apply suitable remedies, which is without doubt the office of the confessor. (5) The confessor must be prudent and circumspect to prevent anything such as a natural affection for him. (6) If religious women desist from the spiritual life they are subject to greater temptations and they need the prudent advice of an experienced doctor to show them the methods of conquest. (7) There are many obstacles in the progress of the spiritual life. Therefore the confessor should be discreet,

23 Bastien, *op. cit.*, n. 336; Brandys, *Rechtsbuch*, p. 159.
24 Hizette, *loc. cit.*, p. 47; ff; Boudinhon, *loc. cit.*
25 Vermeersch, *Per.* VII, p. 92.

sagacious and experienced in the spiritual life. Otherwise he would be like the blind leading the blind with the result that both fall into the ditch.[26] Therefore it is required of the confessor of nuns that he have the knowledge of a judge, for he must make distinctions of sins and give or refuse absolution according to his decision on these, of a physician for he must suggest remedies. He should have the same virtues that he is to form in his penitents, and prudence in asking only opportune questions and applying due remedies. He should have zeal for souls and although the hearing of nuns' confessions is laborious, yet he should look upon it as a time to bring pious souls closer to God. He should use great tact especially in obtaining confession of more atrocious sins which women naturally fear to mention. He should have patience especially with the scrupulous.[27]

He should be studious in prayer and contemplation that he might form his penitents.[28]

The confessors of religious women should evidently know the duties of the state of life of their penitents, i. e., resulting from their vows and principal rules; this is advisable but not always possible, in order to direct them to the particular spirit of their order or congregation.[29] Confessors of contemplative nuns should have more knowledge of mystical theology than those of ordinary sisters. It should be a special study of the confessor to see that he acquires a greater knowledge of mystical theology, so as to be of benefit to them. These qualities neither can nor should be dispensed with.[30]

B. Required Age—Shortly after the Council of Trent, the Congregation of Bishops and Regulars decided that the ordinary confessor of nuns should be over forty years of age,[31]

26 Pellizzarius, *Tractatus De Monialibus,* Cap. X, n. 153 (ed. Venice, 1651). cf. Joder, *Beichtvateramt in Frauenklöstern,* AKKR, 78, p. 669.

27 ibid. n. 154-162.

28 Fanfani, *op. cit.,* n. 140.

29 Creusen, *op. cit.* n. 160.

30 Boudinhon, *loc. cit.,* p. 338.

31 S. C. EE et RR, *in una Venetiarum,* May 2, 1617; June 7, 1620; Ferraris, v. *Monialis,* V, n. 49, p. 1106; cf. Hizette, Confessions Des Religieuses, p. 51.

and the Congregation of the Council extended this requirement to the extraordinary confessor.[32]

It was on such decision that Benedict XIV[33] prescribed for the extraordinary confessor of a community or the special confessor of an individual, the same qualities. He stated that at no time was it doubted that in such priests there should be maturity of years, integrity of morals and the light of prudence, as is admitted by all. What he says of the extraordinary confessor applies "a fortiori" to the ordinary confessor,[34] although it was disputed as to whether the maturity of age of the extraordinary after the constitution "Pastoralis Curae" was the forty years of the ordinary confessor.[35] But this age has been retained without question as the rule for all confessors of religious women, even of simple vows.[36] The discipline of the Church was constant in this matter and the decree, "Cum de Sacramentalibus" explicitly required 40 years, At the same time it gave the right to choose priests below that age if they excelled in other qualities.[37] This decree settled the dispute as to the age. It also freed the Ordinary from the necessity of obtaining dispensation of the Congregation of Bishops and Regulars to choose priests below that age. But it made the latter a matter of conscience with the bishops. The legislation of the Code is the same on these points.

This age gives the presumption of greater knowledge, and maturer judgment and spirituality necessary for such a ministry.[38] As a presumption, it may not correspond to reality, since these qualities can be anticipated or retarded.[39]

The priest should have attained forty complete years. In computing this time, the first day is not included[40] and the

---

32 S. C. Conc., *in Cosentina,* Nov. 26, 1689; lib. 39, *Decret. fol.* 340; Ferraris, loc. cit.
33 Const. *Pastoralis Curae,* § 9; FJC, n. 388.
34 Hizette, *op. cit.,* p. 51.
35 Boudinhon, *op. cit.,* p. 337.
36 Hizette, *loc. cit.*
37 Art. VIII; AAS V, p. 63.
38 Bastien, *op. cit.,* n. 363.
39 Boudinhon, *loc. cit.*
40 Can. 34, § 3, 3°.

priest would be capable of assuming the office juridically only at midnight of his fortieth birthday. Thus a priest born on April 30, 1900, could not take office until midnight between the 30th of April and the first of May, 1940. For a just motive, however, the Ordinary can dispense from the requirement of age. The present Code does not explicitly make it a matter of conscience for the bishop, as the decree "Cum de Sacramentalibus" did, in using the power to dispense. The Code only requires an exercise of prudent judgment. Sufficient reason for such a dispensation would be the difficulties in sending another, the scarcity of disposable priests and suitable personnel, a variety of languages spoken in the convent, needing a priest who could understand them.[41] In such cases the lack of age must be supplied by good moral integrity and prudence, which even age does not always guarantee.[42] It will be more difficult to appoint a younger priest as a permanent ordinary or extraordinary confessor, than in a passing case, i. e., in time of retreats, in which he will have sufficient integrity and prudence for such an appointment. Neither the age nor the qualities of soul, if lacking, affect the validity of the absolution,[43] to assure the special approbation of the bishop to hear these religious women suffices.[44] A priest validly delegated and appointed by the Ordinary, can acquiesce in the judgment of the latter and hear confessions with a safe conscience, although he seems to himself to be devoid of some of the qualities required for a lawful appointment.[45]

---

41 Boudinhon, *loc. cit.*; Papi, *Religious in Church Law,* p. 60.

42 Bastien, *op. cit.*, n. 263; Augustine, A Commentary on Canon Law, III, p. 165.

43 Vermeersch, *Per.* VII, p. 92.

44 Can. 876, § 1.

45 Vermeersch, *loc. cit.*

CHAPTER XIII.

RULES TO BE OBSERVED BY THE ORDINARY AND EXTRAORDINARY CONFESSOR.

CANON 524.

§ 3. Confessarii religiosarum tum ordinarii tum extraordinarii interno vel externo communitatis regimini nullo modo sese immisceant.

This is by no means a new prescription of the Code. It was the object of many replies of the Congregation of Bishops and Regulars,[1] which decided at various times that the confessor had no right to meddle in the external affairs of a community. It follows from this, that the office of a delegated superior, could not be joined to that of confessor.[2]

The cardinals of this congregation refused September 7, 1797, (1) to approve the practice of a superioress making known the faults of the sisters; (2) to permit the confessor to impose disclipinary punishments upon them; (3) to allow the confessor to be in any way the superior of the convent.[3] In approving the constitutions of the Servants of the Immaculate Heart of Mary of Lerida, a congregation of simple vows, this congregation commanded that a clause, stating that in certain affairs the confessor could be consulted, must be deleted. The reason given was that the confessor should have no part in the administration of the institute.[4]

This constant discipline of this congregation became the existing law which was repeated and reenforced by its incor-

---

1 Bastien, *Directoire Canonique*, n. 365.
2 Joder, *Beichtvateramt*, AKKR, 79, p. 457.
3 Joder, *loc. cit.*
4 S. C. EE et RR, *Lerida*, Aug. 13, 1887, ad. 15; "*Consultatio autem confessarii expugnatur. Confessarius enim administrationi institutis se ingerere minime debet;*" cf. Battandier, *Guide Canonique*, n. 262; Joder, AKKR, *loc. cit.;* Hizette, *Confessions des Religieuses*, p. 54.

poration into the decree "Cum de Sacramentalibus,"[5] which forbade all confessors of nuns and sisters to meddle in the internal or external government of the community. This distinction of internal and external, although contained implicitly in preceding decrees of the Congregation of Bishops and Regulars, was explicitly stated for the first time by the decree "Cum de Sacramentalibus." The Code gives us this decree without change, except for brevity and by adapting it to the terminology of the new legislation.

Purpose of the Law.

1.—The Church does not want the religious to be subject to too many superiors. 2.—The confessor is bound by the most strict seal of the confessional, which should not be betrayed in any manner or even suspected. 3.—Since the bishop gives confessors jurisdiction for the internal forum only their mission is restricted entirely to that forum. Therefore, the authority of which they are depositories does not confer upon them the quality to occupy themselves in the internal or external administration of the house. 4.—The good of souls who are entrusted to them or who entrust themselves to them, requires that they avoid giving the least suspicion of lack of perfect discretion. The religious might otherwise be estranged from having recourse to their ministrations by the thought that in one person are united the confessor and the superior of the house.[6]

The Subject of the Law.

The law makes this prohibition only for the ordinary and extraordinary confessor of Canon 520, § 1, and Canon 521, § 1, respectively, that is, the confessors appointed to hear the confessions of all the community. This is a change from the decree of 1913, which used the words "omnes confessarii." The omission of these words frees from this prohibition the special confessor of a particular religious (Can. 520, § 2) and the supplementary confessors (Can. 521, § 2). The omission is evidently intentional,

5 n. X; AAS V, p. 63; *Confessarii omnes sive monialium sive sororum, caveant se interno vel externo communitatis regimini sese immisceant.*

6 Boudinhon, *op. cit.*, p. 340; Hizette, *op. cit.*, p. 55.

according to the axiom "quod voluit expressit, de quo noluit tacet." The reason for this is evident. Only the ordinary and extraordinary confessors of the community are appointed "ex officio" to the community. It is only before these that the religious must present themselves at least for their blessing. The other confessors are to be chosen by the religious herself and there cannot be the same restriction for them. Thus, any part they might have in the government of the community, might influence the choice of the religious, but in no way would it make the Sacrament of Penance odious to those who freely and spontaneously requested them.

Forbidden Interventions.

A. *Matters which concern the internal government* would be those for the promotion of the observance of the rules and constitutions by other means than those of the internal forum,[7] i. e., the direction of a family of religious, as such, in regard to the daily order to be observed, the distribution of offices or duties, the administration of the temporal goods, etc.[8]

These belong properly to the province of the superioress and not the confessor.[9] The confessor is there primarily to aid individual souls by his attention, help and experience.[10]

If questioned by the religious in regard to the constitutions, he can only state their obligation, for the observance of poverty, etc., will vary with institutes and superiors. Providing the religious superioress does not offend by laxity or severity, the confessor can only state that the religious should abide by the decision of the superioress, even though the confessor might think it more advisable to do otherwise. He cannot hinder the rule of the superioress in any way.[11] The confessor in these matters, should be very careful, for he can get himself into great trouble, because of the seal of the confessional, even in matters of advice given in confession, according to the decree

---

7 Hizette, *Confessions des Religieuses*, p. 55.
8 Biederlack-Fuhrich, *De Religiosis*, n. 49.
9 Brandys, *Rechtsbuch*, p. 160.
10 Leitner, *Handbuch* (*Dritte Lieferung*), p. 361.
11 Brandys, op. cit., p. 160.

of 1915.[12] Internal regime here must not be understood as spiritual direction of an individual religious, which properly belongs to the confessor.[13] If the confessor is asked by the superioress to promote her counsels to the religious, the confessor should use the greatest discretion in carrying out his part and should avoid doing anything in which he would have to take the initiative.[14]

By action contrary to this, experience has proven that he can cause great trouble and diminish the authority of the religious superioress.[15] If a superioress seeks advice in regard to the changing or rejection of a religious, she should always address herself to another priest than the confessor. But if she should have recourse to him then the circumstances of the matter should be explained in such a way that the confessor can form his judgment without knowing the person in question. The superioress should not be surprised if the priest refuses to give any advice whatsoever and advises her to address herself, even if this is done by writing to some other competent person. If a religious should ask about the force of these counsels of the superioress, the confessor should confine himself to the statement of the precise obligations of the counsel resulting from moral theology and canon law. He cannot make disciplinary measures, which agree more with his own temperament or personal views.[16]

The confessor has not the power to dispense from the obligation of going to Mass on Sundays and days of precept, or from ecclesiastical laws of fast and abstinence unless it is evident that he has received the necessary delegation from the Ordinary.[17] This was expressly forbidden before the Code to the

12 *Instr. S. Officii, ad Rev. mos locorum Ordinarios familiarumque religiosarum moderatores super inviolabili sanctitate sigilli sacramentalis;* June 9, 1915; Cf. Vermeersch-Creusen, *Epit.* II, n. 169; Cf. Can. 889, 890.

13 Biederlack-Fuhrich, *loc. cit.;* Lanslots, *Handbook of Canon Law,* p. 157.

14 Boudinhon, CC, 36, p. 310 ff; Hizette, o. c., p. 55 ff.

15 Bastien, *loc. cit.,* n. 365.

16 Creusen, *Religieux et Religieuses,* n. 100.

17 Battandier, *Guide Canonique,* n. 261; *Confessarius non habet facultatem dispensandi a jejuniis ecclesiasticis,* Lanslots, *Handbook of Canon Law,* p. 157.

confessors of the Dominican Tertiaries of Przemysl, March 21, 1885.[18]

This power, in the terms of Canon 1245, § 1, is proper and requires jurisdiction in the external forum. In the first place it belongs to him who has jurisdiction for the community of simple vows, whether of diocesan or pontifical right. That person is the Ordinary. The pastor has equivalent right if the communities are not withdrawn from his jurisdiction. Therefore, if the pastor were the confessor, whether ordinary or extraordinary, he could dispense from these laws. Ordinarily, if the community has a particular chaplain, he should receive the necessary powers from the Ordinary. The confessor surely can, in particular cases, interpret the law and declare that in certain cases they are not obliged in virtue of the circumstances.[19]

Although it seems more preferable that the confessor and not the superioress should excuse from the recitation of the office and should choose their books for spiritual reading, it is more expedient and more in order that this be reserved to the superioress. It is in effect an act of community life passing into dominative power. This was decided by the correction of the constitutions of the Sisters of Our Saviour and of the Blessed Virgin of Limoges.[20] These confessors are also warned not to exercise jurisdiction in the external forum, e. g., by censuring the religious, settling affairs or reserving cases which require ecclesiastical trial.[21]

B. *Matters of the External Government.*—These belong to the province of the local Ordinary, the regular superior or their delegates.[22] Those which are forbidden, would be the extension of the congregation, foundation or suppression of the houses,

---

18 ad. 20. Augustine, III, p. 165.

19 Bastien, *op. cit.*, 368; Battandier, *loc. cit.*

20 *Sóeurs du S. Sauveur et de la Ste. Vierge, Limoges,* Aug. 12, 1891, ad 10; *"Melius confessario quam superiorissae committuntur facultates dispensandi sororum aliquam ab officii recitatione, vel eligendi libros asceticos pro lectione spirituali."* This was corrected in May, 1904; Cf. Battandier, *loc. cit.*

21 Can. 893, § 1; Augustine, III, p. 165.

22 Schäfer, *Ordensrecht,* p. 119, note 2.

etc.[23] This prohibition would not include the ministrations which can be given by the confessor by common law or episcopal delegation, in the quality of chaplain or procurator, etc.[24] These functions concern the entire community and do not, of their nature, cause any indiscreet meddling in the government or affairs of the community.[25] BASTIEN says neither would the confessor, upon request, be prohibited to give counsel in regard to the administration of the goods or the government of the community.[26]

The confessor cannot oblige penitents to receive his direction of their conscience, but only that they fulfill the prescriptions required as conditions for absolution. They retain the liberty to seek this direction, i .e., clearer advice and encouragement, from another priest.[27]

The confessor should respect and make the religious respect the common law and statutes in regard to the place and manner in which confessions are to be heard.[28]

---

23 Hizette, *op. cit.*, p. 55.
24 Schäfer, *Ordensrecht*, p. 119.
25 Boudinhon, *op. cit.*, p. 341.
26 Bastien, *loc. cit.*, n. 231.
27 Creusen, *Religieux et Religieuses*, n. 100.
28 Creusen, ibid.

CHAPTER XIV.

REMOVAL OF CONFESSORS.

CANON 527.

Loci Ordinarius, ad normam Can. 880, potest, gravem ob causam, religiosarum confessarium tam ordinarium quam extraordinarium amovere, etiamsi monasterium regularibus subdatur et ipse sacerdos a confessionibus sit regularis, nec tenetur causam amotionis cuiquam significare, excepta Apostolica Sede, si ab ea requiratur; de amotione autem debet Superiorem regularem monere, si moniales regularibus subdantur.

This canon seems to be new law, as is evident from the fact that the Code contains in its footnotes no sources to this canon. Formerly, however, the bishop was permitted by Gregory XV in the Constitution "Inscrutabili," February 5, 1622, to warn regular superiors for a reasonable cause to remove confessors of nuns subject to them. Upon refusal or neglect, the bishop had the right to remove the said confessors without interference as often as he judged necessary.[1]

Causes for Removal.

The canon requires a grave cause for removal. Such would be, e. g., if the lives of the confessors were a source of scandal or immoral; if they had committed a crime for which, in the reasonable judgment of the bishop, they should be suspended from hearing confessions, since the principal quality of the minister of the Sacrament of Penance is integrity of life and morals. For such causes pertaining to the Sacrament of Penance, the bishop could remove or suspend confessors approved

---

1 Gregory XV, Const. *Inscrutabili*, § 5; FJC n. 199; cf. Augustine, III, p. 169.

by himself, from hearing confessions of nuns and sisters.[2] Other reasons sufficient for removal, would be disregard of an interdict or the discovery of irregularities by the bishop at the time of the canonical visitation;[3] or the abuse of his office by violation of Canon 524, § 3, which prohibits his meddling in the internal or external government of the community.

Since the bishop is the one who grants jurisdiction in all cases for the hearing of the confessions of religious women, his revocation of this jurisdiction is always valid.[4] If, by this revocation, he does an injustice to the confessor, the Holy See can correct him for this abuse. The same principle holds if not the confessor but the community suffers the injustice. This canon is modeled on Canon 454, § 5,[5] whereby pastors who are regulars, can always be removed, either by the bishop or the superior. The one removing must give notification to the other, but the consent of the latter is not necessary. Neither is bound to make known the cause of the removal to the other or in the least to defend it, preserving, of course, the right of the other of making recourse "in devolutivo" to the Holy See. The same principles apply in the removal of the confessor and the Ordinary is not bound to state the cause of removal to anyone but the Holy See, and only when this is required of him by the latter. Therefore, the Holy See will hear appeals if warranted by a removal without sufficient reason. The Apostolic See will probably inquire about the reasons for removal, if any of the interested parties has had recourse to it against the decree of removal. This complaint to the Holy See is, of course, permissible, but has no suspensive effect, i. e., until the Holy See has decided, it does not prevent the local Ordinary from removing the confessor.[6]

The Ordinary must, however, notify the regular superior upon removal of confessors of nuns subject to regulars, for

---

2 Clement X, Const. *Superna*, June 21, 1670, § 6; FJC, n. 246.
3 S. C. P. F., Dec. 11, 1839, ad 4; Col. S. C. P. F. (ed. 1907), n. 892.
4 S. C. EE et RR, Dec. 9, 1740; Bizzarri, p. 350.
5 Augustine, III, p. 169.
6 Papi, *Religious in Church Law*, p. 63; Augustine, III, 169.

the regular superior has, under Canon 525, the right of presenting another confessor to succeed the one deposed.[7]

Simultaneous Removal of All Confessors of a Convent.

CANON 880.

§ 3. Non tamen licet Episcopo, inconsulta Sede Apostolica, si de domo formata agatur, omnibus alicuius religiosae domus confessariis una simul iurisdictionem adimere.

As Augustine states, the bishop "may not remove all confessors of the same religious house at one time, because such a removal would be not only senseless, but injurious to the spiritual welfare of the nuns and the moral character of the priests involved." [8]

---

7 Augustine, IV, p. 280. ff.
8 Augustine, III, 169.

CHAPTER XV.

SUPPLEMENTARY CONFESSORS.

The supplementary confessors had their origin in various responses of the Congregation of the Council from 1665-1672 referred to and confirmed by Benedict XIV,[1] who granted to nuns the right, under certain conditions, to ask for priests approved for the confessions of nuns. This system, however, had its difficulties, to remove which Leo XIII exhorted the bishops to officially designate supplementary confessors, living in the neighborhood, and give them faculties for the different communities near which they resided. His purpose was that the sisters could thus easily have recourse for the Sacrament of Penance.[2] The bishops responded to this and drew up official lists of supplementary confessors for this purpose.[3] The actual use of this right to ask for such a confessor, unfortunately became a dead letter in a great number of communities. This was due not to the opposition of the superioresses, but to public opinion created in the communities in favor of the absolutely exclusive use of one confessor by all. Thus a religious, who requested a supplementary confessor, more or less openly, was considered as rather singular, strange, pretentious or an oppositionist. This moral pressure made many religious timorous of the contemptuous judgments upon their liberty in a matter so delicate.[4] As a result to protect the liberty of conscience, the Holy See in the decree, "Cum de Sacramentalibus"[5] forbade the sisters to speak among themselves, concerning the confessions of particular religious and especially to criticize those who con-

1 Vermeersch, *Per.* V, p. (10).
2 S. C. EE et RR, Decr. "*Quemadmodum,*" Dec. 17, 1890, ad 4; Col. S. C. P. F. (1907), n. 1745; cf. Boudinhon, CC, 36, p. 275; Hizette, *Confessions des Religieuses*, p. 35.
3 Hizette, *loc. cit.*
4 Mothon, *Traite de la Confession Sacramentelle*, p. 25 ff.
5 S. C. De Rel. Feb. 3, 1913, n. 4, n. 12; AAS V, 63.

fessed to a confessor other than the appointed one.[6] Violation of this was to be punished by their superior or the Ordinary, according to the gravity and circumstances. The present Code confirms the anterior legislation intending to extirpate at any price, abuses which, notwithstanding the decree of the Holy See, unfortunately continue to exist despite the danger of interference by the superior, whether General, Provincial or Local.[7]

CANON 521.

§ 2. Ordinarii locorum, in quibus religiosarum communitates exsistunt, aliquot sacerdotes pro singulis domibus designent, ad quos pro sacramento poenitentiae in casibus particularibus recurrere eae facile possint, quin necessarium sit ipsum Ordinarium toties quoties adire.

Appointment by the Local Ordinary.

Even under the decree, "Quemadmodum," it was the local Ordinary, who was to grant these confessors to communities. It was not a matter of obligation, however, until the decree "Cum de Sacramentalibus" of the Congregation for Religious in 1913, upon which the present canon is based. If the Ordinary neglects to do this, the superioress should ask him to appoint two or three priests in the neighborhood, with the necessary faculties to hear the confessions of the religious of the community when called upon. For religious subject to regulars, the Superior General or the Provincial has, on canonical visits, the grave obligation of seeing that these religious have obtained from the local Ordinary the extraordinary and supplementary confessors for every community or house.[8] The local Ordinary alone has the right to appoint the supplementary confessors, even for the nuns subject to regulars.[9] The superioress, of course, cannot appoint, for that is entirely outside of her province and competency.[10]

---

6 Hizette, *op. cit.*, p. 62.
7 Bastien, op. cit., n. 359.
8 S. C. De Rel. Feb. 3, 1913, n. 4; AAS V, p. 62; Hizette, *op. cit.*, p. 36; Mothon, *Traite de la Confession Sacramentelle,* p. 23.
9 Vermeersch-Creusen, *Epit.* I, n. 594.
10 Bastien, *Directoire Canonique,* n. 359.

Faculties of These Confessors.

To determine just how far these extend, the faculties and their wording must be examined. Confessors appointed to hear the confessions of religious of one community cannot hear those of another.[11] If, on the other hand, the Ordinary has granted faculties in some such terms as "*etiam ad monialium*" or better "*etiam ad omnium religiosarum confessiones audiendas*" and has not made a special condition or inserted a restrictive clause, the confessor appointed for a community of Dominicans, could hear the confessions of a community of Benedictines.[12]

Rules for These Confessors.

They are habitually delegated for the particular community[13] or house, but they are not to become the ordinary confessor of the community. The canon requires that more than one be appointed, i. e., at least two "Pluralis locutio, duorum numero est contenta."[14]

There is nothing to prevent each of these from fulfilling this office for several communities if the Ordinary so desires.[15] Thus the deans and regular superiors of the same or another institute could be given faculties as supplementaries for the convents in their territory.[16] Although these supplementary confessors are particularly approved to hear the confession of the religious of the community, it would be well if they would not fulfill this office, unless requested by the religious.[17] They are given the name of supernumerary confessors "Confessarii adjuncti"[18] by the Congregation for Religious.

---

11 Clement X, Const. *Superna*, June 21, 1670, § 4; FJC n. 246; Innocent XIII, Const. *Apostolici Ministerii*, May 23, 1723; FJC n. 280, § 19; S. C. EE et RR, Decr. *Tridentina*, ad 1, Jan. 29, 1847; Bizzarri, p. 116; Aertnys, *Theol. Mor.* (1906) II, n. 234; Marc, *Institutiones Morales* (1885), II, n. 1764.

12 Cf. Augustine, III, p. 160.

13 Cocchi, II, *pars* II, n. 41.

14 R. J. n VI°, Reg. 40.

15 Papi, *Religious in Church Law*, p. 53; Blat, II, *pars* II, n. 584; Prümmer, *Manuale Juris Canonici*, n. 190.

16 Creusen, *Religieux et Religieuses*, n. 94.

17 Creusen, *op. cit.*, n. 94.

18 Instr. S, C, De Rel. Feb. 6, 1924, *De Clausura*, III, 2, g. AAS XVI, 95; *Il Monitore*; XXXVI (1924), p. 70.

These confessors are not bound by the law of the three-year removal.[19] Neither is a definite age nor any other conditions, except those necessary for the right, fruitful and salutary exercise of their ministry, required of them.[20] The confessor for a community should be so situated, that by reason of time, place and distance, the request of the religious would not be hard to fulfill. Otherwise the appointment of such confessors would be useless. The religious could protest against such appointment. It is very evident that if the Ordinary makes a list of such supplementary confessors, it should be made known to the community.[21]

It is the superior who is to regularly call the confessor, but this should not be urged too strictly.[22] If a religious desires to benefit by the ministry of one of these supplementary confessors, she should not then address the bishop herself, but present her request through the superioress of the house in which she resides.[23]

Confession made in the convent to such priests unknown to the superioress, are certainly valid. Considering Canon 522, where the permission of the superioress is not necessary for a licit confession to a simple confessor, "a pari" such a confession to a supplementary confessor is also lawful.[24]

Sufficient Reason to Ask for This Confessor.

It would seem from the wording of the law "*pro sacramento poenitentiae*" that the religious should have recourse to the supplementary confessor only for matters connected with the Sacrament of Penance. Therefore, religious could not request a supplementary confessor merely for direction and counsel in other matters not touching upon the sacrament.[25] This

19 Mothon, *op. cit.*, p. 23; *Il Monitore*, XVIII, p. 534.
20 Fanfani, *De Jure Religiosorum*, n. 140; Vermeersch-Creusen, *Epit.*, I, n. 594.
21 Hizette, *op. cit.*, p. 37.
22 Genicot, *Theol. Mor.* II, n. 341, note 2.
23 S. C. EE et RR, *Malacitana*, Aug. 17, 1891; ad 1; Col. S. C. P. F. (1907), n. 1763; Choupin, *L'Etat Religieux*, p. 225; Mothon, *op. cit.*, p. 24.
24 Vermeersch, *Per.* VII, p. 90; cf. Choupin, *op. cit.*, p. 226.
25 Blat, II *pars* II, n. 584.

is a privilege, however, and should not be interpreted too strictly. Therefore, the following reasons would seem to be sufficient; (1) if the sister had not gone to the ordinary confessor at the proper time and cannot go to him now. This, however, should not become the rule, so as to make the supplementary confessor almost the ordinary confessor; (2) if the religious had greater confidence in a religious confessor; (3) the fear that a priest of her own order would not be impartial in his decision; (4) the desire for greater spiritual consolation or progress.[26] If the confessor realizes that he has been called without sufficient reason of spiritual necessity or utility, he cannot legitimately exercise his office. He is bound in conscience to refuse to hear the confession of the religious, whom he should prudently dismiss,[27] although he would be justified in arousing in the penitent the required dispositions.

In Particular Cases. These would occur when a religious wishes to call such a confessor for the purpose of confession in a particular instance, i. e., not habitually, and with sufficient reason.[28] Brys infers from these words "in casibus particularibus" that the supplementary confessor could not be called in to hear the confessions of the entire community. He claims that this interpretation is more in conformity to the history of this canon, admitting, nevertheless, the serious probability of the other opinion. A particular case may, however, exist not only for the individual but for the community, e. g., if the ordinary confessor is sick or impeded from coming. In such circumstances the superioress could call a supplementary confessor to hear the confessions of the community.[30] This follows from (1) the fact that he is appointed for the confessions of these religious; (2) and for

---

26 Fanfani, *op. cit.*, n. 136; cf. Cocchi, II *pars* II, n. 42.

27 S. C. EE et RR, Feb. 1, 1891, ad 2; Col. S. C. P. F. (1907), n. 1781; cf. Vermeersch-Creusen, *Epit.* n. 594; Vermeersch, *De Rel.* II, n. 231; S. C. De Rel. *Cum de Sacramentalibus*, Feb. 3, 1913, n. 13, AAS V, 64; Boudinhon, CC, 36, p. 410; Mothon, *Traite de la Confession Sacramentelle*, p. 26.

28 Fanfani, *loc. cit.*

29 *Collationes Brugensis* (1923), p. 474; quoted by Creusen, *op. cit.*, n. 94, note (1).

30 Fanfani, *op. cit.*, n. 136; Vermeersch-Creusen, *Epit.*, I, n. 594.

each house. (3) The religious can have recourse to his administrations on all occasions without the intervention of the Ordinary each time. (4) The terms of the canon do not limit the use of this faculty to one or many religious in particular. (5) The superioress should furnish the religious with the occasion to confess at least once a week (Can. 595, § 1, 3°). (6) The intervention of the supplementary confessor does not constitute an assuming of the office of ordinary confessor, who is presumed to be, for some reason, temporarily prevented from performing it.[31] In these cases there would be no necessity of having recourse to the Ordinary.

Removal of Abuses.

The obligation of removal rests upon the bishop, but if necessary, he should warn the religious that the faculty to call in a supplementary confessor is an exception to the law of the Church. The law of Trent and Benedict XIV still retain their obligatory force in regard to one confessor for each community.[32]

It would certainly be an abuse if all and every religious in a community had recourse habitually to the right of confessing to supplementary confessors. Thereby the law of one confessor for a community would be practically nullified.[33]

Obligations of the Superioress.

Benedict XIV [34] had made provisions for the refusal or neglect upon the part of the regular superior and bishops to give such confessors. The trouble, however, did not arise on that score, but from the superioresses of the individual houses. They assumed to themselves the right to restrict the use of this right by prohibition or irksome inquiry into the motives of the re-

---

31 Creusen, *op. cit.*, n. 94; Chelodi, *Jus De Personis*, n. 257; Prümmer, *Manuale Juris Canonici*, n. 190.

32 Can. 520 § 1. S. C. EE et RR, Feb. 1, 1892, ad 4; Col. S. C. P. F. (1907), n. 1781; S. C. De Rel., *Cum de Sacramentalibus*, Feb. 3, 1913, n. 13, AAS V, 63.

33 Mothon, *Traite de la Confession Sacramentelle*, p. 26.

34 Const. *Pastoralis Curae*, §§§ 6, 7, 8; FJC n. 388.

quest.[35] They sometimes refused to call a supplementary confessor, even in cases where the religious needed these confessors badly for their conscience sake. Such actions and even the manifestation of displeasure, at the request, were forbidden by Leo XIII.[36] The Congregation of Bishops and Regulars cleared up many difficulties on this matter.[37] Its prescriptions were reenforced by the decree "Cum de Sacramentalibus"[38] to be incorporated by the Code in Canons 521, § 3, 522, 523 and 2414, which contains the punishment for such violations.

CANON 521.

§ 3. Si qua religiosa aliquem ex iis confessariis expetat, nulli Antistitae liceat nec per se nec per alios, neque directe nequeindirecte, petitionis rationem in-neoue directe neque indirecto, petitionis rationem inratione ostendere se id aegre ferre.

If the religious asks for one of the supplementary confessors, the superioress cannot refuse, etc. VERMEERSCH-CREUSEN,[39] CREUSEN,[40] BASTIEN [41] and PAPI [42] consider that these words "ex iis confessariis" refer to all confessors mentioned in both § 1 and 2 of Canon 521. Therefore, a religious can ask for both the extraordinary and the supplementary confessor of the community. They claim that this is evident from the whole setting of the canon and the wording of § 3.

But the opinion of AERTNYS-DAMEN [43] and KINANE,[44] that these words refer only to the supplementary confessor of § 2 is more in conformity to the true spirit of the law for the following reasons: I—The extraordinary confessor has not *per se*

35 S. C. EE et RR, *Quemadmodum,* Dec. 17, 1890, intro.; Col. S. C. P. F. (1907), n. 1745.

36 S. C. EE et RR, ibid., ad 4.

37 S. C. EE et RR, Aug. 17, *in Malacitana;* Col. S. C. P. F. (1907), n. 1763; Feb. 1, 1892, ibid, n. 1781; Aug. 5, 1904, ibid., n. 2204.

38 S. C. De Rel., Feb. 3, 1913, n. 11; AAS V, 63.

39 *Epit.,* I, n. 594; *Periodica,* IX, p. 12.

40 *Religieux et Religieuses,* n. 94.

41 *Directoire Canonique* (1923), n. 359.

42 *Religious in Church Law,* p. 53.

43 *Theol. Mor.,* II, n. 374.

44 *Irish Ecclesiastical Record* (1923), 5th Series, vol. XXII, p. 641 ff.

jurisdiction as special confessor of a particular religious. II—The first paragraph of this canon refers to the extraordinary confessor, who is to visit the convent to which he is appointed, at least four times a year. On the occasion of each visit every member of the community must present herself to him at least for his blessing. In the second paragraph it is stated that certain confessors, residing in the neighborhood, are to be appointed to whom the religious can have recourse in individual cases, without applying to the Ordinary. It is the natural interpretation of the words of the third paragraph which states, that if a religious asks for a confessor of this kind, the superioress cannot refuse, etc., to consider them as applying only to the second paragraph. This seems logical since the second paragraph is the only one in which the religious are given the right to make such a request. It is only the supplementary confessors that are appointed to be granted on demand of the religious. III—If it was intended that the extraordinary confessor could also be demanded by the individual religious the first paragraph, which defines his functions, should have stated so.[45]

The superioress is not to designate the confessor, for the religious has the right to choose anyone of those approved by the Ordinary.[46] On the other hand, the religious could hardly ask for one from a distant place.[47] If she should ask for one not appointed for her community, then it will be necessary to have recourse to the Ordinary to obtain faculties for him. This can be made either by the superioress[48] or the confessor himself. The bishop should accede to the reasonable demand of the religious, but he retains the right and obligation of

45 Kinane, *loc. cit.*

46 S. C. EE et RR, *in Malacitana*, Aug. 17, 1891, ad 1; Col. S. C. P. F. (1907), n. 1763.

47 Creusen, *Religieux et Religieuses*, n. 94.

48 Benedict XIV, Const. *Pastoralis Curae*, § 6; FJC n. 388 Battandier, *Guide Canonique*, n. 359; S. C. EE et RR, *In Malacitana*, loc. cit., ad 3; Choupin, *op. cit.*, p. 225.

49 Boudinhon, CC, 36, p. 277.

examining the priest requested to see if he satisfies all the required conditions.[49]

Prohibition to the Superioress.

Refusal of the request of a religious is forbidden. The superioress must acquiesce, even though she feels certain that there is no necessity for the recourse and that the demand is based upon scruples or depression, etc., that makes the religious apprehend it as true necessity.[50]

Inquiry into the motive just as refusal is also forbidden for all superioresses, whether major or minor.[51] Such inquiry cannot be made either directly or personally or indirectly, i. e., through others. Thus neither the counsellors, nor the mistress of novices, nor any other official or unofficial third party can do this.[52]

Displeasure at the request cannot be shown in any way, either directly by asking the reason for the petition or indirectly by asking what the sister may have done; where she was; who spoke to her; who was in the parlor, etc., even as a joke. The superioress should not shrug her shoulders at the request; use uncharitable words; make faces at the petitioner; ridicule her or let her feel it afterwards.

Prevention—The superioress may not prevent the religious from fulfilling her wish either by not calling the priest requested, but another or by sending the religious on an errand or giving her work to do at that time or in a distanct place.[53]

The superioress, having a motive of the external order, e. g., the intervention of this confessor weakens her authority or causes discord in the community, etc., cannot even then oppose the exercise of his ministry if he is appointed for the community and demanded by a religious. But if there are grave and well founded reasons for stopping this ministry the superioress

---

50 S. C. EE et RR, Aug. 17, 1891, *in Malacitana,* ad 2; Col. S. C. P. F. (1907), n. 1763; Choupin, *L'Etat Religieux,* p. 226; Mothon, *op. cit.,* p. 24.

51 Blat, II *pars* II, n. 584.

52 Augustine, III, n. 584.

53 Augustine, III, p. 161, 163.

should submit them to the Ordinary and abide by his decision.[54] By this canon the legislator has very prudently provided for the timidity of women, especially in regard to matters of conscience.[55]

Punishment for Violations by Superioresses.

The origin of these prohibitions is found in the decree "Quemadmodum"[56] of Leo XIII, but it was not until the decree "Cum de Sacramentalibus"[57] of the Congregation of Religious that sanctions were added for their violation. These sanctions, however, referred only to the refusal of the supplementary confessor. The Code goes further and extends them in its last canon to violations of the prescriptions in regard to the confessor for the peace of conscience (Canon 522) and of the sick (Canon 523).

CANON 2414.

Antistita quae contra praescriptum can. 521, § 3, 522, 523 se gesserit, a loci Ordinario moneatur; si iterum deliquerit, ab eodem officii privatione puniatur, illico tamen certiore facta Sacra Congregatione de Religiosis.

For the first offense the local Ordinary should give a canonical warning, either personally or through another, advisably the chancery.[58] This need not be given publicly, and in fact, it is preferable that it be given secretly. Even in this case the fact of the first warning should be evident from some document, which is to be kept in the secret archives of the Curia.[59] Since this warning must be given by the "local Ordinary," there is to be noticed the change over the decree "Cum de Sacramentalibus," which had the words "proper ordinary."

54 S. C. EE et RR, Aug. 5, 1904; Col. S. C. P. F. (1907), n. 2204; cf. Mothon, *Traite de la Confession Sacramentelle,* p. 24; Battandier, *Guide Canonique,* n. 259.

55 Blat, II *pars* II, n. 584.

56 S. C. EE et RR, Dec. 17, 1890, ad 4; cf. Col. S. C. P. F. (1907), n. 1745.

57 S. C. De Rel., Feb. 3, 1913; n. 9; AAS V, 63.

58 Can. 2307.

59 Can. 2309, § 5.

This term included, at that time, exempt regular superiors, as Ordinaries of the nuns subject to them.[60]

For the second offense the law of the decree "Cum de Sacramentalibus" required the deposition of the superioress by the Ordinary only after the matter had been referred to the Congregation of Religious.[61] The Code reverses the process commanding the deposition of superioresses violating the prescriptions of these canons with the subsequent notification of the same congregation. There is the obligation of making this notification immediately. This is due, no doubt, to the fact that the Code makes no distinction here between superioresses.[62]

It is evident that if it is a question of a General or a Provincial Superioress, an institute or province may find itself seriously embarrassed. This it should attempt to remedy without delay.[63] The canon requires for the deposition of the superioress that she be twice guilty of violation of this law. But the complaints on the two occasions need not be made by the same religious. The Ordinary should send to the Congregation of Religious the statement of the facts of the case. This would include the first warning, which was disregarded; the two complaints; the results of the two inquiries as to the abuses and should then conform himself to any subsequent decision of the congregation.[64] Suspicion[65] suffices to give the canonical warning. Prudence, however, demands that the Ordinary make serious inquiry by questioning both the complainant and the superioress before he gives such a warning.[66]

It is certain that if the Ordinaries will show themselves severe on the points indicated in these canons, the abuses which may have continued until the Code will cease.[67]

---

60 S. C. De Rel., Feb. 3, 1913, n. 9; AAS V, 63.
61 ibid. n. 11.
62 Hizette, *Confessions des Religieuses* (Supplement, 1920), p. 15; Bastien, *op. cit.*, n. 359.
63 Bastien, ibid.
64 Hizette, *op. cit.* (1914), p. 61.
65 Can. 2307.
66 Hizette, *op. cit.*, p. 60.
67 Bastien, *op. cit.*, n. 359.

CHAPTER XVI.

SPECIAL ORDINARY CONFESSOR OF AN INDIVIDUAL RELIGIOUS.

CANON 520.

§ 2. Si qua religiosa, ad animi sui quietem, et ad maiorem in via Dei progressum, aliquem specialem confessarium vel moderatorem spiritualem postulet, eum facile Ordinarius concedat; qui tamen invigilet ne ex hac concessione abusus irrepant; quod si irrepserint, eos caute et prudenter eliminet, salva conscientiae libertate.

The Subject of the Law.

This canon applies to all women religious without distinction, whether of solemn or simple vows, whether of diocesan or pontifical right. It also includes novices, although they are not religious properly so-called, because, in virtue of Canon 566, § 1, they are to have the same discipline in regard to confessors and confession as religious. For like reasons members of societies of women living in community even without vows, come under this canon, according to Canon 675.[1]

The Use of This Canon.

Necessity of conscience is not required that the religious might ask for such a confessor or that the Ordinary can grant him,[2] but only peace of soul or greater progress in the spiritual life, the way of God. The motives for which a religious can request such a confessor should be taken in a wide sense.[3] These

---

1 Cf. Treatment on Can. 522, p.

2 Blat, II, pars II, n. 583.

3 Choupin, *L'Etat Religieux*, p. 223; Brandys, *Rechtsbuch*, n. 145; Shäfer, *Ordensrecht*, p. 112; Leitner, *Handbuch* (*Dritte Lieferung, Das Ordensrecht*), p. 354.

can be motives of conscience, e. g., trouble because of a doubtful confession or motives of spiritual advancement.[4]

In the latter class can be included the lack of confidence in, or the repugnance to, the ordinary confessor; the difficulty of revealing their sins or faults to him; the impossibility of obtaining frequent and necessary counsels from him; a special situation or condition such as scruples or temptations, which are grave or frequent; extraordinary graces to be received by confessing to the special confessor. These causes would all justify the demand for and the grant of a special confessor, since these things are all obstacles which hinder spiritual progress.[5]

A religious can request such a confessor, even though she does not confess to him,[6] for he may be called only for the purpose of spiritual direction. It is to be remembered, however, that the Ordinary cannot offer such a confessor, for the Code requires that the religious first request him.

The Special Confessor.

He can be either a secular or a religious priest and it is not necessary that he be presented by the religious superior if it is a question of religious subject to regulars.[7]

This confessor could also be the extraordinary or the supplementary confessor of the community (Canon 521, § § 1, 2).[8]

The rule before the Code was that the ordinary confessor of a community could not become the special confessor of an individual religious until after a lapse of a year from the completion of his three-year term. Even then, this was permitted only for the cases mentioned in the constitution "Pastoralis Curae" of Benedict XIV.[9] These cases were (1) in grave sickness; (2) repugnance to the ordinary confessor and refusal to confess to him; (3) confessor requested for peace of conscience

---

4 Battandier, *Guide Canonique*, n. 259.
5 Choupin, *op. cit.*, p. 223.
6 Blat, II, *pars* II, n. 583; Shäfer, *Ordensrecht*, p. 112, note 5.
7 Vermeersch-Creusen, Epit., I, n. 593; Shäfer, loc. cit.
8 Mothon, *L'Etat Religieux*, n. 174; Battandier, *op. cit.* n. 259; Shäfer, *op. cit.* p. 112 ff.
9 §§ 5, 7; FJC, n. 388; S. C. EE et RR, *Majarien et Civitatis Plebis*, Dec. 7, 1906, ad 3; Vermeersch, *Per.* III, n. 172.

and greater progress in the spiritual life. This restriction no longer exists under the Code, for the Congregation for Religious[10] extended it to include all cases where there were sufficient reasons. Sufficient reason would be that religious women might thereby have the "copia confessarii," which is proper and conducive to their liberty of conscience. This end is perfectly obtained if the ordinary confessor at the end of his three-year term is retained as the special confessor of a particular religious.[11] This confessor is not bound by the law of the three-year term and his office perdures as long as the necessity or utility for which he was given, lasts.[12] The responses upon which this deduction is based, were given before the Code, but they are declarative rather than extensive of the law and it seems that they can be lawfully followed and applied at the present.[13] The religious can make use of his ministrations habitually or occasionally and if she is given a special confessor, she no longer has to confess to the ordinary confessor of the community.[14]

The special confessor need not be of the canonical age of forty years,[15] which is required by the Code only for the ordinary and extraordinary confessors of a community.

Obligation of the Ordinary.

If a religious should request one of these confessors, the Ordinary should be very willing to grant him. The sovereign Pontiffs have more than once insisted upon the facility with which the Ordinary should accede to this demand, when it is

---

10 S. C. De Religiosis, Apr. 20-22, 1917; AAS IX, 276. ad II.

11 Vermeersch, *Per.* VIII, p. 230.

12 S. C. EE et RR, Dec. 7, 1906, ad 5; Vermeersch, *Per.* III, n. 172.

13 Fanfani, *De Jure Religiosorum* (ed. 1925), n. 137; Vermeersch-Creusen, *Epit.* I, n. 593; Blat, II *pars* II, n. 583; Bastien, *Directoire Canonique,* n. 356; Mothon, *Etat Religieux,* n. 174; Prümmer, *Manuale Juris Canonici,* n. 190; Cocchi, II *pars* II, n. 39 (b); Chelodi, Jus De Personis, n. 257 (a).

14 Aertnys-Damen, *Theol. Mor.* II, n. 372; Mothon, *Traite de la Confession Sacramentelle* (1913), p. 28; also *Etat Religieux* (1922), n. 174; Choupin, *Recents Decrets du St. Siege* (1913), p. 48.

15 Can. 524, § 1; Cocchi, *loc. cit.;* Bastien, *loc. cit.;* Vermeersch-Creusen, *Epit.,* I, n. 593.

justified.[16] The Ordinary here referred to is the Ordinary of the place in which the confessions are to be heard, for he alone can grant jurisdiction for the confessions of religious women.[17] Thus the Code differs from the decree "Cum de Sacramentalibus." This decree used the words "proprio Ordinario,"[18] which were less definite than the words of the Code. He is to be freely appointed[19] by the Ordinary. It is not necessary that the consent of the superiors be had, for the special ordinary confessor for those religious women subject to them, nor that they present the confessor. These superiors, on the other hand, can demand that they be informed of his appointment. Moreover, if they judge it opportune they may submit their observations upon the subject to the Ordinary.[20]

Abuses—can arise from this concession on two scores:

I—*From the religious*—such as a too frequent recourse to such a confessor or at a time that is ill-chosen for the confessor or the penitent; also if the confidence of the religious in the confessor of her choice is the result, not of the desire of greater progress in the spiritual life and religious perfection, but of too frequent resorts to him from human affection, which is sensible and may become carnal.[21]

II—*From others*—lest the demands for such a confessor multiply without measure.[22] It would be such an abuse if all and every sister were to ask for a special confessor. As a result the law of one confessor for a community prescribed by the Church, would be practically abrogated for this particular community.[23]

---

16 Creusen, *op. cit.*, n. 93.

17 Can. 876.

18 S. C. De Relig. Feb. 3, 1913, n. 5; AAS V, 62.

19 Vermeersch-Creusen, *Epit.*, I, n. 593.

20 Creusen, *Religieux et Religieuses*, n. 93.

21 Hizette, *Confessions des Religieuses*, p. 40 ff.

22 Creusen, *op. cit.*, n. 93; in a house of 12 religious there were counted 13 confessors, since one sister wanted two confessors to direct her conscience.

23 Mothon, *Etat Religieux*, n. 174; Hizette, *loc. cit.*

Evidently, the local Ordinary should be very prudent in granting an exception, which can degenerate into an abuse or become manifold because of the fact of one concession.[24]

The office of watching, lest such abuses should creep in, rests primarily on the bishop, at least in the external forum. In the internal forum, however, the special confessor should take care of this matter. He should prudently dismiss the religious who has requested him without a just cause.[25] This concession should not be taken away immediately when abuses arise, but every effort should be made to remove them in some manner.[26] If this should fail, they should be eradicated with kindness, but at the same time firmly, cautiously and prudently.[27] In doubt as to the abuse, the liberty of conscience prevails.[28]

It is the bishop who, in all cases, is to judge about these things. The religious superioress, when asked by a religious for such a confessor, should not show opposition, even though she feels that the recourse is not justified. If the superioress believes that there is a notable abuse, she can, if it seems opportune, send her observations on the matter to the bishop when she notifies him of the request of the religious.[29]

---

24 Bastien, *op. cit.*, n. 356.

25 S. C. EE et RR, Feb. 1, 1892, ad 2 cf. Vermeersch, *De Rel.* II, n. 231; S. C. EE et RR, Aug. 5, 1904, ad 3 cf. Vermeersch, *Per. II*, n. 29; S. C. De Rel., Feb. 3, 1913, n. 13, AAS V, 64; Chelodi, *Jus de Personis*, n. 257.

26 Papi, *Religious in Church Law*, p. 53; Vermeersch-Creusen, *Epit*, I, n. 593.

27 Augustine, III, p. 159.

28 Chelodi, *loc. cit.;* Augustine, *loc. cit.*

29 S. C. EE et RR, Aug. 17, 1891, Col. S. C. P. F. (1907) n. 1763; Aug. 5, 1904, ibid. n. 2204. cf. Choupin, *op. cit.*, p. 224.

CHAPTER XVII.

THE CONFESSOR FOR PEACE OF CONSCIENCE.

The concession to confess to priests, not approved for nuns, was given for the first time by the Congregation of Bishops and Regulars on August 27, 1852,[1] to nuns who were outside of their convent in habit for a short time for their health or any other reason. They were permitted to go to any priest approved by the Ordinary for both sexes, although not for nuns. The restrictions in regard to the retention of the habit, the reason for being outside and the length of their stay outside, were removed in the permission of the same congregation to school sisters. Those sisters who, in community outside of the cloister, received the sacraments and assisted at Mass, etc., in the parish church, could confess outside of their house to any confessor approved by the Ordinary.[2] Therefore, the congregation in particular instances forbade the inclusion in the constitutions of any clause prohibiting the use of this faculty by a sister.[3]

Approbation for nuns' confession was no longer required in practice from the viewpoint of the general law.[4] The Sacred Penitentiary, Feb. 7, 1901,[5] stated that absolutions given to religious not having permission to go out to confess, were valid. Moreover, there was no obligation upon the confessor to inquire, whether she had permission, unless he had a prudent suspicion

---

1 S. C. EE et RR, Bizzarri, p. 129; Vermeersch, *De Religiosis* II, n. 227; Ballerini, *Opus Theologicum Morale*, V, n. 409, (ed. 1900); Genicot, *Theol. Mor.* II, n. 340.

2 S. C. EE et RR, *Atrabaten*, Apr. 22, 1872, ad 3; Col. S. C. P. F., (1893) n. 433; Aertnys, *Theol. Mor.* (1906) II, n. 236; Marc, *Institutiones Morales Alphonsiae* (1885) II, n. 1765.

3 S. C. EE et RR, to Sisters of Third Order of St. Francis, Angers Feb. 22, 1875, ad 11; cf. Vermeersch, *Per.* V, p. (8); quoted by Battandier, *Guide Canonique* (1923), n. 260.

4 Battandier, *loc. cit.*

5 *S. Poenitentiariaa, Tornaoen et Mechlinien.;* Vermeersch, *De Rel.* II, n. 223.

that she confessed to him illicitly. The "Normae" of 1901[6] granted to religious the right of confession in public churches to any priest, approved by the Ordinary. The Congregation for Religious[7] in 1913 gave nuns and sisters, outside of their convent for any reason, the right to use this faculty not only in churches but even in oratories, including those which were only semi-public. The congregation added for the superioresses the prohibition to inquire even indirectly in regard to the use of this faculty. The religious were, moreover, in no way bound to report to the superioress, when they confessed in virtue of this decree. The Code has reproduced the law of 1913 in the following canon, but with some further mitigations.

CANON 522.

Si, non obstante praescripto can. 520, 521, aliqua religiosa, ad suae conscientiae tranquilitatem, confessarium adeat ab Ordinario loci pro mulieribus approbatum, confessio in qualibet ecclesia vel oratorio etiam semi-publico peracta, valida et licita est, revocato quolibet contrario privilegio; neque Antistita id prohibere potest aut de ea re inquirere, ne indirecte quidem; et religiosae nihil Antistitae referre tenentur.

Article I.

The Subject of This Law.

The legislator in the word "religiosa," which is a generic term, includes in this privilege all religious women without distinction, whether of solemn or simple vows, whether of diocesan or pontifical right.[8] Under the old law this concession was granted in the beginning to nuns only,[9] but later extended

6 June 28, S. C. EE et RR, June 28, 1901. att. 149.

7 Decr. "*Cum de Sacramentalibus,*" Feb. 3, 1913, n. 14; AAS V, 64.

8 Can. 488, 7°—, which defines terms applied to religious, uses this word in reference to both nuns and sisters; cf. Goyeneche, CpR (1921), II, p. 14.

9 S. C. EE et RR, Aug. 27, 1852; Bizzarri, p. 129; S. C. EE et RR, Apr. 22, 1872, ad 3; Col. S. C. P. F., (1893), n. 433.

to sisters by the decree "Cum de Sacramentalibus."[10] The Code must be interpreted in the same way.[11]

Nuns observing papal cloister, certainly have the right to use this canon, but due to the restrictions of the cloister, will not be able to use it as frequently as sisters.[12] Novices, although not religious properly so-called, for they have no vows,[13] can also use this canon. By the prescription of Canon 566, § 1, novices are to follow the same discipline as religious in regard to confession and confessors. This is a change from the "Cum de Sacramentalibus," in which the novices were not included, since it was considered more favorable to them to regard them as secular persons, for whose confessions common approbation and jurisdiction sufficed.[14] For similar reasons, according to Canon 675, members of pious societies of women living in community, even if without vows, enjoy this right.[15] Canon 522 then extends to all women leading a religious life in community. This is the unanimous opinion of recent commentators.[16] There is no need of extending this to postulants, since they can confess to any priest, approved for the faithful.

Article II.

Necessary Conditions for the Use of This Canon.

This canon is burdened with many difficulties and has been the subject of more written articles than any canon in the Code.[17] The wording of the canon often seems equivocal with the resultant difficulty of determining just what conditions are necessary for validity and liceity.

10 loc. cit.

11 Can. 6, 4°.

12 Can. 601, 604, 607.

13 Can. 488, 7°.

14 Lehmkuhl, *Theol. Mor.* (1914), II, n. 5118.

15 Blat, II, *pars* II, n. 585 (1921).

16 Goyeneche, CpR, (1921) II, p. 14; Blat, II *pars* II, n. 585; Vermeersch, *Per.* IX, p. (13); *Il Monitore* I, series IV, (1919) p. 158; Arregui, *Summarium Theol. Mor.* (1919), n. 605; 2°; Prümmer, *Manuale, J. C.,* (ed. altera) p. 297, note, 5; Leitner, *Handbuch,* (*Dritte Lieferung*), *Das Ordensrecht,* (1919) p. 336; Augustine, III, p. 163; Chelodi, *Jus de Personis,* n. 258; Noldin, De Sacramentis, n. 349; and others.

17 cf. Chelodi, Jus de Personis, n. 258.

Even the affirmation that all these conditions are necessary for validity seems to be supported by certain reasons. 1.—The law makes no distinction between them and neither should we.[18] It must be remembered, however, that the interpretation of law is the declaration of the genuine sense of the law, according to the mind and will of the legislator.[19] The historical survey of the question has shown that the tendency of the legislator has always been towards further liberty of conscience for religious women in confessional matters. Moreover, the fact that the wording of the canon is not clear in places gives to authors the right of advancing views on these points. Therefore, any opinions founded on good reasons, tending toward leniency, are consistent with the doctrine and practice of the Church in this matter. Otherwise confession might become odious to religious, a calamity which the Church wishes to avert.[20]

2.—Some authors think that Canon 522 is an exception to the general law of Canon 876 which requires that all confessors of religious women and their novices have special jurisdiction. But according to Canon 19, laws containing an exception to the general law must be subjected in all their clauses to a strict interpretation. Therefore a confession to a simple confessor in virtue of Canon 522 is subject to four conditions and if one of them is missing there is a case outside of the concession, outside of which the confessor can not, due to a defect of this peculiar jurisdiction required by common law, absolve a religious.[21] This interpretation does not seem to be justified since Canon 876 explicitly mentions Canon 522 not as an exception, but as a prescription of law ("Salvo praescripto Can. 239, § 1, n. 1, 522, 523.") On the contrary it would be better to say that Canon 876 is not a general law and also that Canon 522 can not become an exception to it, since it is explicitly mentioned

---

18 *Ubi lex non distinguit, nec nos distinguere debemus;* cf. Wernz, *Jus* Decretalium, (1913), n. 131.

19 Maroto, *Institutiones* J. C., I, n. 235.

20 *Odia restringi, et favores convenit ampliari;* R. J. in VI°, Reg. 15.

21 Goyeneche, CpR, II, p. 16.

and confirmed by Canon 876. Moreover in Canon 522 it is not a question of a later law derogating a former one, but only of a definite article of one law or legal rule for the confessions of religious women. Otherwise Can. 239, § 1, which treats of a privilege of Cardinals and Canon 523, which grants the choice of a confessor to sick religious women, should also be strictly interpreted since they too are enumerated in Canon 876. This interpretation of Canon 876 can not be said to make it a "res odiosa" on the ground that the prudence of those who are destined for the confessions of female religious is guaranteed by this special approbation. Rather should Canon 520, which takes away the ordinary choice of a confessor granted to the faithful in Canon 905 and assigns only one ordinary confessor to houses of religious women, be considered as the "res odiosa."[22]

I. *The Motive.*

The confession must be made for the peace of conscience of the religious. This requirement was not contained in the decree, "Cum de Sacramentalibus." Although the Code permits religious women to confess within their own oratory to confessors not approved for religious, at the same time to safeguard the rule of regular confessions to the ordinary confessor appointed for that purpose, it requires that these confessions be made for peace of conscience. Nevertheless the very evolution of the law, which, as shown above, was always towards leniency, demands that these words: "*Ad suae conscientiae tranquillitatem*" must be taken in a broad sense.[23] This motive of peace of conscience may be defined then as any cause, which is at least subjectively serious, tending to procure for the religious a greater interior tranquillity.[24] In other words the religious are to confess with the sincere desire of purifying their conscience or relieving it to advantage.

---

22 Vermeersch, *Per.*, XI, p. (14): Vermeersch-Creusen, *Epit.* (1921) I, n. 59, n. 498.

23 Creusen, *Religieux et Religieuses*, n. 95.

24 Bastien, *Directoire Canonique*, n. 360.

A.—*This motive is not necessary for validity.* Most authorities now agree upon this although there was an opinion that the "peace of conscience" is a "conditio sine qua non." Appeal was made to a comparison of phrasing, e. g., Article VII of the decree "Ne Temere"[25] contains the words "ad consulendum conscientiae," accepted by authors as a condition imposed under penalty of invalidity.[26] AUGUSTINE takes issue with this opinion proving that this could not be a "conditio sine qua non" and is at the most a motive cause, which does not affect the validity of the confession.[27]

I. If the phrase "ad suae conscientiae tranquilitatem" were changed into a dependent clause it would read "ut consulatur conscientiae tranquilitati." Here the motive is expressed by the *ut finalis.* Even if it be taken as the *causa finalis* and not merely an impulsive cause it can not be construed as a "conditio sine qua non" for the purpose or end of the law does not fall under the law (finis legis non cadit sub lege) unless expressed in the law itself.[28] Neither does the phrase of the "Ne Temere"[29] imply a "conditio sine qua non." The main point of the decree is the imminent danger of death, in which there is generally disturbance of mind, and during which marriage could be contracted before any priest and two witnesses. In these cases the priest did not have to ask the contracting parties if they wished to appease their consciences as a condition without which they could not contract marriage. It is evident that here too the appeasing of the conscience is the impulsive or motive cause, the "conditio sine qua non" being the danger of death. The present Code (Can. 1098) has omitted this clause.

---

25 S. C. C. Aug. 2, 1907; ASS, XL, 591 ff.

26 Kinane, *Ir. Ecc. Rec.*, (1919) vol. XIII, p. 239. 414; Stettner, *Am. Ecc. Rev.* (1919) vol. LXI, p. 446.

27 Augustine, *A Commentary on Canon Law,* IV, p. 269-273; cf. *Am. Ecc. Rev.* (1920), LXII, p. 58.

28 Cf. Can. 11, cf. Augustine, *loc. cit.*

29 Art. VII—"The phrase is accepted as meaning a reason for admitting the extraordinary form of contracting marriage, the non-existence of which would invalidate a marriage informally contracted." Augustine, *loc. cit.*

The preposition *ad* has several meanings, but as a rule is only used to denote a condition when a contract or stipulation is involved, e. g., faculties granted "ad beneplacitum nostrum." i. e., as long as it is the pleasure of the one delegating.[30]

II. Incongruity of the opposite opinion. If this phrase is considered as a condition necessary for validity then the religious would administer the material for a valid confession, not only by her confession and dispositions of souls such as true sorrow, etc., but even by her "peace of conscience." That is contrary to the principles of theology.[31]

III. This has been the constant interpretation of similar clauses in past legislation. Benedict XIV advised indulgence, by the bishops and superiors, to the desires of the individual nuns when they reasonably seek anything that confers greater security and peace of conscience.[32] Benedict XIV used the phrases "pro animi quiete" and "ad earum conscientiae quietem et securitatem." The wording of this text is clear and a strict interpretation of it would be foreign to the mind of the legislator. In order not to torture the nuns in conscience he gave them the right to call in another confessor than the ordinary of the community, even if they had to apply to the Sacred Penitentiary This was a motive cause but not a condition properly so-called.[33]

IV. To subject the validity of confession to a condition which is entirely subjective and about which the legislator would have great difficulty in judging, would argue for grave imprudence upon the part of the legislator.[34] BARBOSA [35] defines conscience as something hidden in the soul which can not be easily

---

30 Augustine, IV, *loc. cit;* Father Augustine discusses this question very well and it will suffice to synopsize his treatment here.

31 Augustine, *op. cit.*, p. 272.

32 Benedict XIV, Const. *Pastoralis Curae;* § § 7, 8; FJC n. 388; cf. Augustine, loc. cit.

33 Augustine, loc. cit.

34 Goyeneche, CpR, (1921) II, p. 16.

35 *Tractatus Varii, Axiomata* 52, (ed. London 1660) p. 34; *Conscientia nihil aliud est quam sensus animae cognoscentis bonum et malum et quid intrinsecus latens in mente, quod probari non potest directa*

proven in the external forum. This could hardly be made a "conditio sine qua non" for the validity of confession.[36]

V. The words "for the peace of conscience" if taken in the wide sense, will almost always be verified in a sincere confession. Every serious confession and the serious choice of a confessor is directed in some way to putting the conscience at ease.[37]

If the strict interpretation is insisted upon it will be impossible to determine the limits beyond which the confession, which is made, may be null.

VI. Stettner[38] requires the "peace of conscience," as a distinct motive. But the result of that requirement is to defeat the purpose of the law. It imposes upon the religious the previous judgment as to the gravity of the reasons for which she can address a confessor in virtue of this canon. In many cases this decision would trouble consciences, which are not clear, or well formed, or which are given to anxiety and scrupulosity.[39] Therefore, the concession granted by the legislator for the peace of conscience of religious women would lead to nothing else but confusion and anxiety.[40] It is true that the legislator makes laws for normal persons and not the scrupulous. Yet it is reasonable to deduce that the mind of the legislator, who wishes to promote quietude of conscience, is, that a condition in regard to such a thing should not open the door to scruples for normal persons.[41] It would also be very difficult in individual cases to judge whether the confessor would be useful for the peace of conscience or not. Thus instead of facilitating approach, the consciences of the religious by the above mentioned faculty would be thrown into more and more difficulties.[42]

---

36 Augustine, IV, p. 271; Vermeersch-Creusen, *Epit.* I, n. 595.

37 Vermeersch-Creusen, *Epit.* n. 595; n. 588; Fanfani, *De Jure Religiosorum*, n. 127, *dubium* I; cf. p. 155; Chelodi, *Jus de Personis*, n. 256; Choupin, *L'Etat Religieux*, p. 228; Goyeneche, CpR, II, p. 16; Leitner, *Handbuch* (*Dritte Lieferung, Das Ordensrecht*) p. 358; Stettner, *Am. Ecc. Rev.*, (1919) XLI p. 446 ff.

38 *Am. Ecc. Rev.* ibid.

39 Creusen, *Religieux et Religieuses*, n. 95.

40 Goyeneche, CpR, II, p. 17.

41 Vermeersch-Creusen, *Epit.* I, n. 588, n. 595.

42 Fanfani, *op. cit.* n. 127, dubium 1, cf. p. 155. (ed. 1925); n. 102, (ed. 1920).

Therefore the motive of tranquillity of conscience can not be required for validity but, at the most, only for the liceity of the confession made in virtue of Can. 522. This interpretation is held today by almost all commentators.[43]

B.—*Sufficient Reasons* to use this canon present themselves more frequently in persons of delicate or anxious consciences and in certain passing circumstances and periods of the spiritual life. This is especially so in communities, which are less favored in the choice and quality of confessors.[44] Such motives can not be given taxatively for many of them can be found. Demonstratively they would be as follows: a doubt of conscience in regard to a sin, a fault, a temptation or some obligation,[45] whether imposed or freely assumed; the ability to confess more freely to another priest than to the ordinary confessor; the involuntary omission of confession on the customary day; the desire to purify herself of a fault, even if light and much less deliberate than a habit; the occasion to confess to a priest particularly learned or experienced;[46] or the desire to continue the practice of weekly confession, since such regularity contributes to the interior peace.[47] These reasons suffice to make the confession licit.

C. *Conclusion*—A religious who seriously desires to reconcile herself should not worry as to having made an invalid confession. If the confession is sincere it is also valid,[48] since such confessions tend to appease the conscience. If there were no reason whatsoever, the confession would be valid but unlawful. But any confessor is certainly justified in arousing in the religious the proper dispositions. Therefore he would not have to refuse

43 Vermeersch-Creusen, *Epit.* I, n. 588, 595; Fanfani, *loc. cit.;* Goyeneche, CpR, II, p. 17; Creusen, *op. cit.*, n. 95; Augustine, IV, p. 269 ff; Chelodi, *Jus de Personis*, n. 256; Choupin, *op. cit.*, p. 228; Leitner, *op. cit.*, p. 358; Cocchi, *op. cit.*, II, pars II, n. 42; Bastien, *op. cit.*, n. 360; Papi, *Religious in Church Law*, p. 55; Aertnys, *Theol. Mor.* III, § 378; Mahoney, *Am. Ecc. Rev.* LXXIV (1926), p. 43; Grosam, *Linzer Quartalschrift* (1923), LXXVI, p. 111.

44 Creusen, *op. cit.*, n. 95.

45 Cocchi, *op. cit.*, n. 41.

46 Vermeersch, *Summa*, n. 189; Creusen. *loc. cit.*

47 Choupin, *op. cit.*, p. 227.

48 Vermeersch-Creusen, *Epit.* I, n. 588, 595 (1923); Choupin, *loc. cit.*

to hear that particular confession, but should tell her to go to the ordinary confessor[49] in the future.

A confessor in a public church hearing the confessions of all who come to him may observe the regularity of a penitent and know his or her profession. He has no right, however, to interfere with their liberty unless they are guilty of an abuse on other grounds.[50] It is the religious and not the confessor who is to judge as to the quieting of her conscience[51] and therefore there is no obligation on the confessor of inquiring as to her motive.[52]

The confessor must, however, be guided by the rules of prudence. He could not by the request of a religious assume the permanent direction of her conscience unless he receives special faculties from the Ordinary, as her special ordinary confessor. The religious herself would, of course, have to request this. In that case he would go to hear her confession in the convent. Unless there is a manifest misuse of this canon the confessor in the public church can in all other circumstances disregard the frequency of the penitent's approach to the holy tribunal. This seems to be the spirit as well as the letter of the law and protects both the penitent and the confessor.[53]

II. *The Approach.*

The words "*si adeat confessarium,*" which were not contained in the law of 1913, are therefore an innnovation.

That the religious approach the confessor is a condition necessary for the validity of the confessions made in virtue of this canon.

I.—The general rule laid down in Canon 876 is that all priests who hear the confessions of religious women and their novices should have special jurisdiction, "salvo praescripto, Can. 522." Canon 522, however, is not granted in favor of

---

49 S. C. EE et RR, Feb. 1, 1892, ad 2; AAS XXX, 121, 122; cf. Col. S. C. P. F. (ed. 1907), n. 1781; Vermeersch, *De Rel.* II, n. 231.
50 *Am. Ecc. Rev.* vol. (1923) LXIX, p. 538 ff.
51 Augustine, *Am. Ecc. Rev.* LXVI, p. 417.
52 Choupin, *op. cit.*, p. 229.
53 *Am. Ecc. Rev.* (1923) LXIX, 538.

the confessor but the religious. Therefore, the confessor can hear these confessions only when the religious approach him for that purpose.[54] Thus the initiative must be taken by the religious and not the priest and it must be a spontaneous and free approach.[55]

II.—This clause "si adeat" since it restricts the liberty of the religious should be strictly interpreted and the words taken in their direct and primary significance. "*Adire*" has the primary meaning "to go to," or when used in reference to a person "to go up to, to approach." FACCIOLATI[56] defines it in these words "*adeo . . . . accedo ad aliquem vel aliquid eo . . . cum de persona usurpatur, significat convenire, visere . . . etiam consulendi causa et auxilium ab alio petendi.*"[57] It is used in this sense in Canon 530, § 2, "*Expedit ut ipsi filiali cum fiducia Superiores adeant,*" where there can be no doubt that it means personal approach by the religious.

III.—This interpretation is confirmed by the anterior legislation which permitted a religious to go to a simple confessor only when she was able to approach him outside of the religious house.[58]

IV.—If any priest, not approached or requested by the religious, could absolve in virtue of this canon then Canon 876, § 1, which requires peculiar jurisdiction for all priests who hear the confessions of religious women and their novices, would become vain and useless.[59]

V.—The religious must make the approach since the simply

---

54 Goyeneche, CpR, II, p. 18; Bastien, *op. cit.*, n. 360; Vermeersch, *Per.* XI, p. (14).

55 Vermeersch-Creusen, Epit. I, n. 595.

56 *Totius Latinitatis Lexicon*, I, p. 38. (London 1826).

57 ibid. *Secundam, Tertiam Editionem*, (Schneebergae, 1831); cf. Andrews, *Latin-English Lexicon*, p. 28; Forcellini, *Lexicon Totius Latinitatis*, v. *adeo;* Burt's *Latin-English Dictionary*, p. 3; Cassell's *Latin-English Dictionary*, p. 11; cf. Creusen, *op. cit.*, n. 95.

58 S. C. EE et RR, Aug. 27, 1852; cf. Bizzarri, p. 129; Apr. 22, 1872, ad 3, Col. S. C. P. F. (1893) n. 433; *Normae*, June 28, 1901; S. Penitentiaria, *Tornacen. et Mechlinen.*, Feb. 1, 1901, cf. Vermeersch, *De Rel.* II, n. 223; S. C. De Rel. Feb. 3, 1913, AAS V, 64; Goyeneche, CpR, II, p. 18.

59 Goyeneche, *loc. cit.*

approved priest is not numbered among those confessors who can be called by the religious.[60]

VI.—This view is supported by the majority of authors.[61]

Conclusion.—In order that the simply approved confessor may validly hear the confessions of religious in virtue of Canon 522, the religious must approach him for that purpose. A religious truly approaches the confessor not only when she seeks him when outside of her religious house, e. g., in a public church, but also when she seizes the opportunity of his presence, within her convent, to request him to hear her confession.[62] On the other hand, since the initiative must always be taken by the religious, a simple confessor can never go to a church or convent of religious and offer to hear their confessions or invite them to confess.[63] Moreover, he could not, without being requested by a religious, sit in the confessional of a church or the domestic chapel of the religious and wait for them to come to confession. Otherwise the prescription of Canon 522 would be useless. In these cases he would act unlawfully and invalidly.[64]

It is to be remembered, however, that the offering of oneself, is quite different from going upon the request of the penitent, whether made personally or through another, to the confessional where the penitent is kneeling.[65]

Questions—

I.—Can a community of religious make use of Canon 522?

A.—If the religious approach as individuals and each one

---

60 Vermeersch, *Per.* IX, p. 14.

61 Vermeersch, *loc. cit.;* Vermeersch-Creusen, *Epit.* I, n. 595; Goyeneche, CpR, II, p. 18; Biederlack-Fuhrich, *De Religiosis*, p. 189; Fanfani, *De Jure Religiosorum* (1920) n. 110; Blat, *Commentarium in Textum C. J. C.*, II *pars* II, n. 585; Augustine, *A Commentary on Canon Law*, IV, p. 163; Cocchi, *Commentarium in Codicem J. C.*, II *pars* II, n. 42; Bastien, *Directoire Canonique*, n. 360; Ramos, CpR, (1922) p. 32; Kinane, *Ir. Ecc. Rec.*, 5th Series (1923) vol. 22, p. 643.

62 Vermeersch, *Per* IX, p. (14); Biederlack-Fuhrich, *loc. cit.;* Goyeneche, *loc. cit.*

63 Goyeneche, CpR, II, 181; Bastien, *op. cit.*, n. 360; Vermeersch-Creusen, *Epit.* n. 595.

64 Biederlack-Fuhrich, *op. cit.*, p. 189.

65 *Monitore Ecclesiatico,* (1921) XXXIII, p. 160.

enters for the peace of her conscience, even though the whole community might approach in this manner, he could hear their confessions, since the canon grants this right to *"aliqua religiosa"* for the peace of her conscience. This case is similar to that of a pastor who may, in virtue of Canon 1245, § 1, dispense individual subjects from the law of fasting and abstinence. This dispensation may be granted to all parishioners taken individually until the whole parish is dispensed.[66]

B.—When requested by the superioress to hear the confessions "of some of the religious," can he do so? He can, for the same reasons, hear their confessions in a church, semi-public or public oratory or a place legitimately destined for the confessions of women. The canon requires an approach, but that can be made "per se" or "per alios" and by asking, through the superioress, to go to confession, the religious are fulfilling the prescriptions of Canon 522.[67]

C.—Could he hear the community at the request of the superior on the grounds that each sister is "aliqua religiosa?" (1) The canon was granted for the peace of conscience of the individual, of which she alone is the judge. Nevertheless, the confessor could hardly assume that the whole community wished to have its conscience quieted.[68] (2) The word "aliqua" is indefinite in meaning and can be translated as "some, someone, any or anyone" or the indefinite article "a." BARBOSA[69] defines it as a general term comprising the whole species, but also supposing distribution into parts. Although, as AUGUSTINE states, it refers to individuals, it does not comprise the totality of persons as such, but only the individuals. Again, although it is used in the singular, it may comprise many and therefore equals the plural. Therefore, in the strict sense of the words, the simply approved priest cannot hear the confessions of "the" community, since such an expression signifies the community

66 Augustine, *Am. Ecc. Rev.* vol. (1922) LXVI, p. 417; Father Augustine's treatment of these questions is followed here.

67 Augustine, ibid; *Il Monitore Ecclesiastico, loc. cit.*

68 Augustine, loc. cit.

69 *Tractatus Varii, Dictiones Usufrequentes, Dictio,* XXII, p. 648 ff (ed. London 1660).

in its totality. For such confessions he needs special jurisdiction and the presumption of this would not justify his action.[70] He can, however, state that he is willing to hear the confessions of those who wish to avail themselves of his presence. If any then express the desire to confess, he can hear them licitly and validly.[71]

If the sisters should do this "in fraudem legis," i. e., it is arranged among them that one sister should request confession in order to bring the confessor into the confessional and then all intend to follow as a community, the bishop should correct this abuse.

II.—Can they ask him to come to the convent to hear their confessions?

Before the publication of the decisions of the Pontifical Commission for the interpretation of the Code in regard to Canon 522, on November 23, 1920,[72] it was the common and almost certain opinion, sponsored by VERMEERSCH,[73] that the approach by the religious to the simply approved priest, since he is not enumerated among those who could go to the religious, was necessary for validity. Otherwise the principle of Canon 876, § 1, would be destroyed. After the reply of the Pontifical Commission for the Authentic Interpretation of the Code to the following question: "*Utrum verba canonis* 522: '*Confessio in qualibet ecclesia vel oratorio etiam semi-publico peracta valida et licita sit' ita intelligenda sint, ut confessionem extra ea loca peracta non tantum illicita, sed etiam invalida sit,*" which was couched in the following words: "*Canon* 522, *ita est intelligendum, ut confessiones, quas ad suae conscientiae tranquilitatem religiosae peragunt apud confessarium ab Ordinario loci pro mulieribus approbatum, licitae et validae sint, dummodo fiant in ecclesia vel oratorio semi-publico, aut in loco ad audiendas confessiones mulierum legitime destinato,*"[74] omits the words

70 Augustine, *loc. cit.;* Vermeersch-Creusen, *Epit.* I, n. 595.
71 Augustine, *loc. cit.*
72 AAS XII, 575, ad 3.
73 Periodica, IX, p. (14); Vermeersch-Creusen, *Epit.* I, p. 221 (ed. 1921).
74 Com. PP ad CC Auth. Interpret., Nov. 24, 1920, *de religiosis* ad III; AAS XII, 575; cf. L. Q. S. (1920); LXXIV, 150.

of the canon *"si adeat"* VERMEERSCH and CREUSEN [75] granted probability to the opinion that confession made to a priest simply approved for women, even when called for that purpose, is valid. Other authorities appealing to the admission of Vermeersch in support of their opinion state (1) that the opposite opinion is too rigid; (2) it does not conform to the spirit of the law; (3) there is no difference or at least a negligible one between the two expressions "to summon a confessor" and "to seek one;" (4) it is not reasonable that the validity of the absolution should depend upon such a secondary circumstance.[76]

The better opinion is that the confessor cannot be summoned to hear the confessions of the community, in virtue of Canon 522, for the following reasons:

I.—The response of the commission left this condition of approach by the religious, intact. It is evident from a reading of the text that the omission of these words "si adeat" cannot have any significance since they had no relation to the question asked, which was in regard to the place of confession, i. e., whether the phrase of Canon 522, "*Confessio in qualibet ecclesia vel oratorio etiam semi-publico peracta valida et licita sit*" must be so understood that confessions made outside of these places were not only illicit but invalid. Since the question was not whether these confessions were valid, because made for peace of conscience, or because they were made to an approved priest; or whether the approach by the religious was necessary for the validity and liceity; but only as to the point; whether the validity and liceity of these confessions depended upon the requirement in regard to the place in which they were to be heard, the omission of the words *"si adeat"* in the reply of the Pontifical Commission, has no significance. Moreover, the words of this reply *"confessiones quas . . . peragunt"* show that the answer refers only to the validity and liceity of confessions, the approach to which is presumed as having been made in the prescribed way.

---

75 *Epit.* loc. cit.

76 Choupin, *L'Etat Religieux*, p. 228.

II.—The supporters of the opposite opinion, if their reasoning is right, do not go far enough. According to the wording of the reply these confessions in which the confessor is summoned, would not only be valid but lawful, and therefore these words form merely a directive rubric and not a condition at all as the introductory particle *"si"* implies. This clause then, which is the only one definitely worded as a condition, would be the least important. This is deduced from the fact that the reply even mentions that those confessions made in these places would be valid and licit, if made for the peace of conscience. Yet the motive of peace of conscience, by the common opinion of authors, is had in every serious confession and is, according to some, only an impulsive cause. Such an interpretation, of the clause *"si adeat,"* hardly seems to be in conformity to the prudent mind of the legislator.

III.—The word *"adeat"* cannot be distorted in any way so as to mean the right to summon the confessor. As seen above from its very definition, it always implies that its subject, which in this case is *"aliqua religiosa,"* should make the approach. If summoning was intended by the legislator he should have used here the words of the following Canon 523, *"arcessere possunt,"* whereby sick religious have the right to summon a confessor.

IV.—This opinion is certainly in conformity with the law, for if it were possible to summon a priest, then Canon 876, which requires special jurisdiction for the confessions of religious and their novices, would be entirely destroyed. Any religious could summon any priest at practically any time she desired and the prescriptions of Canons 520, 521, 523 would be useless. Since the Code imposes upon the local Ordinaries the obligation of appointing priests whom the religious can freely call (Canon 521, § § 2, 3) and grants this right to sick religious (Canon 523), it is evidently the intention of the Code that they cannot call others.

Summoning the confessor, then, is not merely an evasion of the law but directly against it. This concession of Canon 522 is a great privilege and since the Holy See must put some limit upon it, the stricter opinion will naturally be considered by some as narrow minded. On the other hand, once authorities begin to extend this faculty for the reasons advanced by the first opinion, the extensions will never cease.

V.—This opinion is supported by the following authorities: BIEDERLACK-FUHRICH,[77] PRUMMER,[78] GOYENECHE,[79] GROSAM,[80] and KINANE.[81]

Conclusions for practice.

Once more the confessor can resort to Canon 209 to settle all qualms of conscience on this point. VERMEERSCH,[82] CREUSEN[83] and CHOUPIN[84] defend the milder opinion and the reasons offered together with their extrinsic authority suffice to create a positive and probable doubt of law. In these circumstances the confessor can follow this opinion with the assurance that the Church will supply him with the necessary jurisdiction.

The superioress is not in the least obliged to summon such a priest at the request of a religious[85] and there is even an obligation on her to refuse.[86] But if she should summon one upon request, there is nothing to prevent the valid and licit confession of the religious,[87] who seizes the opportunity of his arrival to approach him. It is true, as KINANE rightly states, that something else is done which is not permitted by law, but is upon the fulfillment of the prescribed conditions that the jurisdiction depends.[88]

---

77 *De Religiosis*, (1919), n. 49.
78 *Manuale Juris Ecclesiastici*, (ed altera), p. 297.
79 CpR, II, p. 19.
80 L. Q. S. (1923), LXXVI, p. 111.
81 Ir. Ecc. Rec. (1923), XXII, p. 642 ff.
82 *Epit.* (1921), I, p. 221; (1924) n. 595 (e); In the latter edition his words are not as clear as in the first, but it is evident that he accepts the more lenient opinion.
83 *Religieux et Religieuses*, (1924), n. 95; *Am. Ecc. Rev.* (1926) LXXIV, 507.
84 *L'Etat Religieux*, p. 228.
85 Vermeersch-Creusen, *Epit.*, I, n. 595.
86 Kinane, Ir. Ecc. Rec. XXII, (1923) p. 642 ff.
87 Vermeersch-Creusen, *loc. cit.*
88 Kinane, *loc. cit.*

Summoning by telephone the general principles given above must be applied, for it is not a question of the means of summoning, since that makes little difference,[89] but the right, under the canon, to summon him at all to the convent. Moreover, nuns of solemn vows need permission even to have a telephone in the convent. Such an indult was granted to the Bishop of the Canary Islands for his nuns. They were allowed to have a telephone to summon the ordinary confessor. It was required that two nuns of good character be present with the nun at the time of the telephonic conversation.[90]

It is to be noted that during the time of jubilee, the religious has the right to summon the confessor approved by the Ordinary for both sexes for her jubilee confessions,[91] which can be made twice, once to obtain the indulgence for the living and once for the dead.

III. *The Confessor.*

The confessor should be approved for the confessions of women by the local Ordinary. This is a change over the reply of the Congregation of Bishops and Regulars of August 27, 1852,[92] which required that he be approved for the confessions of both sexes. In 1872 the same congregation only required that he be approved by the Ordinary[93] as did the Sacred Penitentiary in 1901[94] and the "Normae" of the same year.[95] But this was changed again to approval for both sexes by the decree "Cum de Sacramentalibus."[96] The Code has made this requirement to read "approved for the confessions of women."[97]

---

89 Goyeneche, CpR, IV, (1923), p. 3, § 7.

90 S. C. EE et RR, *Canarien.* March 20, 1895; Col. S. C. P. F. (1907), n. 1891. Leitner, *Handbuch, (Dritte Lieferung, Das Ordensrecht)*, p. 444.

91 Pius XI, Const. *Universis Christifidelibus,* Dec. 25, 1925; pt. II ad Facultates, n. II; AAS XVII; 614; cf. *Il Monitore Ecc.* (1925) XXXVIII, p. 11.

92 Bizzarri, p. 129.

93 S. C. EE et RR, *Atrabaten.* Apr. 22, 1872 ad 3; Col. S. C. P. F., (1893), n. 433.

94 Vermeersch, De Rel. II, n. 233, Feb. 7.

95 S. C. EE et RR, June 28, 1901, art. 149.

96 S. C. De Rel. Feb. 3, 1913; n. 14; AAS V, 64.

97 Augustine, III, p. 162.

This approbation is necessary for validity of the confession and absolution, for the religious in the case contemplated by Canon 522 are made equal to secular women. But where special approbation is required to hear the confessions of women, this approbation is understood as being necessary for validity. The custom in our country is that priests are approved to hear the confessions of both men and women at once after ordination. But in some countries such as England, Belgium, France and in Rome and certain dioceses of Italy and Spain and, according to AUGUSTINE, even in our own state of Louisiana, the ordinaries give special faculties for the hearing of women's confessions. This is generally done five years after the priest has been approved for the confessions of men.[98] In our country, for the greater part, faculties are granted in some such formula as the following, "*ad audiendas confessiones Christi fidelium.*" Hence, wherever the clause "*pro mulieribus approbatus*" is not in use, the confessor of the faithful of both sexes has the faculty of hearing the confessions of sisters, who approach him in a church, semi-public or public oratory or a place legitimately destined for the confessions of women by the Ordinary.[99]

The general principle of canon law is, that special jurisdiction is required to hear the confessions of religious women and their novices (Canon 876, § 1). Canonical logic demands, therefore, that this confessor be approved at least for secular women. Otherwise the legislator would not be consistent nor would he conform to the discipline of the past if he gave religious greater liberty in this matter than secular women. Under the decree "Cum de Sacramentalibus," this was expressly stated and this approbation was considered by all as necessary for validity.[100]

It might happen that a priest would be given faculties only

98 Innocent XIII, Const. *Apostolici Ministerii*, May 23, 1723, § 19, FJC n. 280; Ballerini, *Opus Theologicum Morale* (ed. 1900) V, p. 296, n. 352, 3°; Augustine, *loc. cit.;* Creusen, *op. cit.* n. 95; Goyeneche, CpR, II, p. 19 ff; Bastien, Directoire Canonique, n. 360.

99 Augustine, III, p. 162.

100 Vermeersch, *Per.* IX, p. (14); Goyeneche, *loc. cit.;* Maroto, CpR II, p. 37.

or a religious priest who has not received the regular diocesan faculties. This would be the case if he is only appointed as confessor to a certain community, as might easily happen to retreat masters. In view of the fact that he has been approved for the confessions of these religious women, he could hear the confessions of any religious woman approaching him in virtue of Canon 522 and he need have no scruples.[101] In regard to the Ordinary, who is to approve the confessor, the same principles apply here as mentioned under Canon 519. It is the local Ordinary of the place where the confessions are to be heard, who alone can grant this approbation and jurisdiction.[102] The priest with maritime faculties is an exception to this general rule. If he has rightly received faculties from his own Ordinary, or the Ordinary of the port from which the boat is to leave, or to which it is going, or any intermediate port, through which he passes, he can hear in virtue of Canon 522 the confession of any religious woman, who is sailing with him or who comes to the boat for any reason, or who approaches him when he is called to land for any other reason. This confessor can hear their confessions despite the fact that on the journey the boat passes through different jurisdictions. He can validly and licitly absolve from cases, even cases reserved to the local Ordinary. Hearing religious women in virtue of Canon 522, he would have to observe the other prescriptions of this canon in regard to the place, approach, etc.[103]

IV. *The Place of Confession.*

The place of confession was not mentioned in the early concessions, for confession outside of the convent. Yet before the Code the religious of the dioceses of Malines and Tours had the right to confess when outside of their convent for some days to any priest approved for the faithful. In solving a case in regard to confessions by these religious, the Sacred Peniten-

101 Vermeersch-Creusen, *Epit.* I, n. 595.
102 Can. 874, § 1; 876, § 2: 883.
103 Can. 883; Blat, III *pars* I, n. 206.; Cf. Can. 519, where these principles are clearly stated in regard to male religious.

tiary[104] presupposed that the confessions which it declares valid were made in a church. The Congregation of Bishops and Regulars in the "Normae" of 1901[105] incorporated this idea into article 149, which gave to the sisters the right to confess to a priest approved by the bishop, if they did so in a public church. The decree "Cum de Sacramentalibus" gave further liberty by extending this to confession made in any oratory, whether public or semi-public, outside of the convent.[106] The Code permits the exercise of this faculty even in the oratories of their convents and the Commission for the Authentic Interpretation of the Code[107] declared that confessions could be heard in virtue of Canon 522 in any place legitimately destined by the local Ordinary for the confessions of women.

A. *General Law on the Place for the Reception of the Confessions of Women.*

(1) The proper place for sacramental confession is a church or a public or semi-public oratory.[108]

(2) The confessional for the hearing of women's confessions, should always be located in an open and conspicuous place and generally in a church, or a public or semi-public oratory destined for women.[109] (3) The confessional should have a fixed screen, containing small perforations, between the penitent and confessor.[110] (4) The confessions of women should not be heard outside of the confessional unless in cases of sickness or some other true necessity. Even then the priest should use those precautions which the local Ordinary has judged opportune.[111] It is to be noted in this regard that the con-

---

104 Feb. 9, 1901; Vermeersch, *De Rel.* II, n. 233, p. 498.
105 S. C. EE et RR, June 28; cf. Boudinhon, CC, 36, p. 412.
106 S. C. De Rel. Feb. 3, 1913, n. 14; AAS V, 64.
107 Nov. 24, 1920 *de religiosis*, ad III; AAS XII, 575.
108 Can. 908.
109 Can. 909, § 1.
110 Can. 909, § 2.
111 Can. 910, § § 1, 2.

fessionals of nuns should be so placed that the confessor is outside of the cloister and the nuns within.[112] This is generally accomplished by having a permanent grating placed in the wall of the sacristy of their chapel.

Therefore, in discussing the question of the validity and liceity in reference to the place, three elements must be considered: (1) the church, which certainly is a suitable place for receiving such confession, since it is destined for the use of the faithful in the exercise of divine worship and the reception of the sacraments.[113]

(2) Public oratories are erected mainly for the convenience of some college or even private persons. The faithful have the right, legitimately proven, of going there at least at the time of divine offices.[114] (3) Oratories are semi-public if erected for the convenience of some community, and the faithful have not the right of going there.[115] Semi-public oratories may be found in major and minor seminaries; hospitals; orphan asylums; homes for the aged; monasteries of religious men and women, whether of solemn or simple vows; in colleges and schools of every kind, even if they are under state control.[116] In all churches and oratories then, except private oratories, which are erected in private houses for the sole use of some family or private person, confessions may be heard in virtue of Canon 522. Unlike the law of 1913, this includes not only all churches and oratories outside of those of the religious, but also those of their own convent or community. This is the universal opinion of canonists and theologians, for the Code

---

112 S. C. De Rel. *Instructio de Clausura,* Feb. 6, 1924, II, 3°; AAS XVI, p. 95.

113 Can. 1161.

114 Can. 1188, §§ 1, 2, 1°.

115 ibid. 2°.

116 Gasparri, *De Eucharistia,* n. 213; Wernz, *Jus Decretalium,* III, n. 457; Choupin, *L'Etat Religieux,* p. 229.

has omitted the words "*extra propriam domum*" of the decree "Cum de Sacramentalibus."[117]

III. *Places legitimately destined for confessions of women.*

Canon 522 only mentiones churches and public and semipublic oratories as the approved places in which the confessions of religious women can be heard. The Pontifical Commission for the Interpretation of the Code was asked whether confessions made outside of these places would be not only illicit but invalid. The commission answered "*Canon* 522, *ita est intelligendum, ut confessiones, quas ad suae conscientiae tranquilitatem religiosae peragunt apud confessarium ab Ordinario loci pro mulieribus approbatum, licitae et validae sint, dummodo fiant in ecclesia vel oratorio semi-publico, aut in loco ad audiendas confessiones mulierum legitime destinato.*"[118]

The right to legitimately designate such places belongs to the Ordinary of the place where the confessions are to be heard. Yet the immediate and the direct intervention of the Ordinary personally in designating individual places does not seem necessary.[119] This can be done through his delegate.[120] The approval of the Ordinary may be explicit, but even his implicit approval seems to be sufficient, e. g., if these places satisfy the prescriptions of the Ordinary in regard to the place of confession; or the precautions to be used; or if, on his canonical visitation, the Ordinary diligently inspects these places. Otherwise it seems that that designation must be considered as legi-

---

117 Genicot, *Theo. Mor.* II, n. 339; Vermeersch, *Summa*, n. 190; Noldin, *De Sacr.*, n. 350; Blat, II, n. 585; Augustine, III, p. 162; Cocchi, II *pars* II, n. 42; Creusen, *Religieux et Religieuses*, n. 95; *Il Monitore*, XXXI (1919), p. 158; Choupin, *op. cit.*, p. 229; Bastien, *Directoire Canonique*, n. 360; Arregui, *Summarium Theol. Mor.* (1923), n. 605; Goyeneche, CpR, II, p. 20; Chelodi, *Jus de Personis*, n. 258; Prümmer, *Manuale J. C.* n. 190; note 4; Papi, *Religious in Church Law*, p. 55; Sabetti-Barrett, *Compendium Theologiae Moralis*, n. 778, in the early editions after the Code restrained the use of this faculty to those churches and oratories outside of the convent in keeping with the Decree "Cum de Sacramentalibus." This has been changed in the edition of 1924.

118 Nov. 24, 1920, *de religiosis* ad III; AAS V, 575.

119 Goyeneche, CpR, II, p. 38.

120 Bastien, *op. cit.*, n. 360; Choupin, *op. cit.*, p. 229.

timate which is made by their proper and immediate local superior or rector.[121]

The following places can be considered as legitimately destined for the confessions of women; (1) confessionals in hospitals, erected in some suitable place outside of the church or oratory, legitimately destined for the convenience or use of sick women; (2) the same kind of confessionals in schools and colleges for hearing the confessions of girls; (3) in retreat houses, in the places appointed legitimately for the confessions of women making the retreats; (4) confessionals in the sacristy or other places adjacent to the church or oratory, legitimately destined for the confessions of deaf women. Even if the sister be not deaf, she can approach the confessor of Canon 522 in the last mentioned confessional.[122]

I. *Question*—Would the words *"loco ad audiendas confessiones mulierum legitimate destinato"* include confessionals, located outside of a church or oratory and reserved exclusively for the confessions of women religious?

First Opinion—replies in the negative since the place of confession must be understood, at least primarily and directly, as the one legitimately appointed for the reception of the confessions of secular women. A.—The word *mulieres* in Canon 522 certainly stands for secular women. Therefore, since it does not expressly refer to religious women, should it not be received in the same sense in the response of the commission making a declaration of the meaning of that canon.[123] B.—The confessor, treated of here, is considered as approved only for the confessions of secular women, since Canon 522 contains an exception to Canon 876, § 1, requiring special jurisdiction for the confessions of religious women and their novices. The quality of the confessor should then correspond to the quality of the place and it would be far fetched to suppose that, when the response referred to a confessor approved for secular women, it did not mean to signify, primarily and directly,

121 Goyeneche, *loc. cit.;* Creusen *op. cit.*, n. 95.
122 Goyeneche, CpR, II, p. 38, § IV.
123 Maroto, CpR, II, p. 37; Fanfani, *De Jure Religiosorum*, n. 137 (1925).

a place also intended for secular women.[124] C.—Religious women, when making confession in virtue of Canon 522, do so not after the manner of religious or inasmuch as they are religious but after the fashion of secular women. Hence, the reason why they can confess their sins to any confessor approved for secular women, is evident. Therefore, the place for hearing confessions of this kind must conform to that in which secular women are wont to make their confessions.[125] D.—If this concession is extended to include the confessional of religious women, the distinct mention in the Code and the response of the Commission, of the church, oratory or place legitimately destined for confessions of women, is useless. They could have said more clearly and briefly, that such confessions would be valid and licit if made in any place legitimately destined for the confessions of secular women or religious.[126]

This opinion is subscribed to by FANFANI,[127] MAROTO,[128] GURY-FERRERES,[129] MAHONEY,[130] COCCHI [131] and CHELODI,[132] and therefore has extrinsic probability at least.

Second opinion—which permits confessions in virtue of Canon 522, even in confessionals reserved to religious, is the better.[133]

Reply to objections.—It does not follow from the fact that the phrase "pro mulieribus approbatum" is used in Canon 522 and the reply of the Pontifical Commission taken in conjunction with the phrase of this same reply "loco ad confessiones mulierum legitime destinato" that the word "mulierum" must be taken in exactly the same sense, thereby excluding the confessionals of religious women. The generic term *mulier* is used in both Canon 522 and the reply in which the commission did

124 Maroto, *op. cit.* II, p. 36. ff.
125 Maroto, *loc. cit.*
126 Fanfani, *op. cit.* n. 137.
127 *loc. cit.*
128 CpR, II, p. 36 ff.
129 *Casus Conscientiae*, II, n. 573 (1921); claims that it would be invalid.
130 *Am. Ecc. Rev.* LXXIV, (1926), p. 43.
131 *Commentarium in C. I. C.*, II, pars II, n. 42.
132 *Jus de Personis*, n. 258.
133 Creusen, *op. cit.*, n. 95.

nothing else but accommodate the words of Canon 909, § 1, "oratorio semi-publico mulieribus destinato" and the word *mulieribus* in this canon certainly has an extensive sense.[134]

The arguments of the other opinion are not exact. A.—The word *mulieres* does not necessarily apply to secular women alone, for it is a generic term and includes religious women. Therefore, a priest approved only for the confessions of the religious of a convent, and having no other jurisdiction, can hear the confessions of religious who approach him in virtue of Canon 522.[135] As stated above, the word *mulieres* is used to show that approbation for the confessions of men alone would not suffice. It seems a strange deduction to exclude from the office of hearing the confessions of religious women in virtue of Canon 522, the very priests who have received special approval for the confessions of some religious women from the local Ordinary. Therefore, since this word in the canon does not exclude religious women, it should be received in the same sense in the reply of the Pontifical Commission. B.—As proven above,[136] Canon 522 is not an exception to Canon 876, § 1, but a prescription of law recognized and confirmed by that very canon. Canon 876 states that in the circumstances of Canon 522, the confessor of women religious need not have the special approbation of the local Ordinary for such a confession, but it does not, by any means, say that a priest endowed with such special faculties could not act in virtue of Canon 522. Therefore, the only argument that can be drawn from the word *mulierum* in the response of the commission is that it applies indiscriminately to all women and thus confessions can be heard in virtue of Canon 522 in confessionals of women, whether secular of religious. C.—Neither is it exact to state that they confess like secular women. They are similar to them only inasmuch as they can choose their confessor, but they are restricted in the exercise of this choice by many conditions of motive, approach, etc.,

---

134 *Il Monitore Ecclesiastico,* (1921), XXXIII, 160.
135 cf. Vermeersch-Creusen, *Epit.* I, n. 595 (f).
136 p. 226; Vermeersch, *Per. XI,* p. (14); Vermeersch-Creusen, *Epit.* (1921) I, n. 59, p. 498.

with which secular women are not burdened. No valid argument can be drawn, therefore, from the fact that they can choose a confessor, that they must confess only in confessionals used by secular women. If female religious have so many conditions to fulfill in using Canon 522, why must they be prevented from complying with these requirements in the place where one would naturally expect this to be done, i. e., their own confessionals? D.—The fourth argument of the first opinion that the extension of this reply to include confessionals of religious argues for a useless distinction in the Code and the reply of the Commission between churches and oratories and places legitimately destined for the confessions of women, proves too much. It would be just as logical to conclude that, since the reply of the Commission has the phrase "loco ad confessiones mulierum legitime destinato," the explicit mention in the Code and the reply of the Commission of churches and oratories is useless since these are places legitimately destined for confessions and are comprised in the broader term.

Arguments.

I. Creusen states well, "*confessionals approved for secular women*" [137] do not exist. The Code merely states that without a grave reason, one cannot hear women's confessions except in a confessional which has a fixed screen, is accessible to all and in sight . . . (cf. Canon 909). Evidently this confessional is a legitimate place in which to hear the confession of a nun, who legitimately presents herself.

To use the words of Creusen "the confessionals in convents satisfy all the conditions required that a woman of the world should be able to confess there; without that a nun could not confess there. For, after all, a nun is a woman. If any difference had to be made, more guarantees would have to be demanded for nuns' confessionals than for those of secular women." [138]

There can be no doubt that the confessionals erected for

137 Creusen, *Am. Ecc. Rev.* (1926), LXXIV, 507 ff.
138 Creusen, *Am. Ecc. Rev.* (1926), LXXIV, 507 ff.

cloistered nuns are to be considered as true confessionals suitable for the confessions, not only of women living in the convent, but even any secular woman legitimately within the enclosure,[139] when the following reply of the Holy Office of November 25, 1874 is consulted.

1.—*An loca in quibus excipi solent confessiones monialium habenda sint ut loca destinata ad audiendas confessiones, vel ut vera confessionalia.*

2.—*An idem dicendum sit de locis constructis ad formam eorum, in quibus excipi solent confessiones monialium claustralium, in quibus excipiuntur confessiones mulierum degentium in locis quae vulgo dicuntur conservatorii, ritiri.*

3.—*Quatenus habenda sint ut vera confessionalia, utrum talia censenda sint solum quoad moniales et alias degentes in praedictis locis, an etiam quoad alias mulieres extraneas.*

Resp. Ad tria dubia prout exponuntur; Affirmative.[140]

II. The restriction of the other opinion, without serious foundation, deprives all nuns, against the evident intention of the legislator and with grave detriment, of the right conferred by Canon 522, since they cannot leave the cloister.[141] That nuns have this right is evident from the words of Canon 522, which confers it upon "aliqua religiosa," and the reply of the Commission, which repeats the word "religiosae." But as has been proven above,[142] the word "religiosa" is a generic term including all religious women without distinction.[143] Fanfani tries to solve this difficulty by saying that the Code realizing this, gives them a special spiritual director for their peace of their conscience in Canon 520, § 2.[144] But it must be remembered that this director is given for a permanent need or utility. The purpose of Canon 522, on the contrary, is to meet the temporary and passing needs of the individual religious. It may

139 Creusen, *loc. cit.*
140 Col. S. C. P. F. (1893), n. 435; (1907), n. 1424; cf. Vermeersch-Creusen, Epit. I, n. 595.
141 Creusen, *Religieux et Religieuses*, n. 95.
142 p. .
143 Can. 488, 7°; cf. Goyeneche, CpR (1921), II, p. 14.
144 Fanfani, *op. cit.*, n. 137.

easily happen that a nun has some very urgent reason for going to confession at the time and place that the priest's presence offers and it would be a great difficulty for her to wait until the spiritual director was called. To refuse nuns the use of Canon 522 in their own confessionals, is to snatch from the strictly cloistered the greatest benefice that the history of confessional discipline has granted to them, since only the most extraordinary occasions warrant their leaving the convent.[145]

IV. Extrinsic probability can certainly be claimed for this opinion since it has the support of VERMEERSCH-CREUSEN,[146] the "IL MONITORE ECCLESIASTICO,"[147] CREUSEN,[148] GENICOT-SALSMANS[149] and PAPI.[150]

Conclusion.—This is very well presented in the words of CREUSEN,[151] "Hence only by openly abusing the context or the literal sense of the words can one deny to nuns the right to confess in their confessional within the limits of Canon 522."

II. *Question.*

Is the clause in Canon 522 and the reply of the Pontifical Commission for the Authentic Interpretation of the Code in regard to the place of confession necessary for validity, so that confessions heard and absolutions given in other places than a church, oratory or place legitimately destined for the confessions, would be invalid?

First opinion.—Such confessions would be invalid. This is based on the reply of the Commission, "*Canon* 522, *ita est intelligendum, ut confessiones . . . licitae et validae sint dummodo fiant in ecclesia vel oratorio semi-publico aut in loco ad audiendas confessiones mulierum, legitime destinato.*"[152] The

---

145 Vermeersch-Creusen, *Epit.* I, n. 595.
146 *Epit.* I, n. 595.
147 (1921) XXXIII, 162.
148 *Religieux et Religieuses*, n. 95; cf. *Am. Ecc. Rev.* (1926), LXXIV, 507 ff.
149 *Theol. Mor.* II, n. 339, p. 304, note 3.
150 *Religious in Church Law*, p. 57.
151 Am. Ecc. Rev. loc. cit.
152 Com. Pont. ad CC Auth. Inter. Nov. 24, 1920, *de religiosis*, ad 3; AAS XII, 575; cf. LQS (1920) LXXIV, 150.

"dummodo" clause is rigorously interpreted as having the sense that these confessions are valid and licit, provided they are heard in these places. Appeal is made in proof of this to Canon 39 *"Conditiones in rescriptis tunc tantum essentiales pro ecrumdem validitate sunt, cum per particulas, si, dummodo, vel asliam ejusdem significationis exprimantur."* Therefore, the studious insertion of this *"dummodo"* clause which was omitted in Canon 522, was equivalent to the explicit declaration that this clause contains a condition essential for validity in the concession made by the Pontifical Commission by way of a general rescript to Canon 522. This "dummodo" clause implies a condition "sine qua non."[153]

This opinion has the support of the following authorities, Blat,[154] Fanfani,[155] Il Monitore Ecclesiastico,[156] Bastien.[157]

Second opinion—that the circumstance of place is only required for liceity is the better.

1. The nullity of such confessions is neither expressly or equivalently decided anywhere in the Code (Canon 908-910) as would be required by Canon 11.[158]

2. The question asked of the Commission was whether confessions made outside of a church, or semi-public oratory were not only illicit but also invalid. The Commission, by answering this question directly, could have easily settled the doubt, but it evidently was unwilling to declare invalid those confessions made in virtue of Canon 522 outside of the places mentioned. The reply just stated that confessions made according to the prescriptions of Canon 522, provided that they were made in

153 Oesterle, AKKR (1923), LXXVII, p. 138 ff; synopsized by Schweiger, CpR, V, 58; Bastien, states (*Directoire Canonique*, p. 228, note (1)) he has sufficient authority for believing that the Commission intended the "dummodo" clause to be abrogating. Such an assertion has no juridical value, his conviction unsubstantiated by his reason has no force.

154 II *pars* II, n. 585.

155 *De Jure Religiosorum*, n. 137.

156 vol. XXXIII, p. 160.

157 *loc. cit.*

158 *Can.* 11—*Irritantes aut inhabilitantes eae tantum leges habendae sunt, quibus aut actum esse nullum aut inhabilem esse personam expresse vel aequivalenter statuitur*; cf. Hecht, *Theologie und Glaube* (1924) 16, p. 482-491 as synopsized by Schweiger, CpR, V, 59.

churches, semi-public oratories or places legitimately destined for the confessions of women, are valid and licit, but it did not refer to the validity of confessions made outside of these places.[159] It cannot be definitely determined whether the "*dummodo*" clause refers to both words "*licita*" and "*valida*" or only the former. Therefore, the reply might be interpreted as follows: the confessions which religious women make for their peace of conscience to a priest approved by the local Ordinary for women, are valid and provided they are made in a church, etc., are even licit. The Commission, as is evident, borrowing the words of the response from Canon 522, transcribes the same ambiguity under which they labor in the canon. Therefore, it must be deduced that the interpretation of this question is left to the students of the law.[160]

3.—This is further strengthened by the response given before the Code to the bishop of Linz by the Congregation for Religious on July 3, 1916,[161] which stated that the word "*liceat*" of the decree "Cum de Sacramentalibus" no. 14, "*liceat in qualibet ecclesia vel oratorio etiam semi-publico*" did not affect the validity of confessions made by religious women to a simply approved priest when outside their convent. Neither did it prohibit the making of such confessions outside of a church or semi-public oratory, but in some fitting place. This clause of the decree of 1913 has been transcribed into Canon 522, in which the discipline of the old law is not restricted but extended. Therefore, this clause in Canon 522 must be interpreted in the light of the decree of 1913,[162] as not affecting the validity of the confession or absolution, but only the liceity.

3. *Extrinsic probability.* The majority of commentators have allied themselves in accepting this view. Brandys[163] and

---

159 Goyeneche, CpR, II, 21, 22 note (26); Mahoney, *Em. Ecc. Rev.* (1926), LXXIV, p. 42; Papi. *Religious in Church Law*, p. 57.

160 Goyeneche, CpR (1921), II, p. 21; Hecht, *loc. cit.*

161 ad 1, *Verbum "liceat" numeri 14 Decreti "Cum de Sacramentalibus" neque respicit validitatem confessionum neque prohibitionem confessionem peragendi in alio decenti loco;* (not officially edited); cf. Vermeersch, *Per.* IX, p. (14); AKKR, 97, p. 85.

162 Can. 6, 2°, 3°, 4°; cf. Hecht; as synopsized by Schweiger, *loc. cit.*

163 *Kirchliches Rechtsbuch*, n. 151.

GOYENECHE[164] call it solidly probable, while AERTNYS-DAMEN[165] say it is more probable. Others defending this view are CREUSEN,[166] LINDSMAN,[167] PRUMMER,[168] PAPI,[169] LEITNER,[170] CHOUPIN,[171] CHELODI,[172] HECHT [173] and MAHONEY.[174]

VERMEERSCH [175] and the IL MONITORE ECCLESIASTICO [176] formerly held this view, but after the reply of the Commission retracted it, accepting the other view.[177]

Confessions in Places not Legitimately Destined for the Confessions of Women

Confessions of women can be heard in such places in cases of infirmity or any other true necessity, according to

CANON 910.

§ 1. Feminarum confessiones extra sedem confessionalem ne audiantur, nisi ex causa infirmitatis aliave verae necessitatis et adhibitis cautelis quas Ordinarius loci opportunas iudicaverit.

In cases of necessity the priest approved for the confessions women could hear the confessions of religious women approaching him for that purpose in virtue of Canon 522, outside of the confessional. It is solidly probable that the prescription of Canon 522 and the reply of the Pontifical Commission in regard

---

164 CpR, II, 21 ff.
165 *Theol. Mor.* II, n. 378.
166 *Nouvelle Revue Theologique* (1921), p. 55; quoted by Vermeersch-Creusen, *Epit.* I, n. 595, as stating that it is solidly probable and safe.
167 *Nederlandische Katholicke Stemmen* (1924), p. 77; quoted by Vermeersch-Creusen, *loc. cit.* as favoring it.
168 *Manuale J. C.*, n. 190.
169 *Religious in Church Law*, p. 57.
170 *Handbuch*, p. 336.
171 *L'Etat Religieux*, p. 230 footnotes.
172 *Jus de Personis*, n. 258.
173 *Theologie und Glaube* (1924) 16 p. 488 ff. Synopsized by Schweiger, CpR, V, 59.
174 *Am. Ecc. Rev.* (1926) LXXIV, p. 42.
175 *Periodica*, IX, p. (14).
176 (1919) Vol. I, series VI, p. 158, n. 39.
177 Vermeersch-Creusen, *Epit.* I, n. 595; *Il Monitore*, vol. XXXIII, 160.

to the place of confession do not affect the validity of the confession and absolution. Such a priest, in cases of necessity, need not scruple to use this more lenient opinion. The division of commentators in regard to the force of the phrase of the law referring to the place for hearing these confessions, gives rise to a positive and probable doubt of law. In these cases then, the Church supplies the required jurisdiction, according to Canon 209.

It will be impossible to enumerate all the cases in which these principles could be applied, but the following will serve as examples. 1.—If a sister could not go to confession in a public church without very great embarrassment, then her confession could be heard in a room using a grate, if possible, but necessity will excuse even from this. Papi proposes the two next cases which are very likely to happen, i. e., (2) a priest having only faculties for the confessions of women visiting a former penitent, and finds her sick in the infirmary of the convent. Even if the sickness is not grave, provided it prevents the religious from easily leaving the infirmary, and she ask him to hear her confession he can do so validly and licitly; (3) The same holds for the case of a portress, who requests such a priest visiting another religious in the convent to hear her confession. She has, however, a great repugnance to going to the ordinary place set aside for the confessions of the sisters, because owing to her occupation, she would have to make her case public by going there.[178] In such conditions he could hear her confession in the parlor. (4) Thus, for similar reasons, a priest could hear the confession of a cloistered nun who requests it in the parlor of the cloister. (5) The same holds on board ship, if there is not a semi-public oratory or the place used for Mass is locked up or embarrassment as above would arise, then a religious could be heard in the priest's cabin or some other suitable place.[179] Blat is far too strict in stating that such confessions on board ship can be made only in a semi-public oratory. That

---

[178] Papi, *Religious in Church Law*, p. 57.
[179] Blat, III *pars* I, n. 206.

would make confession for religious women on a voyage almost an impossibility.

Grave necessity will excuse in all these cases from using the grate. It is to be remembered that the extreme necessity is not required and sufficient reason would be danger or loss of reputation or defamation of character, embarrassment, or the fact that priests seldom come to the religious house when it would be easy to approach them.[180]

It cannot be stated that this opens the door to abuses, e. g., if a religious would confess in the parlor. The danger of the abuse of liberty does not require that the liberty for that reason should be taken away. This danger cannot be urged too strongly, for what law is there, especially if it favors liberty, which will not give occasion for abuse. Moreover, even if such abuses should arise *"abususnon tollit usum"* and the solution is the proposal by the legislator of the proper remedies for its removal.[181]

Conclusion.—A religious, to assure the lawfulness of her confession should confess in one of the determined places, unless for a just and reasonable cause it can be prescinded from. Therefore, the Ordinary should take sufficient means to prevent abuses.[182]

Some authors propose a seeming difficulty in regard to the liceity of confessions made in that side of a confessional which is reserved for men. There is the custom in some places of hearing the confessions of women from one side of the box and men from the other. GURY-FERRERES[183] and FANFANI[184] claim that if a religious makes a confession in the side reserved to men, the confession is illicit. But as has been shown before, there are no confessionals recognized by law as reserved to men or to women. The only prescription of law is that the con-

---

180 Cf. Kinane, *Ir. Ecc. Rec.* (1921), XVII, p. 639.
181 cf. Goyeneche, CpR (1921), II, p. 23.
182 Goyeneche, *op. cit.*, p. 24; *Am. Ecc. Rev.* (1919), LXI, 447 (1926); LXXIV, 43.
183 *Casus Conscientiae* (1921), II, n. 257.
184 *De Jure Religiosorum*, n. 110.

fessional, in which women's confessions are to be heard, should be always located in an open and conspicuous place and generally in a church, or a public or semi-public oratory destined for women. This confessional should be provided with a finely perforated and fixed screen, between the penitent and confessor.[185] Therefore, if the side of the confessional, which by custom is used solely by men, is in a conspicuous place and can be easily seen and has the required screen, any woman of the world can lawfully confess there, since this confessional satisfies all the conditions required by law for the confessionals to be used by women. Therefore, religious women can "a pari" confess lawfully in such confessionals in virtue of Canon 522.[186]

Suggestions for the Use of This Canon

1.—*By the religious.*

A.—*Within the convent.*—Both nuns and sisters can address themselves, without permission, to a simply approved confessor for the purpose of confessing to him in their chapel, if they observe the regular order of exercises. The superioress has no right to exclude one or the other of the confessors, for the choice rests with the religious. If the religious asks to confess to such a confessor the superioress cannot refuse her even for extrinsic motives, such as the general discipline of the community. The superioress should submit the matter to the Ordinary and accept his decision.[187] In the use of Canon 522 religious are not allowed to violate the rules or constitutions or perform other acts of disobedience, e. g., a teacher could not seriously neglect her work to go to confession, unless there is good reason to excuse this. They should ask permission to leave class, or some common exercise. This permission would of piety held in chapel or during study or free periods. They can make use of this canon unknown to the superioress if the occasion offers.[188]

---

185 Can. 909; cf. Creusen, Am. Ecc. Rev. (1926), LXXIV, 507.
186 Prümmer, *Manuale* J. C., n. 190; Goyeneche, CpR (1921) II, 24.
187 S. C. EE et RR, Aug. 5, 1904; Col. S. C. P. F. (1907), n. 2204.

B. *Outside of the convent.*—All religious outside of the convent for a lawful reason can make use of Canon 522 if they do not thereby neglect some duty.[188a]

1. *Nuns*—This concession has not, however, changed the canons or rules in regard to the cloister.[189] Therefore for nuns bound to the observance of the papal cloister this would not be sufficient reason for leaving it.

2. *Sisters*—They can ask and be given permission to go out for the purpose of confessing in virtue of Canon 522, but they can not demand such a permission when it is contrary to the usages of the community.[190] Neither can they go out without this permission for such liberty would be excessive and would bring about the ruin of community discipline. Violation of this prescription without any other motive constitutes an offense against the rule of not going out without permission. The confessions would, however, be valid and licit.[191]

C. *Frequency of use.*—The Code does not limit the number of times that Canon 522 can be used. On the other hand, although the practice of confessing frequently in virtue of this canon does not seem to be prohibited, it is less in conformity to the mind of the legislator. If necessity urges or great spiritual benefit would be derived from these frequent confessions the religious should ask the local Ordinary for a special confessor. If this request can not be made without grave inconvenience, it is certainly lawful for her to choose the other way.[192] Hence, a religious may choose another confessor in the required circumstances as often as her peace of conscience dictates.[193] She

188 S. C. De Rel. Dec. 1, 1921; cf. Hilling, *CIC Interpretatio*, p. 37 ff.

188a Biederlack-Fuhrich, *De Religiosis*, n. 48.

189 S. C. De Rel. Dec. 1, 1921; Hilling, *CIC Interpretatio*, p. 38; Creusen, *op. cit.*, n. 95; Aertnys-Damen, *Theol. Mor.* II, n. 378.

190 S. C. De Rel. Dec. 1, 1921; Hilling loc. cit; Fanfani, *op. cit.*, n. 141; Choupin, *op. cit.*, p. 230.

191 Choupin, *loc. cit.*

192 Biederlack-Fuhrich, *op. cit.*, p. 89.

193 Augustine, III, p. 157; Vermeersch, *Periodica*, IX, p. (14); Blat, II *pars* II, p. 503; Goyeneche, CpR, II, p. 17.

should also make her regular appearances before the community confessors.[194]

D. *Reporting.*—If sisters when outside of the convent for any reason confess in virtue of Canon 522, neither the religious making use of this faculty, nor those knowing of the fact, even if questioned, are bound to inform the superioress.[195] Therefore no mention need be made of the fact that she has gone or that she intends to go to confession to a priest, who has no special faculties for the confessions of religious women.[196] Sometimes it may be necessary to give this reason to explain her delay. Even in that case the religious need mention no more than the fact that she went to confession. Moreover, it is advisable that she should not say anything until questioned,[197] lest she establish thereby a precedent which other religious may find very irksome.

By the Confessor. The only condition of those mentioned above, which is admitted by all as necessary for validity is that the priest be approved for the confessions of women. All the other points, the motive, tranquillity of conscience, the approach, by the religious; that the confession be made in a church, oratory whether public or semi-public or in a place legitimately destined for women's confessions are all disputed by authorities. As a result on each of these points there is a positive and probable doubt of law. Therefore the confessor can with safety choose the more lenient opinion to act upon, for the Church in these conditions will supply him with the necessary jurisdiction.[198]

The superioress has no power to correct abuses of this faculty and even the bishop, although he can, will not have the opportunity unless scandal arises. Therefore, the confessor is the only one who can correct this if he discovers the lack of sufficient reasons for using the canon. He should prudently tell the

---

195 Blat, II *pars* II, n. 585.

196 Papi, *Religious in Church Law,* p. 58.

197 Choupin, *op. cit.,* p. 230.

198 Can. 209.

religious to confess to the ordinary confessor, or make application to the Ordinary for a special confessor, lest the law of the unity of confessor be evaded.[199]

3. *Obligations of the Superioress.*—The one who has the right to grant or deny a confessor is the one who has appointed him and not the head of the house whether a man or woman.[200]

(A) *Before Confession* the superioress can not in any fashion restrain or limit the liberty of the religious in the legitimate use of this canon, either by prohibition or inquiry as to motives. When the superioress knows the reason why the religious intends to go out and that her request can not be satisfied by calling the ordinary or a supplementary confessor to the house, a true and weighty reason is needed to refuse permission. Such a reason may be the general discipline of the community but even for such causes the spiritual welfare of the individual must not be lightly set aside.[201] She does not have to give permission every time, but it would be more in conformity with the spirit of the Church to do so.[202] Of course, if going out is against the rules of the community, the superioress is the one to judge whether in the case an exception can or must be made.[203]

There is no obligation upon the superioress or the Ordinary of offering occasions to use this canon and much less are they bound to change anything in the cloister discipline or the constitutions.[204]

Choupin[205] thinks that a superioress should not be blamed who places obstacles in the way of a religious, who she knows is the manifest victim of scruples and clearly abusing the patience of the priest. But even in this case the superioress should

---

199 Cocchi, II *pars* II, n. 43.
200 S. C. EE et RR, Aug. 17, 1891 ad 1; Malacitana; Col. S. C. P. F. (1907), n. 1763.
201 Papi, *op. cit.*, p. 58; p. 51.
202 Choupin, *op. cit.*, p. 231.
203 Creusen, *Religieux et Religieuses*, n. 95; cf. Treatment on Can. 521, § 3, p.
204 S. C. De Rel. Dec. 1, 1921, Reply to the Bishop of Innsbruck; Hilling, *CIC Interpretatio*, p. 37 ff.
205 *l'Etat Religieux*, p. 231.

not interfere, for if such extensions are conceded, where will their use in practice cease? The liberty of conscience of the religious must be safeguarded. If she is scrupulous the confessor, trained for that purpose, is the best judge of what is to be done. This is in conformity with the old law which demanded that the superioress should always send for a supplementary confessor, requested by the religious, even though she realized that the need was feigned or arose from scruples or any other defect of mind whereby a religious considered such a confessor to be necessary.[206]

After Confession. The superioress cannot joke about it, show displeasure, ask whom the religious spoke to or ridicule her, etc.[207]

4. *Obligations of the Ordinary.* He must warn superioresses violating the prescriptions of this canon. Upon repetition of the offense he is to depose them and then immediately notify the Congregation for Religious.[208]

The statement of MAHONEY[209] " . . . the faculties should be used in each place according to the interpretation of the Ordinary, or failing this, according to the custom observed in the locality. The matter is still further involved in dioceses where faculties for hearing confessions are restricted by a clause excluding their use in the semi-public oratories of nuns. In delegating faculties the Ordinary can certainly restrict them in any manner he pleases. A priest who holds faculties of this kind cannot invoke Can. 522 in these oratories, since he is not 'approved' for hearing confessions there," can not be admitted.

It is true that delegated jurisdiction can be granted circum-

---

206 S. C. EE et RR, Aug. 17, 1891, *Malacitana,* ad 2; Col. S. C. P. F. (1907), n. 1963.

207 Cf. explanation of Can. 521 § 3, where these things are fully explained.

208 Can. 2414. This fully explained above.

209 *Am. Ecc. Rev.* (1926), LXXIV, 44.

scribed by certain limits,[210] whether in regard to time,[211] persons,[212] or territory, e. g., a parish.[213] "But," to quote CREUSEN [214] who very ably takes issue on this question with MAHONEY, "if a restriction *contradicts* an article of the Codex, it becomes *ipso facto illicit* and sometimes even invalid. Thus an Ordinary could not delegate jurisdiction uniquely for lay people of the masculine sex, to the total exclusion of men in religious orders. In virtue of Can. 519, any man in a religious order can occasionally go to a confessor 'approved of by the Ordinary of the place.' If the delegation is accorded for all laymen, the restriction is formally contrary to a right accorded by the Codex; it is therefore invalid . . . .

"Similarly, an Ordinary cannot delegate jurisdiction for all secular women, but with the addition that the confessor cannot hear the confession of a nun who comes to him within the limits of Can. 522.

"Once the jurisdiction is given, the *use* of it cannot be declared invalid in the circumstances when the Codex gives it formal authorization. Thus an Ordinary can not declare that he gives authority to hear women's confessions only in churches and not in semi-public oratories. Once all the conditions prescribed by the Codex are present, the faithful are using a right accorded by the Holy See—a right which the Ordinaries can not restrict."

Conclusion. Since Canon 522 uses the words "*in qualibet ecclesia vel oratorio etiam semi-publico*" the Ordinary can not grant jurisdiction to a confessor to hear the confessions of secular women and at the same time restrict him from acting in

---

210 Can. 878 § 1.

211 "several of the pontifical documents, quoted as sources of Can. 878, § 1, speak exclusively of this restriction," Creusen, *Am. Ecc. Rev., loc. cit.*, 508.

212 Can. 522, 875, 876.

213 Creusen, *loc. cit.*

214 *loc. cit.*

virtue of Canon 522 in the semi-public oratories of nuns. Therefore religious constitutions [215] and diocesan statutes, which contain a contrary or restrictive prescription lose all their obligatory force.[216]

---

215 S. C. De Rel. Normae, March 6, 1921; Cap. IV, *De excludendis e textu constitutionum.* (e) *omnia ea quae respiciunt munera et officia Episcoporum et confessariorum; cum pro his non scribantur constitutiones, sed pro religiosis*; (this is not officially published) quoted by Fanfani, *De Jure Religiosorum*, p. 552, App. 1; *Am. Ecc. Rev.* (1921), LXV, 594 ff.

216 Blat, *Commentarium in Textum* CIC (1919), II, *de Personis*, p. 503 ff; Boudinhon, CC, 36, p. 277; Choupin, *op. cit.*, p. 230.

CHAPTER XVIII.

THE CONFESSOR OF THE SICK.

A special confessor granted to sick religious dates from the time of Benedict XIV. This confessor was to be given to nuns by the Bishop or Regular Superior to whom they were respectively subject.[1] Such confessors were conceded only in danger of death and this was the basis for the formal confirmation of the text of this concession by the "Normae" of the Congregation of Bishops and Regulars.[2]

The decree "Cum de Sacramentalibus" extended to both nuns and religious of simple vows the far greater concession by which even outside of the danger of death they could, when gravely sick, choose any confessor simply approved for confessions. Special approbation for religious women was not necessary. This right to choose a confessor was to last as long as the gravity of the sickness perdured and during that period the religious could make use of it as often as she wished.[3]

This has been incorporated in the Code with a few slight changes in wording and an added prohibition to superioresses violating the prescriptions of the law.

Grave Sickness.

CANON 523.

Religiosae omnes, cum graviter aegrotant, licet mortis periculum absit, quemlibet sacerdotem ad mulierum confessiones excipiendas approbatum, etsi non destinatum religiosis, arcessere possunt eique, perdurante gravi infirmitate, quoties voluerint, confiteri, nec Antistita potest eas sive directe sive indirecte prohibere.

1 Const. *Pastoralis Curae,* Aug. 5, 1748, § 5; FJC n. 388.
2 June 28, 1901; art. n. 148.
3 S. C. De Rel. Feb. 3, 1913; n. 15; AAS V, 64; cf. Vermeersch, *loc. cit.;* Boudinhon, *loc. cit.*

Subject of the Law.

The words "*moniales et religiosae*" of the law of 1913 have been designated in the new terminology of the Code by the words "*religiosae omnes,*" which being generic have practically the same force. Therefore this right is granted to all religious women, whether nuns or sisters, whether cloistered or not, whether of solemn or simple vows, whether of pontifical or episcopal (diocesan) right.[4] Only what is expressly stated of nuns must be applied to them alone since juridically nuns are on a plane distinct from sisters.[5] Novices, by virtue of Canon 566, § 1, and women of pious societies living in community, even without vows, by reason of Canon 675, are included in this right.[6]

Gravity of Sickness Required.

Previous to 1913, as has been seen, danger of death was required, but this is no longer necessary. The determination of grave sickness outside of the danger of death offers difficulty. Therefore since the Code requires grave sickness it is evident that a cold, or a simple indisposition,[7] old age, or a general exhaustion or weakness, etc., are not usually in the sense of the law, grave sicknesses.[8] In all cases the judgment of a physician as to the gravity will suffice, whether the person is confined to bed or not.[9] It will often be very difficult for the confessor alone to determine what constitutes gravity, where it begins and where it ends, and when it becomes "periculum mortis." Canonists differ on this point and to make it clear the following distinction is made.

A. *Absolutely Grave* sicknesses are those which are very weakening or of such gravity that although the danger of death

4 Can. 488, 7°; cf. Noldin, *De Sacramentis*, n. 349; Cocchi, II *pars* II, n. 43.

5 Fanfani, *De Jure Religiosorum*, n. 7; n. 137.

6 Cf. Commentary on Canon 522 p. ; Noldin, *loc. cit.;* Goyeneche, CpR, II (1921), p. 14.

7 Hizette, *Confessions des Religieuses*, p. 88.

8 Salsman, cf. Vermeersch, *Per.* VII, p. 95; Choupin, *op. cit.*, p. 223.

9 Bastien, *op. cit.*, n. 362.

is not present it is likely to induce it.[10] The confessor can certainly act in virtue of this canon in such cases. On the other hand to restrict the confessor, as FANFANI [11] does, to these cases, seems too severe. Every grave sickness which can considerably weaken the strength of the sick and give rise to dangerous complications would be sufficient. Therefore pneumonia, rheumatism (but not merely pains concomitant with a chronic case of this), pleurisy, a bad case of grippe, etc.[12] would be serious enough to warrant the use of this canon. The fact that the religious is confined to bed for a week or so may be an indication of a grave sickness. Yet it can not be the only norm for judging nor a required condition for the use of this canon for there are grave sicknesses in which a person is not confined to bed and, in some cases, cannot lie down. On the other hand, a religious might be confined to bed or her room by reason of a sprain, which would not be sufficient since the Code says expressly "when they are gravely sick." [13]

B. *Relatively Grave* sicknesses are those which because of certain special circumstances weaken the powers of resistance of the sick. This would be the case in less malignant sicknesses which have attacked a person of a temperament or constitution, debilitated by age, privations or previous or concomitant sickness, etc.,[14] although these of themselves without the added presence of some other illness would not be sufficient reason for using this canon.[15]

In these cases of relatively grave sickness it seems that the confessor would be justified in absolving. The solution of the difficulty seems to lay in the word, "*arcessere.*" This word gives to a gravely sick religious the right to summon a confessor approved for women's confessions. It implies upon her part

---

10 Fanfani, *op. cit.*, n. 137; Vermeersch, *Per.* VII, p. 95; Vermeersch-Creusen, *Epit.* n. 596; Cocchi, II *pars* II, n. 43.

11 *Loc. cit.*

12 Choupin, *L'Etat Religieux*, p. 232; Vermeersch, *loc. cit.*

13 Creusen, *Religieux et Religieuses*, n. 96.

14 Creusen, *loc. cit.*

15 Vermeersch, *Per.* VII, p. 95.

the inability to go to the confessional or any place legitimately destined for that purpose.

In Practice. It is true that sickness is required not only for the liceity but even the validity of a confession made to a priest lacking special approbation for religious,[16] for by the fact that he is called by a gravely sick religious he gets faculties from the common law for this case. Therefore, if the religious is not in danger of death but due to sickness can not approach the confessional, the priest should form a probable judgment as to the gravity. This judgment will be sufficient to act upon. The confessor should remember that this is a privilege and should be given a wide interpretation according to the axioms of law "*Odia restringi, et favores convenit ampliari*"[17] and "*Quum in beneficiis plenissima sit interpretatio.*"[18] In order then that the religious can demand a priest and that he might acquiesce, it is not necessary to have certitude in regard to the gravity of the sickness. The appearances of a grave sickness and the probable judgment to that effect suffice.[19]

The priest need not be too severe in acting in virtue of Canon 523. There is a doubt of law here, as is evident from the dispute of authors as to the gravity of the disease required to use this canon, which is positive and probable. On the other hand the priest may have a doubt as to whether this particular case is sufficiently grave, i. e., a doubt of fact. It he has good reasons for thinking the disease is grave he can make the probable judgment in favor of granting absolution and act upon it. In both of these cases of positive and probable doubt of law and of fact the church will supply him with the necessary jurisdiction.[20]

It is worthy of note that a confessor acting in such conditions need not worry about reservations of sins. Reservations of

16 Fanfani, *op. cit.*, n. 137; Biederlack-Fuhrich, *De Religiosis*, p. 89.
17 R. J. in VI°, Reg. 15.
18 c. 22, X, *de privilegiis*, V, 33; cf. Wernz, *Jus Decretalium*, I, n. 161; cf. Canons 68, 50.
19 Choupin, *op. cit.*, p. 223; Hizette, *loc. cit.*; cf. Index to the Code of Canon Law, the word "privilegia."
20 Can. 209.

sins *ratione sui* cease for these religious women, according to the prescriptions of Canon 900 § 1, when they are unable to leave the house. Sufficient reason for this would be a broken foot, etc.[21] All that is necessary for the cessation of reservation is that the illness prevents the religious from leaving the house.

Qualifications of the Confessor.

The Code is stricter on this point than the law of 1913 [22] which stated "*quemlibet sacerdotem ad confessiones excipiendas adprobatum.*" The Code requires that he be approved for the confessions of women. This approbation for women's confessions is necessary for validity as explained under Can. 522. Faculties are commonly given in our country simultaneously for the confessions of men and women. On the other hand, in some countries of Europe faculties are first given for men and only after some time extended to include the confessions of women. But by the very fact that a priest approved for the confessions of women is demanded by the sick religious, he is authorized by the Holy See to receive her confession.[23]

Question.—Canon 522 uses the words "*confessarium adeat ab Ordinario loci pro mulieribus approbatum,*" while the present canon states "*quemlibet sacerdotem ad mulierum confessiones excipiendas approbatum.*" Does the omission of the phrase "*ab Ordinario loci*" imply that any priest approved by any Ordinary for the confessions of women could act in virtue of this canon anywhere in the world?

First opinion—in the negative.

I.—When taken alone, Canon 523 might warrant this conclusion, but this is a question of approbation, which after the Code is synonymous with jurisdiction.[24] But delegated jurisdiction to receive the confessions of anyone whatsoever, whether

21 Vermeersch-Creusen, *Epit.* II, n. 179; Dargin, *Reserved Cases according to the Code of Canon Law,* p. 33.

22 n. 15; AAS V, 64; Hizette, *op. cit.,* p. 89 (Supplement of 1920), p. 14; Boudinhon, CC, 36, p. 413.

23 Bastien, *Directoire Canonique,* n. 361; Choupin, *op. cit.,* p. 232.

24 Biederlack-Fuhrich, *De Religiosis,* n. 50; Vermeersch-Creusen, *Epit.,* II, n. 143.

secular or religious is conferred by the Ordinary of the place in which the confessions are heard.[25] Therefore, the delegation of another Ordinary would not suffice.

II.—A local Ordinary has Ordinary jurisdiction only for his own territory,[26] therefore his delegates cannot exercise their jurisdiction outside of his territory. For the Ordinary cannot grant more power than he has.

III.—This would destroy the principle that, "the place determines the act." [27]

IV.—Except in danger of death the Church has always had stricter regulations for confessions of religious women than for secular women. But even lay women when confessing in grave sickness outside of the danger of death can only confess to a confessor approved by the local Ordinary. Surely, then, in this matter the Church does not grant to religious greater privileges than she does to secular women.

This question is not treated at length by many authors and Papi [28] seems to be the only one directly sponsoring the view just mentioned. He, at the same time, grants probability to the opposite view.

Second Opinion—which is the better, considers approbation by any local Ordinary as sufficient for the use of this canon.

I. The first three arguments of the other opinion are all based upon the supposition that this confessor hears confessions in virtue of the approbation of the Ordinary by whom he is approved, i. e., in virtue of delegated jurisdiction from the Ordinary. That does not necessarily follow from the words of the canon. If that were true one would have to admit that the confessor of Canon 522, who hears the confessors of religious women when they approach him for the peace of their conscience, does so in virtue of delegated jurisdiction from the local Ordinary. This could not be true, for special approbation is required for the confessions of religious. Therefore, he hears

25 Can. 874, § 1; Can. 876.
26 Can. 873, § 1.
27 Vermeersch, *Per.* VII, p. (26).
28 *Religious in Church Law*, p. 59.

in virtue of a supplement of jurisdiction or at least the presumed approbation for such religious women granted by the Code. Before the Code under the decree "Cum de Sacramentalibus" of 1913[29] in regard to confessions of sick religious, which could be heard by a priest without special approbation, authors considered that he received some such supplement of jurisdiction or presumed approbation.[30] Therefore, since the Code, and not the local Ordinary, extends the jurisdiction in these particular cases, it cannot be held that a confessor cannot hear such confessions, because of the fact that he has not been approved by the local Ordinary for the confessions of women. It is evident, then, that in Canon 522, the requirement that he be approved for women's confessions by the local Ordinary and in 523 that he likewise be approved by an Ordinary, are but "conditiones sine qua non," without which this extension of jurisdiction or presumed approbation is not granted. But it cannot be inferred from the wording that this canon and Canon 876 are opposed, because of the fact that that priest is approved by any Ordinary in the world. It seems to be the intention of the Holy See to assure itself that the priest is qualified to hear the confessions of women in order that he might act in virtue of Canon 523. Being certain of that by the fact of approbation by any Ordinary the Code thereby extends to him the faculty to hear the confessions of sick religious.

II. There is quite a difference between the circumstances of Canons 522 and 523. In the former the priest is to hear the confessions in a church or a public or semi-public oratory, or even in a place legitimately destined for the confessions of women. Here the place is expressly mentioned and therefore the delegation by the Ordinary, to receive the confessions of women in these places in his diocese, is naturally to be expected. In Canon 523, on the other hand, the place is not mentioned and the faculty is given to a religious who is presumed to be incapable of fulfilling the requirements of the

29 S. C. De Rel. Feb. 3, 1913; AAS V, p. 64.

30 Boudinhon, CC, 36, p. 413; Vermeersch, *Per.* VII, p. 95.

place of confession. This, then, is a direct privilege granted to a sick individual.

III. Canon 18 states that in the interpretation of the law the words must be accepted in their true and proper signification contained in the text and the context. But in Canon 523 it is only required that he be approved by any Ordinary and neither does the context demand otherwise.

IV. If the strict opinion is held, how can the omission of the words "*ab Ordinario loci*" be explained? The mere assertion that Canon 523 should be accepted in the same way as Canon 522, proves nothing. The very omission argues for the validity of the more lenient opinion and the burden of the proof to the contrary rests upon its opponents.

This omission is *positive* and *intentional,* as is evident from a comparison of these canons with the different parts of the decree "Cum de Sacramentalibus" upon which they are based. Number 14 of this decree, speaking of the confessor, whom the religious could approach when outside of their house, states "*confessionem peragere apud quemvis Confessarium pro utroque sexu adprobatum,*" while in Canon 522 these words have been changed to read "*confessarium adeat ab Ordinario loci pro mulieribus approbatum.*" On the other hand, number 15 of this decree, speaking of the confessor of the sick, contains this wording: "*quemlibet sacerdotem ad confessiones excipiendas adprobatum,*" which becomes in Canon 523 "*quemlibet sacerdotem ad mulierum confessiones excipiendas approbatum.*" The legislator has made changes in both cases over the original phraseology. In the first case he has practically changed the entire wording and inserted the words "*ab Ordinario loci,*" while in the second case the only change was the insertion of the word "*mulierum.*" The legislator found it necessary to use the words "*ab Ordinario loci*" in Canon 522 to convey the meaning that he had in mind, i. e., that the confessor must be approved by the Ordinary of the place in which the confessions are heard. Therefore, he should have used the same or equivalent words in Canon 523, if he intended that exactly the same meaning should be received in both canons in regard to the same point. It would be imputing to the legislator a serious lack of prudence to state, in regard to two successive canons, that the wording of Canon 523 is just a relic of the decree of 1913, when he was so meticulously careful about the wording of Canon 522. This seems true, especially since the conditions of sick religious seem more urgent than those of the religious who would use Canon 522. Why, the very fact that the legislator studiously inserted the one word "*mulierum*" in Canon 523, shows that this canon received his close attention. The only conclusion, therefore, that can be drawn from this omission, is that the legislator intended it.

V. It is true that before the decree of 1913, except in the danger of death, there were stricter regulations for the confessions of religious women than for secular women. But it cannot be deduced from the fact that lay women, when confessing in grave sickness, outside of the danger of death, can confess only to a priest approved by the local Ordinary, that religious women, in the same circumstances, must also confess to such a priest approved by the local Ordinary for secular women. This is evident from the fact that the decree of 1913, which was a co-ordination and revision of previous laws for the confessors of female religious permitted gravely sick religious to confess to any priest approved for confessions. It did not require that this approbation be given by the local Ordinary.[31] "*Quemlibet sacerdotem ad confessiones excipiendas approbatum arcessere possunt.*"

Therefore, since the present canon is based on this part of the decree of 1913, it should be interpreted in the light of the old law.[32]

The extrinsic probability of this opinion is vouched for by the fact that it is supported by Brandys[33] and Wouters,[34] while Mahoney[35] sanctions it as a conclusion which can be

---

31 S. C. De Rel. Feb. 3, 1913, n. 15; AAS V, 64.
32 Can. 6, 2°, 3°, 4°.
33 *Kirchliches Rechtsbuch*, p. 158.
34 *Nederlandische Katholicke Stemmen* (1918), p. 200—Quoted by Creusen, *Religieux et Religieuses*, n. 96.
35 *Am. Ecc. Rev.* (1926), LXXIV, p. 39.

drawn from the omission and PAPI[36] claims that it is not void of all probability, although he chooses the opposite opinion.

Practical Conclusion—Both opinions are theoretically probable and so for the practical solution of the individual case the confessor can make use of Canon 209. The division of authors, on this point, gives rise to a positive and probable doubt of law, in which case the confessor can act in virtue of the jurisdiction which the Church supplies in such cases. A priest of the Archdiocese of New York, therefore, could safely make use of Canon 523 to hear upon request the confession of a sick religious in the diocese of Monterey and Fresno, California, in virtue of the faculties to hear women's confessions which he has received from the Archbishop of New York.

Manner of Obtaining Such a Priest.

In the constitution "Pastoralis Curae" of Benedict XIV, the religious was to address the regular superior or the bishop with her request.[37] But in the law of 1913 and the Code she is given the right to summon (*arcessere*) or directly address the confessor whom she desires. This should be regularly done by submitting her demand to the superioress. It is not, however, "per se" necessary that this application be made to the superioress.[38] The latter should always receive such a request favorably and immediately ask the priest to come.[39] Only the manifest abuse upon the part of the superioress would make it necessary to have recourse to the Ordinary. It is advisable that when a sister is gravely sick, the superioress should ask her if she desires a special confessor. In fact, the Sacred Congregation of Bishops and Regulars advised the Sisters of the Third Order of St. Benedict of Nancy, France, on the tenth of September, 1894, to insert this in their constitutions.[40]

It is to be noted that the words "for the peace of her con-

---

36 *Religious in Church Law*, p. 59.

37 FJC, n. 388, § 5.

38 Cocchi, *op. cit.*, II, *pars* II, n. 43.

39 Hizette, *Confessiones des Religieuses*, p. 89; Choupin *L'Etat Religieux*, p. 223.

40 Hizette, *op. cit.*, p. 87.

science," are missing in this canon and therefore the confession is lawful if there be no particular reason for the request of a sick religious.

Duration of the Confessor's Jurisdiction.

The confessor's jurisdiction is co-extensive with the duration of the grave sickness, even though there is never the danger of death. It ceases, however, at the evident beginning of convalescence,[41] from a grave disease or surgical operation if the religious is confined to bed only for the purpose of healing the wound of the operation.[42] There is no restriction as to the number of times a religious may use this right while gravely sick. Moreover, she is not obliged to address the same confessor every time, provided those chosen are approved for the confessions of women.[43] In regard to the termination of the sickness, the judgment of the physician can always be followed. It is in accordance with the spirit of the law to interpret this canon rather widely.

Obligation of the Superioress.

The superioress, although she can maintain the rule and legitimate customs, cannot in any way, either directly or indirectly, prohibit the use of this privilege. Violation of this prohibition would make her liable to a warning by the bishop for the first offense and deposition for the second as explained above under Canon 521, § 3, Canon 2414.[44] Abuses on the part of the inferiors are in many ways possible. If a superioress judges the conduct of a confessor or a penitent, is imprudent or reprehensible, she cannot refuse to call the confessor, but should submit her observations to the Ordinary.[45]

In Danger of Death.

"A fortiori" from the first moment of the "article" of death or even the probable danger of death, in virtue of the concession *"Pie admodum"* of the Council of Trent,[46] which

---

41 Creusen, *Religieux et Religieuses,* n. 97.
42 Vermeersch, *Periodica,* VII, p. 95.
43 Hizette, *loc. cit.*
44 II, cf. p.
45 S. C. EE et RR, Aug. 17, 1891, ad 2; Col. S. C. P. F. (1907), n. 1763; Aug. 5, 1904, ibid. n. 2204; cf. Creusen, *op. cit.,* n. 97.

has been incorporated by the Code, a simple priest without faculties could absolve female religious.

CANON 882.

In periculo mortis omnes sacerdotes, licet ad confessiones non approbati, valide et licite absolvunt quoslibet poenitentes a quibusvis peccatis aut censuris, quantumvis reservatis et notoriis, etiamsi praesens sit sacerdos approbatus, salvo praescripto can. 884, 2252.

This *periculum mortis* is to be determined, as is evident from a reply of the Holy Office to a former Bishop of Cincinnati, from the teachings of approved authors among whom St. Alphonsus is explicitly mentioned.[47]

This danger of death, according to St. Alphonsus,[48] Ballerini,[49] Aertnys,[50] Noldin[51] and Augustine[52] and others may be not only from an internal cause, such as grave disease, but even when it is induced by an external cause. Thus there can be included in the latter class the danger of death arising where the penitent could not find another approved priest.[53] To these might be added the danger which exists for a person condemned to capital punishment and the danger of becoming perpetually insane.

All that is required in these cases is the probability of death, even though it be more probable that the religious will live. In any of these cases and similar ones, a woman religious could call for any priest to hear her confessions, even if he have no faculties to hear confessions, and moreover, even though

46 *Sess. XIV, ch. 7, "Verumtamen pie admodum, ne hac ipsa occasione aliquis pereat, in eadem ecclesia Dei custoditum semper fuit ut nulla sit reservatio in articulo mortis; atque ideo omnes sacerdotes quoslibet poenitentes a quibusvis peccatis et censuris absolvere possunt.;"* cf. Mansi, 33, p. 96.

47 S. Officii, Sept. 13, 1859, ad. l. Col. S. C. P. F. n. 1181 (1907).

48 *Theol. Mor.* VI, n. 560.

49 *Opus Theol. Mor.*, Tract. X, de Poenitentia, n. 363 (ed. 1900).

50 *Theol. Mor.*, II, n. 223.

51 *De Sacramentis*, n. 345.

52 *A Commentary on Canon Law*, IV, p. 287.

53 Noldin, loc. cit.

an approved priest endowed with special jurisdiction to hear her confession as a religious, is present

Outside of a case of necessity the *"absolutio complicis"* would be illicit on the part of the confessor.[54] A religious can, in danger of death, be absolved by a priest not having special faculties, from a censure reserved *"ab homine"* or *"specialissimo modo"* to the Holy See. In this case the penitent is bound after recovery by the obligation of recurring, under pain of reincidence of the same censure specifically, to him who imposed the censure if *"ab homine"* and to the Sacred Penitentiary or the bishop or in fact anyone else endowed with the required faculty, for censures imposed *"a jure."* The penitent must then observe their commands.[55]

---

54 Can. 884.
55 Can. 2252.

CHAPTER XIX.

ENTRANCE OF THE CLOISTER OF NUNS BY THE CONFESSOR.

During the eighth century, regulations, in regard to the entrance of the cloister by the priest, were laid down. Yet to the ninth century and the period of Charlemagne as Emperor of the Holy Roman Empire is owed most of the early legislation on the entrance of the cloister.[1] These regulations were not definitized until the Council of Aix-la-Chapelle in 816, in the time of Pope Stephen V.[2] This council stated that the confessor could hear the confessions of nuns only in the church and in the presence of witnesses, i. e., generally a deacon and a subdeacon, whom he brought with him. The latter were to be out of hearing and yet capable of bearing witness to the conduct of the confessor and the nun. The confessions of the sick, however, could be heard in any house whatsoever, but with the same requirement in regard to witnesses. This was incorporated by many local councils[3] and religious rules, as is evidenced in that of the Order of Fontevrault.[4] This rule would not permit the hearing of the confessions of sick nuns at their bedside, but

1 *Statuta S. Bonifacii Archiepiscopi Mogunt.*, c. 14; cf. Hefele, *Conciliengeschicte* III, 584; *Conc. Foriorliense* (791), c. 12; S. S. Conc. (Labbeus et Cassertius-edition, *Florence* 1767) p. 850; Conc. *Turonense, III* (813), c. 29, cf. Mansi, XIV, p. 87; Conc. *Cabilonense II* (813), c. 60; Mansi, XIV, p. 106; *Arlatense VI* (813), c. 7, Mansi, XIV, 60; cf. Schaaf, *The Cloister*, p. 42. (This is the best work that we know of in english on the canonical regulations for the cloister.)

2 Conc. *Aquisgranense*, lib. II, c. 27, Mansi, XIV p. 276; *Capitularia Regum Francorum* (*circa* 837) *Additio* 2; Mansi XVII bis, 1141.

3 Conc. *Parisiense* VI, c. 46; Mansi XIV, 565; Harduin, IV, 1323; cf. Hefele, *Conciliengeschicte* IV, p. 15, 16.

4 *Regulae Sanctimonialium Fontis Ebraldi, Vetusta Statuta*, n. 16, MPL, CLXII, 1086; cf. Lea, *A History of Auricular Confession*, I, 201.

demanded that they be brought into the chapel. The nuns of the Gilbertine Order (1139),[5] on the other hand, had a confessional of the modern form, i. e., in the cloister wall, so that the confessor would not have to enter the cloister. Confessions of these nuns were heard while two discreet nuns stood at a distance from the "confessional window" and watched the conduct of the penitent.

The Congregation of the Council, although it permitted the entrance of the confessor to the sick room, required that two nuns should accompany him and remain at the door of the cell, which was to be left open.[6]

It was left to Alexander VII in his constitution "Felici" October 20, 1664[7] to define the law more clearly. He permitted the ordinary and extraordinary confessors to enter the cloister to administer the Sacraments of Penance, the Holy Eucharist and Extreme Unction to sick nuns or others living there, and also to pray over the dying. Yet the confessor was never to enter without a companion of exemplary life and mature age, who was always to remain in that part of the monastery where he could see the confessor and be seen by him.[8]

This law applied only to the regular confessor, but was extended during the next century to other confessors.[9] It was from these prescriptions and others similar to these that our present canon has developed.

CANON 600.

Intra monialium clausuram nemo, cuiusvis generis, conditionis, sexus, aetatis admittatur sine Sanctae Sedis licentia, exceptis personis quae sequuntur:

2°. Confessarius vel qui eius vices gerit potest, cum debitis cautelis, ingredi clausuram ad ministranda Sacramenta infirmis aut ad assistendum morientibus.

---

[5] *Regulae Ordinis Sempringensis,* Ch. V; Holsten, *Codex Regularum,* II, 471.

[6] Pellizarius, *Tractatio de Monialibus,* X, n. 174.

[7] FJC n. 240.

[8] Pellizarius, *op. cit.*, n. 218.

[9] Benedict XIV, *Opera Omnia,* XIII, 264; cf. Schaaf, *op. cit.*, p. 117; Bastien, *Directoire Canonique,* n. 369.

Confessors Who Can Enter the Cloister.

I. *To Hear Confessions of the Sick.*

The ordinary confessor is he who has the special jurisdiction *per se* required to hear the confessions of nuns.[10] The confessor referred to in this canon then, is the ordinary confessor of the community.[11] But the extraordinary should take care of these things at the time of performing his office if the sick nun does not ask for the ordinary, supplementary or other confessors.[12] The substitute or vice-gerent would be not only the priest appointed by the bishop to supply his absence during sickness, etc.,[13] but all confessors of religious (except the one to whom the religious approaches under Canon 522 for her peace of conscience), who have the right to enter the cloister at the request of the sick nun to hear her confession. They include 1—The special confessor appointed by the local Ordinary for an individual nun at her request (Can. 520, § 2). 2—The supplementary confessors, residents of the vicinity (called "*adjuncti*" by the Instruction of 1924), appointed by the local Ordinary as those to whom the nuns can have recourse in particular cases without applying to the Ordinary (Can. 521, § 2). 3—Any confessor approved to hear confessions of women by a local Ordinary, whom a gravely sick nun requests, according to Canon 523, although she is not in danger of death.[14] 4—In danger of death any priest whatsoever, even though he has no faculties to hear confessions.[15] 5—The jubilee confessor, approved for both sexes, whom the nun requests during the first year of the jubilee, while it is reserved to the Eternal city,[16] or

---

10 Vermeersch-Creusen, *Epit.* n. 706; Schäfer, *Ordensrecht*, p. 252.

11 S. C. De Rel. *Instructio de Clausura*, III, 2°, f; Feb. 6, 1924; AAS XVI, 95; cf. Can. 520, § 1.

12 S. C. EE et RR, Dec. 16, 1836; cf. Mothon, *Traite de la Confession Sacramentelle*, p. 98.

13 Schaaf, *op. cit.*, p. 117; Brandys, *Kirchliches Rechtsbuch*, n. 73, p. 67.

14 S. C. De Rel., Feb. 6, 1924. *Instructio de Clausura*, III, 2°, g; AAS XVI, 99; cf. *Il Monitore Ecclesiastico* (1924), XXXVI, 70.

15 Can. 882.

16 Pius XI, Const. "*Apostolico munere*," July 30, 1924; AAS (1924), XVI, 317 ff.

when it is extended to the world during the second year [17] can enter the cloister. This can happen twice each year, for the nun can gain the indulgence once for the living and once for the dead.[18] 6—Bishops also have the right of entering for the purpose of hearing the confession of a sick nun upon her request and even if that be only out of mere devotion.[19] Any of these confessors can enter the cloister to hear the confession of a nun, even if the ordinary confessor or his substitute is at hand [20] and as often as she asks for him.[21] Outside of these cases if a nun is confined to her room, but is not gravely sick only the ordinary, extraordinary or supplementary confessor can enter to hear her confession.[22]

II. *For the Administration of the Other Sacraments.*

The administration of Communion, both as Viaticum and out of devotion, and of Extreme Unction, together with the assisting of the dying, is reserved by Canon 514, § 2, to the ordinary confessor or his substitute,[23] even if one of the other confessors mentioned above has heard the confession. If the administration of the last sacraments is to be concomitant with that of confession, they may permit this administration to the other confessors. Although this seems advisable, yet the ordinary confessor can rightfully insist upon attending to these duties personally.[24] In the absence of the ordinary confessor or his substitute, any of the above enumerated priests can, after confession, administer the other sacraments or even if the nun's

---

17 Pius XI, Const. "*Servatoris Jesu Christi,*" Dec. 25, 1925; AAS XVII, p. 615 ff.

18 Intro. to Const. *Servatoris.*

19 S. C. Conc. in *Mazarien,* May 10, 1727, ad. 4; Benedict XIV, *Opera Omnia,* XIII, q. DLI, p. 263-265.

20 Schaaf, *op. cit.,* p. 118; cf. Papi, *Religious in Church Law,* p. 117; Blat, II, n. 675, 668.

21 *Instructio de Clausura* (1924), III, 2°, g. AAS XVI, 99; cf. Creusen, *op. cit.,* n. 234.

22 Creusen, *op. cit.,* n. 234.

23 *Instructio de Clausura* (1924), III, 2°, f; AAS XVI, p. 99.

24 Schaaf, *op. cit.,* p. 118; Papi, *op. cit.,* p. 117; Blat, II, n. 675.

confession is not to be heard.[25] In the same circumstances Communion of devotion can be brought to sick nuns by the chaplain (Canon 529) and in the event of his concomitant absence by any priest with the permission of the bishop. The bishop can authorize the superioress to designate a priest and grant the latter permission in his name.[26]

III. *Required Precautions.*

The Code does not mention these and therefore they must be gathered from the Instruction on the Cloister, given by the Congregation for Religious on February 6, 1924[27] and the anterior legislation, all the points of which the Code has not renewed, but which may serve as a guide.[28]

1.—*For the administration of Holy Communion*—The decree of the Congregation for Religious of September 1, 1912[29] must be observed, i. e., the priest should be accompanied from the time that he enters the cloister until he leaves by four elderly nuns if that is possible. Regulars no longer are bound to have a companion of their own order.[30]

2.—*For hearing confessions*—Two nuns should accompany the confessor to the cell of the sick nun and wait at the open door of the cell, but out of earshot, while he hears the confession, and then accompany him back to the monastery door.[31]

3.—*For the administration of the last Sacraments and to*

---

25 S. C. Conc. *in Mazarien.* May 10, 1727; Benedict XIV, *Opera Omnia,* XIII, 263-265; S. C. EE et RR, *in Fossanen,* Feb. 1743, Bizzarri, 329 ff; cf. Ferraris, *v. Monialis,* V, 82; Leitner, *Handbuch (Dritte Lieferung, Das Ordensrecht),* 337; Blat, *loc. cit.;* Bastien, *Directoire Canonique,* n. 369; Pellizarius, *op. cit.,* n. 217.

26 S. C. De Rel. Sept. 1, 1912, AAS IV, 625-626; *Instructio de Clausura,* Feb. 6, 1924 III, 2°, h, AAS XVI, 99; Blat, II, n. 675; Leitner, *op. cit.,* p. 336; Creusen, *op. cit.,* n. 234; Schäfer, *Ordensrecht,* p. 252, Papi, *op. cit.,* p. 117; Schaaf, *op. cit.,* p. 118 ff.

27 AAS XVI, 96 ff.

28 Augustine, *op. cit.,* III, 316; Blat, II *pars* II, n. 588-599; Leitner, *loc. cit.;* Papi, *op. cit.,* p. 118.

29 AAS IV, 625-626.

30 S. C. De Rel. *Instructio de Clausura,* Feb. 6, 1924, III, 2°, h; AAS XVI, 99, cf. Schaaf, *op. cit.,* p. 119; Blat, *op. cit.,* n. 675; Leitner, *op. cit.,* p. 336; Schäfer, *Ordensrecht,* p. 252.

31 ibid. III, 2°, i.

assist the dying—The Instruction of 1924 makes no specific regulations for these cases as for the administration of the Eucharist and the hearing of confessions. Speaking of all these offices together, it states, that immediately after his ministry is completed, the priest should leave the monastery.[32] Therefore, for those offices of administering the last Sacraments and assisting the dying, the prescriptions of the old law will have to be applied.

The confessor can enter the cloister to assist dying nuns during the night and the bishop can grant permission for that purpose even to the extraordinary confessor.[33]

The custom of confessors, whether secular or regular, of staying within the enclosure over night, if in the opinion of the physician a nun is about to die, can be tolerated.[34] In protracted agony of death the bishop can, if he judges it prudent, tolerate the custom of a chaplain relieving the confessor and he in turn being relieved by a third priest.[35] But only in cases of a long stay or necessity are the confessors permitted to eat within the enclosure.[36] The confessor must always be vested in surplice and stole when he enters the cloister.[37]

Reasons for Entrance.

1. *Sufficient reason*—would be only to administer sacraments to sick and assist the dying.[38] By the sick are meant not

32 ibid. III, 2°, k.

33 S. C. EE et RR, *in Algaren*, July 1736, Bizzarri, 347-348; Sept. 13, 1583, Ferraris, v. *Monialis*, V, 57; Lucidi, II, 159; cf. Schaaf, *loc. cit.*

34 S. C. EE et RR, *in Aesina*, May 29, 1846, ad. 1; Bizzarri, 546 ff; Lucidi, *De Visitatione SS. Liminum*, II, 158; Pennachi, I, 730, 731; says that to tolerate this (1), the custom must be of long standing (2) no scandal (3) the abolition of this custom would give rise to suspicions; cf. Schaaf, *op. cit.*, p. 120.

35 S. C. EE et RR, *in Fossanen*, Feb. 1743, Bizzarri, 329 ff; Pennachi, I, 729; Lucidi, II, 159.

36 S. C. EE et RR, Sept. 13, 1582; Nones of May, 1590; Lucidi, II, 160; *in Pistorien et Praten*, March 2, 1855, Lucidi, ibid.; Pennachi, I, 732.

37 S. C. EE et RR, *in Cajetana*, Jan. 29, 1627; *Lucien*, March 28, 1589; Dec. 22, 1602; cf. Ferraris, *v. Monialis, V*, 64; Lucidi, II, 159; Bastien, *op. cit.*, n. 369; Schaaf, *loc. cit.*

38 Alexander, VII, Const. *Felici*, § 5, l. c.; S. C. Conc. *Mazzara*, May 10, 1727; Benedict XIV, *Opera Omnia* XIII 263-65.

only those nuns who are in danger of death, but even those who cannot go to the confessional and the Communion window.[39]

The term includes nuns, postulants, novices and all others lawfully residing within the convent, e. g., pupils, who are sick.[40] Reverence to the Blessed Sacrament, however, taking precedence over the cloister rule, permits his entrance to pick up a consecrated host that has fallen through the Communion window.[41]

2. *Insufficient Reasons* would be as follows: (1) to celebrate Mass;[42] (2) to exorcise a nun;[43] (3) to hear the confession of a nun who can approach the confessional window; or on the pretext of accompanying doctors and laborers, etc.;[44] (4) for the burial of a nun;[45] (5) to give spiritual consolation to the sick unless he administers a sacrament,[46] except where in individual cases such a custom is tolerated by the Ordinary.[47] (6) Lately toleration was extended to entrance on like occasions of other priests, both regular and secular, besides the confessor.[48] The prohibition to confessors of entering to bless the cells of

---

39 S. C. de Rel. Sept. 1, 1912; AAS, IV, 625-626; S. C. EE et RR, Sept. 13, 1583; Ferraris, *v. Moniales,* 58; Pellizarius, *op. cit.* Cap. X, n. 220; Blat, n. 675, p. 669.

40 Can. 514, §§ 1, 2; Alexander VII, Const. *Felici,* § 5, loc. cit.; Augustine, III, 141-145; Biederlack-Fuhrich, *op. cit.,* 90; Fanfani, *op. cit.,* 53-54; Blat, *loc. cit.*

41 Ferraris, v. *Moniales,* V. 63; Pennachi I, 732; Lucidi II, 159.

42 S. C. EE et RR *in Lucianen, et Pestor,* July 16, 1685; *In Mantuorin,* June 13, 1591; *In Bononien,* Jan. 2, 1601; Ferraris, *loc. cit.,* V. 62; Lucidi, II, 159; Pennachi I, 732.

43 S. C. EE et RR, July 1, 1616; Ferraris, v. *Monialis,* V, 61; Pennachi, I, 732; Lucidi, II, 159; cf. Schaaf, *op. cit.,* p. 122.

44 S. C. EE et RR, Sept. 13, 1583, Ferraris, *v. Monialis,* V, 59; Lucidi, II, 159; Pellizarius, *op. cit.,* Cap. X, n. 220.

45 S. C. EE et RR, March 10, 1577; ASS XXXVII, 441, *ad calcem; in Una Dominican,* June 30, 1852; *Ulissiponen,* Aug. 11, 1610; Lucidi, II, 158.

46 S. C. EE et RR, Sept. 17, 1779, June 1, 1841; cf. Mothon, *Traite de la Confession Sacramentelle,* p. 96.

47 S. C. EE et RR, *in Pestorien et Pratesi,* March 2, 1855, ASS, XXVII, 441; *in Bononien,* Aug. 20, 1599; Ferraris v. *Monialis* V, 52, 53; Lucidi, II, 158; Pennachi I, 732.

48 S. C. EE et RR, *in Zamoren,* Apr. 24, 1903, ASS, XXXVI, 203-205; *Ursulinarium,* Nov. 12, 1904, ASS, XXXVII, 441-442. These no longer contain the prohibition for them to take refreshment within the cloister, Pennachi, I, 732.

49 S. C. EE et RR, Sept. 4, 1596, Ferraris v. *Moniales,* V, 60.

nuns admits of toleration of a contrary custom by permission of the Ordinary[49] to be asked each time.[50]

Penalty for Violation of a Cloister.

Those violating the cloister of nuns incur "ipso facto" an excommunication simply reserved to Holy See, if they enter without legitimate license and those introducing or admitting them. If they are clerics, they are also to be suspended for a length of time determined by the Ordinary, according to the gravity of the blame.[51]

---

50 Pennachi, I, 732; Lucidi, II, 159.
51 Can. 2342, 1°.

APPENDICES.

APPLYING TO BOTH MALE AND FEMALE RELIGIOUS.

Appendix I.

Frequency of Confession.

During the first centuries of the Church the practice of weekly confession existed both in the East[1] and the West.[2] Previous to the Council of Trent, there was no definite rule in regard to the frequency with which religious were to approach the Sacrament of Penance. This lack of uniformity continued down through the centuries and the statutes of local bishops and councils and religious rules sometimes prescribe confession only at death,[3] sometimes annually,[4] or monthly.[5] Clement V in the Council of Vienna (1311-1312),[6] made monthly confession obligatory for all monks.

The majority of religious rules and councils, however, had the precept of weekly confession.[7]

The Council of Trent striving to bring about uniformity in this matter for nuns, accepted the same rule as the Council of Vienna above mentioned and commanded bishops and regular superiors to insert in the constitutions of their nuns the rule of monthly confession.[8]

Weekly confession—The prescription of the Council of Trent was the normal rule from that time on as enforced by the

1 The Oriental monks of the 4th, 5th and 6th centuries habitually confessed every seven days and were obliged not to have an interval of more than fifteen days between two successive confessions. cf. Marin, *Les Moines de Constantinople,* 95, 96.

2 The rule of the monastery of Kilros (Culros) Scotland (about 448), which was observed by these monks, as Holsten says, from the beginning of Christianity, prescribed confession to their spiritual father every Sunday. cf. Holsten, *Codex Regularum,* II, 65; *index* pp. XXXI.

3 The Order of Fontevrault (about 1116); *Praecepta recte vivendi,* ch. XXII; MPL CLXII, 1084; Rule of the Grandmontines, approved by Adrian IV 1150); cf. Holsten, op. cit., III, p. 307, n. 5, 30.

Pontiffs[9] and the Congregation of Bishops and Regulars,[10] until the decree "Singulari" of March 27, 1896[11] prescribed weekly confession for sisters of simple vows engaged in collecting alms. This has become the basis of our present legislation which holds for both male and female religious. The "Normae" of 1901[12] placed the obligation on the religious, but poses it upon the superiors.[13]

The weekly confession, which is now a matter of law in Canon 595, § 1, Curent Superiores ut omnes religiosi: 3° Ad poenitentiae sacramentum semel saltem in hebdomada accedant. The superiors are to see to it that their religious observe these rules. This canon then is directed towards superiors primarily, but no real obligation can be derived from it and hence, the superiors cannot force religious to go by punishments or censures.[14]

---

4 St. Egbert, Bishop of York, England (732-73) commanded clerics in monasteries to confess at least within the twelve days before Christmas, claiming that this was the custom from the time of Pope Vitalian, i. e., 570; cf. *Egberti Dialogus, Interr.* XVI; Mansi XII; Hadden and Stubbs, *Councils and Ecclesiastical Documents relating to Great Britian and Ireland,* III, 413; MPL, LXXXIX, 442; cf. *Concilium Lateranense* IV, cap. XXI, cf. Mansi XII, 1008, which made annual confession a matter of obligation for all the faithful.

5 *Synodus Londoniensis* (1268) n. 54; Mansi XXIII, 1258; Hefele, VI, p. 112.

6 c. 1, III, "*Ne in agro,*" 10, *in Clem.*

7 St. Chrodegang, Bishop of Metz (742-766), compelled his clergy to live in community giving them the name of *Canons Regular; "Monachi in unaquoque Sabbato confessionem facient, cum bona voluntate, Episcopo aut priori suo;"* Harduin, op. cit., IV, 1187; MPL LXXXIX, 442; Rule of the Cistercians (founded 1092) prescribed weekly confession for both abbots and monks; cf. *Liber Institutorum Capituli Generalis Ordinis Cisterciensis,* Dist. 6, cap. 14; Martene, *Regula Benedicti Commentata, Commentary* MPL XLVI, 697; The Rule of the Carthusian Order, cf. *Consuetudines Guigonis (Stat. cap.* 7) Martene; *op. cit.,* MPL, LXVI, 696.

8 Sess. XXV, *De Regularibus* c. 10; Ehses, *Concilium Tridentinum,* 9, p. 1082.

9 Clement VIII, *Decree to Order of Servites,* July 25, 1599, "*Nullus omnino,*" § 25; FJC, 187.

10 S. C. EE et RR, *Encycl. Lit. Episcopis Italiae,* Oct. 9, 1622; Bizzarri, p. 374; Aug. 22, 1814 n. XI; Bizzarri, p. 44.

11 N. 8; Col. S. C. P. F. (1907), n. 1924. "*. . . in singulis hebdommadis Poenitentiae et Eucharistiae sacramentis reficiantur.*"

12 S. C. EE et RR, June 28, 1901.

13 Battandier, n. 247, p. 207.

14 Blat, II, n. 62, p. 80, 81, Chelodi, *Jus de Personis,* 1922, n. 114, p. 182, note (1).

Then can, however, enforce the constitutions by penal remedies (Canon 2306 ff.) At the most, the superior can only see to it that the religious appears at the confessional, that is, approaches it. He cannot require that the subjects make confession.[15] AUGUSTINE states that the custom of going to confession every other week in large communities can be tolerated.[16] But this cannot be conceded, for Canons 518, § 1, 520, § 1 require that there should be confessors appointed sufficient in number to meet the demands of the community in the observance of Canon 595. The canon confirms indirectly for inferiors the obligation of the rule, but imposes no new obligation under pain of sin.[17]

The superiors then have the obligation of giving their subjects (1) the time and means to make at least weekly confession; (2) to notify the Ordinary if the ordinary confessor refuses or neglects to offer himself once a week for the disposition of the penitents; (3) to exercise surveillance and to warn the religious who neglect weekly confession.[18] Therefore, religious superiors can inquire as to the observance of this prescription, for it is a question of an external act or, at least, a mixed act about which the superiors have the strict right of inquiring as to whether it was placed or not.[19] Just as superiors can ask as to the frequency, so also they can indirectly inquire as to who is the confessor of each religious. They can exact testimony of the approach to confession and thus come indirectly to the knowledge of the confessor. Canons 519 and 522 do not take away from the superiors the right of seeing that their subjects are diligent in the observance of the laws of the church or the order on frequent confession. The obligation imposed upon the superior by the Code presupposes the permission to

---

15 Vermeersch-Creusen, *Epit.* I, n. 700.

16 Augustine, III, p. 3, note (20).

17 Creusen, *Religieux et Religieuses*, n. 204. Biederlack-Fuhrich *op. cit.*, n. 142.

18 Creusen, *loc. cit.*

19 Fanfani, *op. cit.*, n. 322, 352, Dub. 1.

use legitimate means to obtain that end,[20] especially if the violation of this law by a subject is causing scandal to the community. One or two omissions of confession at the regular time can be prudently disregarded by the superior. These prescriptions, of course, apply also to all religious.[21]

---

20 Cf. Fanfani, *loc. cit.* dub. III.
21 Canon 490.

Appendix II.

Cardinal Confessors.

Besides the other privileges contained in the Code, cardinals from the time of their promotion in consistory enjoy the following faculty.[1]

CANON 239.

§ 1. 1°. Audiendi ubique terrarum confessiones etiam religiosorum utriusque sexus et absolvendi ab omnibus peccatis et censuris etiam reservatis, exceptis tantum censuris Sedi Apostolicae specialissimo modo reservatis et illis quae adnexae sunt revelationi secreti S. Officii.

This privilege of hearing the confessions of all religious and absolving from all sins and censures, except those most specially reserved to the Holy See and those connected with the violation of the Holy Office, was first granted to cardinals by Pius X.[2] By virtue of this, cardinals can absolve without any episcopal approbation religious anywhere in the world.[3] This is vicarious jurisdiction and it cannot be delegated. It is evident that the legislator is opposed to extending this fullest ordinary power which the cardinal has received to hear confessions to the conferring of jurisdiction. The legislator cannot be considered to have given them this incredible power of delegating all over the world any priests whatsoever to hear the confessions of any person and of absolving even from cases especially reserved to the Holy See. The privilege of cardinals of choosing a confessor for themselves would be useless if they could make all priests capable of receiving confessions.[4]

---

1 Canon 239, § 1.

2 Ex audientia, SSmi, D. N. Pii PP X. Dec. 20, 1911; Vermeersch, *Periodica* VII, n. 737, p. 251.

3 Vermeersch, *loc. cit.* p. 252.

4 Vermeersch-Creusen, *Epit.* II, n. 146.

Appendix III.

Jubilee Confessors.

Under the old law the choice of a confessor granted to a religious during a Jubilee, was a great concession, but after the decree of 1913 and that of May 3, 1914, the provisions of which, with some few changes, have been adapted into the Code of Canon Law,[1] it is no longer a noticeable exception.

Religious Who Can Gain the Jubilee Indulgence During the Holy Year.

1. All nuns who live in monasteries, in which perpetual enclosure is observed;[2] novices, postulants and secular women who live in such monasteries for the sake of education or for any other legitimate reason and even though these latter reside in the monastery merely for the greater part of the year; also lay sisters who, in the discharge of their duties or for the purpose of collecting alms, leave the religious enclosure.

2. All religious sisters, i. e., females who take simple vows and who belong to a congregation, either of pontifical or of diocesan right, although they are not bound by the strict law of the enclosure as nuns, as well as their novices, postulants, female pupil boarders—externs not included—and other females who live with the religious, sharing their table and residence.

3. Oblates or pious women who live in common, even though they take no vows, as well as their novices, postulants, resident female pupils and others, women who live with them. However, in order that oblates enjoy the privilege conveyed in the apostolic constitution, it is necessary that their institute shall have been approved of by ecclesiastical authority, either permanently or as an experiment.

---

1 Can. 519, 874, § 1, 521, § 2; 522; 523.
2 Can. 488, § 7.

4. All women belonging to any of the Third Orders Regular, provided they live in community under one and the same roof with ecclesiastical approbation as well as women who live with them, as in the case of nuns, sisters and oblates or tertiaries.

5. Certain classes of hermits and anchorites. The privilege is not meant for those who bound by no law of enclosure, live either in community or as solitaries under the direction of Ordinaries and observe certain laws, but only for such hermits or anchorites as live in continuous—although not absolutely perpetual—enclosure, lead a life of contemplation and make profession of a Monastic or a regular order as the Reformed Cistercians of Our Lady de la Trappe, the Camaldolese and the Carthusians.[3]

With this exception of certain classes of hermits and anchorites, male religious as such are not included among those privileged to gain the Jubilee this year without the Roman visits. Some male religious may come, however, under the next two numbers.[4]

6. The faithful of either sex who are held captive in the power of enemies or who are confined to prison or who have been exiled or deported or who have been condemned to labor in penal institutions; also ecclesiastics and male religious who are confined in monasteries or other houses for the purpose of correction.

7. The faithful of either sex, by illness or poor health; those in hospitals taking care of sick; old persons over seventy; if they cannot go to Rome or if in Rome itself cannot make visits. (Those in hospitals is new concession of this year).[5]

During the second year of the jubilee—The faculty to gain

---

3 Pius XI, *Const. Apostolico Munere,* July 30, 1924, AAS, 1924, Vol. XVI, p. 317, ff; Cf. Am. Ecc. Rev. (1924), Vol. 71, p. 494, Cf. n. 490, 501. The translation of this constitution is taken from that made by Rev. Joseph McCarthy; *Am. Ecc. Rev.* (1925) LXXII, 14, 15.

4 McCarthy, Ibidem, p. 16; Numbers 7 and 8 apply directly to the faithful but in "favorabilibus" religious would be included in this term; cf. Maroto, Institutiones J C, n. 236.

5 ibidem, p. 15; (clements not applicable to religious have been omitted).

the indulgence is granted to all religious who were incapable of going to Rome during the first year and also to those who could make the Jubilee during the first year.

Special Faculties of Confessor of Religious Who Make the Jubilee Either Year.

Commutation of Vows and Dispensation.

Vows of Nuns.

The Jubilee confessor, chosen by a nun, can dispense from all private vows made after solemn profession and which are in no way opposed to the regular observance.[6] By C. 1315 vows made before religious profession are suspended as long as the one who made it remains in religion. A vow made after religious profession and which interferes with regular observance, would be invalid and no need of dispensation. A just cause is necessary to grant dispensation and no other work need be substituted, since power granted in favor of nuns is a power of dispensing.

The Holy See grants to the Jubilee confessor the power to commute even by dispensation all private vows, except those reserved to the Holy See, with which sisters belonging to congregations of simple vows (which is the case in all communities of female religious in the United States with the exception of the four convents of the Order of the Visitation, at Georgetown, D. C., Baltimore, Md., St. Louis, Mo. and Mobile, Ala.,[7] as well as oblates, tertiaries of a regular order, girls and women living with any of these or in a school or colleges intended for females, have bound themselves. He can, moreover, having made a commutation, absolve from the observance of vows confirmed by oath.[8]

Private vows reserved to Holy See are vows of perfect and perpetual chastity and the vow to enter a religious order in which solemn vows are taken, made unconditionally and after

[6] Const. *Apostolico munere,* ibid.
[7] S. C. EE et RR, *Americana Votorum,* Sept. 2, 1864; Bizzarri, p. 736.
[8] Const. *Apostolico munere,* n. VIII; AAS XVI, 320.

the completion of one's eighteenth year (Canon 1309). Power of commuting even by dispensing, implies the confessor can substitute a work of notably less moral value than the original work vowed.

Vows of Male and Female Religious—When the jubilee is extended to the whole world, the jubilee confessor can, for a just and probable cause, but only in the jubilee confession itself, by dispensation, commute into other pious works all and every private vow and even those reserved to the Holy See. He can likewise for a just and probable cause by dispensation commute into other pious works the vow of perfect and perpetual chastity. This can be done; even if this vow was publicly taken in religious profession, and this vow remains firm and entire, although the other vows of his profession were taken away by dispensation. This cannot be done, however, if, on the contrary, the penitent was in Holy Orders and bound by the law of celibacy. Vows accepted by a third party cannot be remitted or commuted, unless he, who is concerned, freely and expressly consents. The vows of not sinning and other penal vows he cannot commute into a work, which will be not less effective in restraining from sin than the vow itself.[9]

Choice of Confessors—Nuns and other women, for whose confessions from the prescription of the Code special approbation of the Ordinary is required, have the right for the Jubilee confession to confess to any confessor approved for the faithful by the same Ordinary of the place for both sexes. Once this is completed, the confessor no longer enjoys jurisdiction over that penitent unless, according to the laws of the Code.[10] The words "once completed" must not be taken in a strict numerical sense, that is, that once he has heard the confession he cannot be summoned again. They should be understood in an integrative sense, that is, until the religious has completed the works necessary to gain the jubilee indulgence, so that during this time she could

---

9 Const. *Servatoris,* Dec. 25, 1925, n. VIII; AAS XVII, 616 ff; Pius XI, Const "*Si unquam,*" July 15, 1924; n. VII, p. 312.

10 Const. *Servatoris* Dec. 25, 1925, AAS, 1925. Vol. XVII, p. 615, ad facultates n. II.

again summon a priest approved for both sexes and confess to him. The clause "si adeat" of Canon 522, is suppressed for this occasion and she can summon him to the convent and neither is there any prescription in regard to the place for confession as under this same canon just mentioned.[11]

---

[11] *S. Penitentiaria,* June 5, 1901; Cf. ME, 13, 202, ad. III; Cf. also ME 38, p. 11.

Appendix IV.

Power of Confessor in Regard to Reception of Communion.

To the confessor alone is reserved the right to permit or refuse the approach to the Holy Table. This was first stated by Innocent XI, February 12, 1679,[1] and repeated constantly since. The letter of the S. C. EE et RR, August 4, 1888,[2] which excluded the consent of the superioress as necessary, advised them to go as often as there was no reasonable cause to prevent them.

Nevertheless, abuses crept in and superioresses arbitrarily permitted or refused permission to receive Holy Communion.[3] This caused Leo XIII in the decree "Quemadmodum" to state that the right to permit or refuse reception belonged only to the ordinary or extraordinary confessor. Superiors had no power to mix in this matter, except when a religious had given scandal to community since last confession or was guilty of grave blame. In these cases the superior could refuse permission until the religious approached the Sacrament of Penance again.[4] One getting permission to go frequently and daily to Communion from the confessor, was to notify the superioress. If the latter has grave objections she could manifest them to the confessor, to whose supreme judgment she had to acquiesce.[5]

The same thing was repeated by Pius X in his decree "Tridentina" on frequent Communion, December 20, 1905.[6]

---

1 Decr. S. C. *Concilii, "Cum ad aures"* Col, S. C. P. F. (1907) n. 219.
2 Col. S. C. P. F. (1893), n. 442.
3 S. C. EE et RR, *"Quemadmodum,"* Dec. 7, 1890, Intro; S. C. P. F. 1907, n. 1740.
4 Ibidem, n. 5.
5 Ibidem, n. 6.
6 n. 5—*Ut frequens et quotidiana Communio majori prudentia fiat uberiorique merito augeatur, oportet ut confessarii consilium intercedat. Caveant tamen confessarii ne a frequenti seu quatidiano Communione quemquam avertant, qui in statu graciae reperiatur et recta mente accedat.;* Col. S. C. P. F. (1907), n. 2225, n. 5.

If it is a question of Communion considered in a general fashion in regard to all consciences, it is the confessor who is to judge of sin and on that title indirectly judge of the possible access to the Holy Table. He will prohibit this in certain circumstances and, according to the rules of moral theology, for those habitually in grave sin.

If it is a question of frequent or daily Communion for souls habitually in the state of grace, here the intervention of the confessor is no more than a counsel for the reception of the Eucharist, merited by obedience and prudence.[7]

If, after the last sacramental confession, a religious was the cause of grave scandal to the community, until he has again approached Sacrament of Penance, the superior can prohibit his approach to Holy Communion.[8]

---

7 Mothon, *Etat Religieux,* n. 180, p. 267. ff.
8 Can. 595, § 3, Augustine III, p. 309.

Appendix V.

Correspondence with the Confessor.

This is rather a delicate question, which frequently arises as to whether the religious can keep up their relations for the sake of spiritual direction by visits or correspondence, either postulants with the confessor they had before entrance or a religious with the ordinary confessor after his term has been completed. This was prohibited for nuns by Benedict XIV in his constitution "Pastoralis Curae"[1] which was reaffirmed by the Cardinal Vicar of Rome December 12, 1708,[2] because experience had demonstrated that such practices engendered trouble, confusion, schism and regrettable divergence in the spirit of the community.[3] And in fact the general rule as laid down in the "Normae" of 1901[4] of the Congregation of Bishops and Regulars, was that all letters of the religious were to pass through the hands of the local superior, who had the right to read them, with prudence and kindness and was to keep them under the natural secret. Some religious constitutions required that letters be brought opened to the superior or superioress.[5]

Under the present law, Canon 611, the confessor is not mentioned as one of those to whom religious, whether male or female, can correspond with immunity from inspection of letters by the religious superior or superioress.[6]

Therefore, the confessor should not request his religious penitents to write to him on matters of spiritual direction or conscience, even if the letters are marked "Matters of Conscience" on the outside, unless he is sure that they will not be

1 Aug. 5, 1748, § 18; FJC N. 388.
2 Ferraris, v. *Monialis*, V, ad 3; p. 1103.
3 Mothon, *Traite de la Confession Sacramentelle*, p. 17 ff.
4 June 28, 1901; art. 179.
5 *Statuta, St. Congregationis Benedictino-Bavaricae*, n. 84; quoted by Leitner, Handbuch, p. 444.
6 Leitner, Handbuch, p. 444.

read by the respective superiors, especially since the perusal of these letters in lay institutes of men and women is not forbidden.[7] If it is a question of letters being sent out by their subjects then the superior could read them, but equity demands as well as charity a more benign way of acting.[8]

---

[7] Leitner, ibidem; Vermeersch, *Periodica,* V, p. (53).
[8] Vermeersch, *Per. V,* p. (54).

BIBLIOGRAPHY

Abbreviations will be found prefixed to the title of the work.

JURIDICAL SOURCES

Codex Juris Canonici Pii X Pontificis Maximi jussu digestus Benedicti Papae XV auctoritate promulgatus, Romae, 1917.

Canonical Legislation concerning Religious, Authorised English Translation Rome, 1919.

AAS=*Acta Apostolicae Sedis*, Romae, 1909-1926.

ASS=*Acta Sanctae Sedis*, 41 Vol., Romae, 1865-1908.

Acta Leonis XIII Pontificis Maximi, 22 vol., Rome, 1881-1893.

BRT=*Bullarum, Diplomatum et Privilegiorum Sanctorum Romanorum Pontificum, Taurinensis editio . . . auspicante Card. Francisco Gaude*, 24 vol., Augustae Taurinorum, 1857-1872.

Bullarii Romani Continuatio Summorum Pontificum, 10 vol., Prati, 1756-1883.

Bullarium Ordinis Praedicatorum, 7 vol., Romae, 1739.

Collectanea in usum Sacretariae Sacrae Congregationis Episcoporum et Regularium, vide Bizzarri.

Col. S. C. P. F.=*Collectanea Sacrae Congregationis de Propaganda Fide*, 2 vol. Romae, 1907.

Concilii Plenarii Baltimorensis II, . . . Acta et Decreta, Baltimorae, 1868.

Concilii Plenarii Baltimorensis III, . . . Acta et Decreta, Baltimorae, 1886.

Concilii Plenarii Australasiae I, . . . Acta et Decreta, Sydney, 1887.

Concilii Plenarii Australasiae II, . . . Acta et Decreta, Sydney, 1898.

Constitutiones Fratrum, S. Ordinis Praedicatorum, Paris, 1886.

Corpus Juris Canonici, editio Lipsiensis secunda post Aemilii Ludovici Richteri curas ad librorum manu scriptorum et editionis romanae fidem recognovit et adnotatione critica instruxit Aemilius Friedberg, 2 vol., Lipsiae, 1922.

FJC=*Codicis Juris Canonici Fontes cura Emi. Petri Card. Gasparri editi*, 3 vol., Romae, 1923-1925.

Statuta Dioecesis Novarcensis, quae in Synodo Dioecesana tertia . . . tulit et promulgavit Ill'mus et Rev'mus Michaelis Augustinus Corrigan, Episcopus., New York, 1878.

Synodus Dioecesana Albanensis IV, Troy, N. Y., 1887.

Synodus Dioecesana Albanensis V, Troy, N. Y., 1890.

Synodus Dioecesana Albanensis VI, Albany, N. Y., 1895.

Synodi Hartfordensis Conn., IV Constitutiones, Hartford, Conn., 1887.

Synodus Dioecesana Manchesteriensis I, Manchester, N. H., 1886.

Synodus Dioecesana Neo-Eboracensis V, New York, N. Y., 1886.

REFERENCE WORKS

AERTNYS, Joseph, C. SS. R., *Theologia Moralis,* 2 vol., 7 ed., Paderbornae, 1906.

AERTNYS-DAMEN, C. A., C. SS. R., *Theologia Moralis,* 2 vol., 10 ed., Buscoduci, 1921.

ANDREWS, E. A., L. L. D., *Copious and Critical Latin-English Lexicon,* New York, 1857.

ARREGUI, Antonius M., S. J., *Summarium Theologiae Moralis,* 8 ed., Bilbao, 1923.

AUGUSTINE, Charles, O. S. B., *A Commentary on The New Code of Canon Law,* 9 vol., St. Louis, 1918-1922.

AZPILCUETA, Martin, *Enchiridion sive Manuale Confessariorum et Penitentium,* Wirceburgi, 1593.

BALLERINI, Antonius, S. J., *Opus Theologicum Morale,* 7 vol., Prati, 1898-1901.

BARBOSA, Augustinus, J. U. D., *Tractatus Varii,* London, 1660.

BASTIEN, Dom Pierre, O. S. B., *Directoire Canonique a l'usage des Congregations a voeux simples,* Troisieme Edition, Bruges, 1923.

BATTANDIER, Albert, *Guide Canonique pour les Constitutions des Instituts a voeux simples,* 16 ed., Paris, 1923.

BENEDICTUS XIV, *Opera Omnia,* 17 vol., Prati, 1839-1847.

BENEDICTUS XIV, *De Synodo Dioecesana,* 2 vol., Romae, 1806.

BESSE, Dom. Jean, O. S. B., *Les Moines d'Orient anterieurs au Concile de Chalcedoine* (451). Paris, 1900.

BIEDERLACK, Josephus, S. J., *De Religiosis Codicis Juris Canonici . . .denuo recognovit Maximilianus Führich, S. J.,* Oeniponte, 1919.

BIZZARRI, Andreas, *Collectanea in usum Secretariae Sacrae Congregationis Episcoporum et Regularium,* edita Romae, 1885.

BLAT, Fr. Albertus, O. P., *Commentarium Textus Codicis Juris Canonici,* 5 vol., Romae, 1921-1925.

BOUIX, D., *Tractatus De Jure Regularium,* 2 vol., 3 ed., Parisiis, 1883.

BRANDES, Dom Charles, O. S. B., *A Commentary on the Rule of St. Benedict and a History of His Life,* Einseideln and New York, 1857.

BRANDYS, P. Maximillian, O. F. M., *Kirchliches Rechtsbuch für die Religiösen Laiengenossenschaften der Brüder and Schwestern nach dem neuen Gesetzbuch der hl. Kirche,* 2 ed., Paderborn, 1920.

BUCCERONI, P. Januario, S. J., *Casus Conscientiae,* 2 vol., 6 ed., Romae, 1913; . . . *Jam Resoluti nunc ad Normam Codicis Juris Canonici Emendati,* Romae, 1920.

BUTLER, Cuthbert, O. S. B., *Benedictine Monachism,* New York, 1919.

CASEY, Rev. P. H. S. J., *Notes on a History of Auricular Confession* (*A Reply to H. C. Lea*), Philadelphia, 1899.

Catholic Encyclopedia, 16 vol., New York, 1907-1914; *Supplement I—Canon Law,* New York, 1918.

CHELODI, Joannes, J. C. D., *Jus de Personis juxta Codicem Juris Canonici,* Tridenti, 1922.

CHOKIER, Erasmus, *Tractatus de Jurisdictione Ordinarii in Exemptos,* Colonia Agrippinae, 1639.

CHOUPIN, Lucien, S. J., *Recents Decrets du Saint Siege concernant les Religieux et Religieuses*, Paris, 1915.
Nature et Obligations de l'Etat Religieux, Paris, 1923.

CLARKE, Wm. K. Lowther, *St. Basil The Great—A Study in Monasticism*, Cambridge, 1913.

COCCHI, Guidus, *Commentarium in Codicem Juris Canonici*, 6 vol., Taurinorum Augustae, 1920-1924.

CREUSEN, J., S. J., *Religieux et Religieuses d'apres Le Droit Ecclesiastique*, 13 ed., Paris, 1924.

CRUSENIUS, Nicolaus, *Monasticon Augustinianum*, (Place not mentioned), 1623.

CURRAN, Thomas, P., *Confessors and Confessions of Religious Women of Simple Vows*, Washington, 1916.

DARGIN, Edward, J. C. D., *Reserved Cases According to The Code of Canon Law*, Washington, 1924.

DE LATTE, Abbot Paul, O. S. B., *A Commentary on The Rule of St. Benedict*, New York, 1921.

DE MEESTER, A., D. J. C., *Juris Canonici et Juris Canonico-Civilis Compendium*, 2 vol., Brugis, 1921-1923.

DENZINGER, Henrico, *Enchiridion Symbolorum, Definitionum et Declarationum de Rebus Fidei et Morum*, 13 ed., quam paravit Clemens Bannwart, S. J. Friburgi-Brisgoviae, 1921.

DU CANGE, *Glossarium ad Scriptores Mediae et Infimae Latinitatis*, 6 vol., Parisiis, 1733-1736.

EHSES, Stephen, *Concilium Tridentinum, Diariorum Actorum, Epistularum, Tractatuum, Nova Collectio edidit Societas Goerresiana*, 10 vol., Friburgi-Brisgoviae, 1911-1916; Tom. 9, compilavit Stephanus Ehses.

FACCIOLATI, Jacobi, *Totius Latinitatis Lexicon*, 2 vol., London, 1826.

FANFANI, Ludovicus, I., O. P., *De Jure Religiosorum, ad Normam Codicis Juris Canonici*, Augustae Taurinorum, 1920; ed altera Taurini-Romae, 1925.

FERRARIS, F. Lucii, O. M. Reg. Obs. Sti. Francisci, *Prompta Bibliotheca Canonica, Juridica, Moralis, Theologica necnon Ascetica, Polemica, Rubristica, Historica.*, 9 vol., Romae, 1885-1892.

FORCELLINI, Aegidii, *Totius Latinitatis Lexicon*, 4 vol., Schneebergae-Lipsiae, 1831-1839.

GASPARRI, Petro, *Tractatus Canonicus de Sanctissima Eucharistia*, 2 vol., Parisiis, 1897.

GAZAEUS, D. Alardi, O. S. B., *Cassiani Joannis Opera Omnia, cum Commentariis*, Lipsiae, 1733.

GENICOT, Eduardus, S. J., *Theologiae Moralis Institutiones*, 6 ed. quam recognovit J. Salsman S. J., 2 vol., Bruxellis, 1909; 10 ed. ibid., 1922.

GENNARI, Casmiro, Card., *Consultazioni Morali*, 2 vol., 3 ed., Rome, 1913-1915, *Quistioni Canoniche*, Rome, 1908.

GIRALDUS, Ubaldus, *Expositio Juris Pontificii*, 3 vol., Romae, 1829-1830.

GURY, P. Joannes, S. J., *Compendium Theologiae Moralis*, 3 ed. 2 vol., Lugduni, 1881.

GURY-FERRERES, P. Joannes, S. J., *Casus Conscientiae*, 4 ed., Hispana. Prima post Codicem, 2 vol., Barcinone, 1920.

HADDAN, Arthur West and Stubbs, Wm.; *Councils and Ecclesiastical Documents relating to Great Britain and Ireland,* 3 vol., London (Oxford), 1869-1871.

HARDUIN, Jean, S. J., *Counciliorum Collectio Regia Maxima,* 12 vol., Parisiis, 1714-1725.

HEFELE, Carl Joseph, *Conciliengeschichte,* 9 vol., 2 ed., Freiburg im Breisgau, 1873-1890.

HEIMBUCHER, Dr. Max, *Die Orden und Kongregationen der Katholischen Kirche,* 3 vol., 2 ed., Paderborn, 1907-1908.

HILLING, Nicolaus, *Codicis Juris Canonici Interpretatio,* Friburg, Breisgau, 1925.

HIZETTE, Chanoine, S. T. D., *Confessions des Religieuses,* 2 ed., Paris, 1913; Supplement, Paris, 1920.

HOLSTENIUS, *Codex Regularum,* 5 vol., Augustae Vindelicorum, 1759.

JANSEN, P. Joseph, O. M. I., *Ordensrecht,* Paderborn, 1920.

LABBEUS Phil. et Cossartius Gabr. S. J., *Sacrorum Conciliorum Nova et Amplissima Collectio,* . . . a Card. Dominico Passioneo, 30 vol., Florentiae-Venetiis, 1759-1792.

LA CROIX, R. F., Claudio, S. J., *Theologia Moralis,* 2 vol. Venetiis, 1766.

LADEUZE, Paulin, *Etude sur le Cenobitisme Pakhomien,* Louvaine, 1898.

LANSLOTS, D. I., O. S. B., *Handbook of Canon Law for Congregations of Women under Simple Vows,* New York, 1909.

LEA, Henry C., *A History of Auricular Confession and Indulgences in the Latin Church,* 2 vol., 1896.

LEHMKUHL, Augustine, S. J., *Theologia Moralis,* 2 vol., 12 ed., Friburgi Brisgoviae, 1914.

LEITNER, Dr. Martin, *Handbuch des Katholischen Kirchenrechts auf Grunde des neuen Codex vom 28 Juni,* 1917, (Regensburg, 1918-1919; (*Dritte Lieferung, Das Ordensrecht,* Regensburg, 1922).

LUCIDI, Angelus, *De Visitatione Sacrorum Liminum Instructio S. C. Concilii edita jussu P. M. Benedicti XIII exposita et additionibus aucta per P. Josephum Schneider,* S. J., 3 vol., 3 ed., Romae, 1883.

MACKEAN, Rev. W. H., D. D., *Christian Monasticism in Egypt to the Close of the Fourth Century,* London, 1920.

MANSI, Joannes Dominicus, *Sacrorum Conciliorum Nova et Amplissima Collectio,* 51 vol., Paris, Arnhem and Leipzig, 1903-1924.

MARC, P. Clement, C. SS. R., *Institutiones Morales Alphonsiae,* 2 vol., Romae, 1885.

MARCHAND, Alfred, *Moines et Nonnes, Histoire, Constitution, Regle, Coutume et Statistique des Odres Religieux,* 2 vol., Paris, 1880.

MARIN, L'Abbe, *Les Moines de Constantinople* (330-898), Paris, 1897.

MELO, Antonius, O. F. M., J. C. L., *De Exemptione Regularium,* Washington, 1921.

MPG=*Migne, Patrologia Graeca.*

MPL=*Migne, Patrologia Latina.*

MONIER, Abbe Leon, *A History of St. Francis, of Assisi,* London, 1894.

MONTALAMBERT, Charles Count de, *Monks of the West from St. Benedict to St. Bernard,* Boston, 1872.

MORISON, B. D., E. F., *St. Basil and His Rule. A Study in Early Monasticism,* London, 1912.

MOTHON, Joseph Pie, O. P., *Traite de la Confession Sacramentelle a l'usage des Communautes de Religieuses,* Lille, 1913.
Traite sur l'Etat Religieux, Paris, 1922.

NOLDIN, Jerome, S. J., *Theologia Moralis (De Sacramentis),* Oeniponte, 1920.

O'DONNELL, Rev. M. J., *Penance in the Early Church,* Dublin, 1908.

PAPI, Hector, S. J., *Religious in Church Law,* New York, 1924.
The Government of Religious Communities, New York, 1919.

PELLIZARIUS, Franciscus, S. J., *Tractatio de Monialibus,* Venetiis, 1651.

PENNACHI, Joseph, *Commentaria in Constitutionem "Apostolicae Sedis" qua Censurae latae sententiae limitantur,* 2 vol., Rome, 1883.

PIGNATELLI, Jacobi, *Consultationes Canoniciae,* 11 tomes, Coloniae Allobrogum, 1700.

POURRAT, Rev. P., *Christian Spirituality from the Time of Christ till the Dawn of the Middle Ages,* New York, 1922.

PRÜMMER, Dominicus, M., O. P., *Manuale Juris Canonici,* 3 ed., Friburgi Brisgoviae, 1922.

RAUSCHEN, Gerhard, PH. D., S. T. D., *Eucharist and Penance in the First Six Centuries of the Church,* St. Louis, 1913.

REIFFENSTUEL, F. Anecletus, *Jus Canonicum Universum,* 6 vol., Antuerpiae, 1733.

RODERICI, F. O. F. M., *Resolutiones Quaestionum Regularium,* Lugduni, 1634.

Rule of St. Benedict, Birmingham, 1844. (Editor not mentioned.)

SABETTI, Aloysio, S. J., *Compendium Theologiae Moralis,* 30 *ed. ad novum Codicem Juris Canonici concinnata a Timotheo Barret, S. J.,* (ed. quarta post Codicem), New York, 1924.

ST. ALPHONSUS, C. SS. R., *Theologia Moralis,* 9 vol., Parisiis, 1834.

SCHAAF, Valentine, O. F. M., J. C. D., *The Cloister,* Cincinnati, 1921.

SCHÄFER, P. Timotheus, O. M. Cap., *Das Ordensrecht nach dem Codex Juris Canonici,* Münster i. W., 1923.

SCHERER, Rudolph R. von, *Handbuch des Kirchenrechts,* 2 vol., Graz und Leipzig, 1898.

SMITH, I. Gregory, M. A., *Christian Monasticism from the Fourth to the Ninth Centuries of the Christian Era,* London, 1892.

SMITH, Rev. S., D. D., *Notes on The Second Plenary Council of Baltimore,* New York, 1874.

STADTMÜLLER, Raphael Maria, O. P., *Das Neue Ordensrecht,* Dülmen i. W., 1919.

SUAREZ, Franciscus, S. J., *Opera Omnia,* vol. 16, Parisiis, 1866.

TANQUEREY, Ad. *Synopsis Theologiae Moralis et Pastoralis,* 3 vol., 8 ed., Rome, 1921.

VAN ESPEN, Zegeri Bernardi J. U. D., *Operum Pars Prima, Jus Ecclesiasticum Universum,* Lovanii, 1732.

VERMEERSCH, A. S. J., *De Religiosis Institutis et Personis Tractatus Canonico-Moralis,* 2 vol., 4 ed., Brugis, 1909.
Summa Novi Juris Canonici Commentariis aucta, 2 ed., Mechliniae, 1919.

VERMEERSCH-CREUSEN, *Epit.*=A. Vermeersch, S. J., J. Creusen, S. J., *Epitome Juris Canonici cum Commentariis ad scholas et ad usum privatum,* 3 vol., Mechliniae (ed. 1921), 1924-1925.

WALDE, Alois Dr., *Lateinisches Etymologisches Wörterbuch*, Heidelberg, 1910.

WATKINS, Oscar D., M. A., *A History of Penance*, 2 vol., London, 1920.

WERNZ, Franciscus X., S. J., *Jus Decretalium*, 10 vol., Prati, 1913.

WERNZ-VIDAL, *Jus Canonicum, auctore P. Francisco Wernz, S. J., ad codicis normam exactum opera P. Petri Vidal ejusdem Societatis sacerdote*, tom. II, Rome, 1923.

WOELFLIN, Eduardus, *Benedicti Regula Monachorum*, Lipsiae, 1895.

Works of St. Francis of Assisi, by a Religious of the Order, London, 1882.

PERIODICALS

Am. Ecc. Rev.=*American Ecclesiastical Review*, Philadelphia, vol. 49, 1913; vol. 52, 1915; vol. 61, 1919; vol. 62, 1920; vol. 66, 1922; vol. 69, 1923; vol. 74, 1926.

An. JP=*Analecta Juris Pontificii*, Rome, vol. 9, 1867; vol. 1, 1855; vol. 4, 1860.

AKKR=*Archiv für Katholischen Kirchenrecht*, Mainz, vol. 78, 1898; vol. 79, 1899; vol. 97, 1916; vol. 100, 1920.

CC=*Canoniste Contemporainle*, Paris, vol. 36, 1913.

ME=*Il Monitore Ecclesiastico*, Rome, vol. 29, 1917; vol. 38, 1926.

Ir. Ecc. Rec.=*The Irish Ecclesiastical Record*, Dublin, (Fifth Series, vol. 1, 1913; vol. 4, 1914; vol. 9, 1917; vol. 12, 1918; vol. 13, 1919; vol. 18, 1921; vol. 22, 1923; vol. 23, 1924.

LQS=*Linzer theologisch-praktische Quartalschrift*, Linz, vol. 70, 1917; vol. 73, 1920; vol. 74, 1921; vol. 75, 1922; vol. 76, 1923; vol. 77, 1924; vol. 79, 1926.

Nouvelle Revue Theologique, Paris, vol. 48 (1921).

Razon y Fe, tomo XXXVII, Madrid, 1913.

Vermeersch, *Per.*=Arthurus Vermeersch S. J., *De Religiosis et Missionariis Supplementa et Monumenta periodica*, edita Brugis, 13 vol. (tom. I-XI) 1911-1925.

Universitas Catholica Americae
Washingtonii, D. C.
Sacra Facultas Iuris Canonici
1926
No. 33

DEUS LUX MEA

THESES

QUAS

AD DOCTORATUS GRADUM

IN

JURE CANONICO

Apud Universitatem Catholicam Americae

CONSEQUENDUM

PUBLICE PROPUGNABIT

ROBERTUS EMMET McCORMICK

SACERDOS ARCHIDIOECESIS NEO EBORACENSIS

IURIS CANONICI LICENTIATUS

HORA IX A. M. DIE XXVIII MAII A. D. MCMXXVI

JUS CANONICUM

I.	De Decreto Gratiani.		
II.	De Libro Sexto Bonifacii VIII.		
III.	De Codificatione Codicis Iuris Canonici.		
IV.	Canones	8-9	De Promulgatione et Vacatione Legum Ecclesiasticarum.
V.	Canones	21-23	De Cessatione Legis.
VI.	Canones	25-30	De Consuetudine.
VII.	Canones	36-37	De Subiecto Rescriptorum.
VIII.	Canones	80-86	De Dispensationibus.
IX.	Canones	87-91	De Personis in Genere.
X.	Canones	92-95	De Domicilio et Quasi-Domicilio.
XI.	Canones	96-97	De Consanguinitate et Affinitate.
XII.	Canon	338	De Residentia Episcoporum in Dioecesi.
XIII.	Canon	339	De Episcoporum Obligatione Missam pro Populo Applicandi.
XIV.	Canones	350-352	e Episcoporum Coadiutorum et Auxiliarium Notione et Potestate.
XV.	Canon	451	De Parochis et iis qui in Iure hisce aequiparantur.
XVI.	Canon	476	De Paroeciali Vicario Cooperatore.
XVII.	Canones	514, 523, 600	De Administratione Sacramentorum Religiosis Aegrotis et Moribundis.
XVIII.	Canones	518, 519, 528	De Confessariis Religiosorum.
XIX.	Canones	520-527	De Confessariis Religiosarum.
XX.	Canon	530	De Conscientiae Manifestatione.
XXI.	Canones	566, 675, 891	De Deputatione Sacerdotum a Confessionibus in tam Virorum quam Mulierum Novitiatibus et Piis Associationibus.
XXII.	Canon	595	De Obligationibus Superiorum quoad vitam spiritualem suorum subiectorum.
XXIII.	Canones	808, 857, 858	De Ieiunio Naturali.
XXIV.	Canones	837-840	De Transmissione Stipendiorum.
XXV.	Canones	875-876	De Iurisdictione ad Confessiones Religiosorum et Religiosarum accipiendas.
XXVI.	Canon	882	De Absolutione in Periculo Mortis.
XXVII.	Canon	883	De Iurisdictione Sacerdotis Iter Maritimum Arripientis.
XXVIII.	Canones	1043, 1044	De Potestate Dispensandi in Periculo Mortis supra Impedimenta Matrimonialia.
XXIX.	Canones	1121-1123	De Interpellationibus faciendis in Privilegio Paulino.
XXX.	Canones	1250-1254	De Lege Ieiunii et Abstinentiae.
XXXI.	Canones	1756-1758	De iis, qui Testes esse possunt.
XXXII.	Canones	1970-1973	De Iure Accusandi Matrimonium et Postulandi Dispensationem super Rato.
XXXIII.	Canones	2195-2198	De Natura et Divisione Delicti.

XXXIV.	Canones	2201-2206	De Causis excusantibus vel minuentibus Imputabilitatem Delicti.
XXXV.	Canon	2229	De iis, quae a Poenis latae sententiae excusant.
XXXVI.	Canones	2236-2240	De Remissione Poenarum.
XXXVII.	Canon	2254	De Absolutione Censurarum reservatarum in Casibus urgentioribus.
XXXVIII.	Canon	2290	De Confessarii Potestate suspendendi Observantiam Poenae Vindicativae latae sententiae.
XXXIX.	Canon	2414	De Punitione Superiorissae agentis contra Praescriptum can. 521, par. 3, 522, 523.

ROMAN LAW

A. Justinian Law

XL. Enslavement.
XLI. Manumission from Slavery.
XLII. Origin, Duties and Rights of *Colonus*.
XLIII. Origin, Effects and Loss of Citizenship.
XLIV. The Juridical Concept of the Roman Family.
XLV. *Patria Potestas*.
XLVI. Origin and Cessation of *Cura*.
XLVII. Guarantees of *Tutela* and *Cura*.

B. The Institutes of Gaius

XLVIII. Forms of Marriage in Classical Law.
XLIX. The Juridical Meaning of *Manus*.
L. *Tutela* and *Cura* of the Classical Period in Roman Law.

INTERNATIONAL LAW

LI. The Meaning and Character of International Law.
LII. Sources and Fundamental Principles of International Law.
LIII. General Rights and Obligations of States.
LIV. Immunity.
LV. Extradition.
LVI. Consular Agents.
LVII. The Monroe Doctrine.
LVIII. The Drago Doctrine.
LIX. Jurisdiction over Vessels.
LX. Piracy.

Vidit Facultas:

Philippus Bernardini, S.T.D., J.U.D., Decanus.
Ludovicus H. Motry, S.T.D., J.C.D., a Secretis.
Valentinus T. Schaaf, O.F.M., S.T.B., J.C.D.
Franciscus Lardone, S.T.D., J.U.D.
Manoel De Oliviera Lima, L.H.B.

Vidit Rector Universitatis:

✠Thomas J. Shahan, S.T.D., J.U.L., LL. D.

VITA

Robert Emmet McCormick was born on March 29, 1901, at Kingston, New York. His primary education was received in Public School No. 4 of that city and St. Columba's Parochial School, New York City. Having completed the courses at St. Francis Xavier's High School (1917) and Cathedral College (1919) he entered St. Joseph's Seminary at Dunwoodie, N. Y., in September of that year. Ordained to the priesthood, on September 20, 1924, by His Eminence P. Cardinal Hayes, he registered in the School of Canon Law of the Catholic University of America, at Washington. He takes this opportunity to express his gratitude for the kind assistance he has received, not only from the Faculty of Canon Law, but also from the Reverend Joseph McCarthy and the assistant librarian of the University.

www.ingramcontent.com/pod-product-compliance
Lightning Source LLC
LaVergne TN
LVHW050253080826
844660LV00012B/632